WITHDRAWN

THE PRESENCE
OF THE PAST

THE PRESENCE OF THE PAST

POPULAR USES OF HISTORY IN AMERICAN LIFE

Roy Rosenzweig and David Thelen

COLUMBIA UNIVERSITY PRESS ♔ NEW YORK

147360

Columbia University Press

Publishers Since 1893

New York   Chichester, West Sussex

Copyright © 1998 Columbia University Press

All rights reserved

Library of Congress Cataloging-in-Publication Data

Rosenzweig, Roy.

   The presence of the past : popular uses of history in American life /
Roy Rosenzweig and David Thelen.

     p. cm.

   Includes bibliographical references and index.

ISBN 0–231–11148–7

   1. United States—History—Philosophy. 2. Memory—Social aspects—United States.
3. National characteristics, American. 4. United States—Social life and customs.
5. Interviews—United States.

   I. Thelen, David P. (David Paul) II. Title.

   E179.5.R67 1998

   973.'01—dc21   97-47535

Casebound editions of Columbia University Press books are printed on permanent and
durable acid-free paper.

Printed in the United States of America

c 10 9 8 7 6 5 4 3 2 1

Contents

Acknowledgments

Two names appear on the title page of this book, but this particular partnership rests on a much broader collaboration with dozens of others to whom we are in profound debt. As the introduction explains, the project emerged out of a set of meetings in Indianapolis supported by the Indiana Humanities Council in 1989 and 1990, as well as the follow-up activities by participants in those meetings who called themselves "The Committee on History-Making in America" (COHMIA). We would like first of all to thank the various people who took active roles in those meetings and that organization—especially Jo Blatti, John Bodnar, Steve Brier, Barbara Franco, Mike Frisch, John Gillis, Ken Gladish, Henry Glassie, D. D. Hilke, Katherine O'Donnell, Philip Scarpino, Thomas Schlereth, Lois Silverman, Allie Stuart, John Kuo Wei Tchen, and Jamil Zainaldin. Starting in the fall of 1990, Indiana University established and funded the Center on History-Making in America to support the committee's projects, which came increasingly to center on the survey that became the basis for this book. From the start Lois Silverman served as director of this center. In coordinating the committee's and the center's activities, she played a crucial role in helping to lay the groundwork for this survey—including shaping its methodology and overseeing the preparation of the grant proposals. We are deeply grateful to Lois and to her assistant, Lynne Hamer, for their dedication to this and other COHMIA projects. And we are deeply indebted to administrators at Indiana University, particularly George Walker, for believing in the project, supporting the center, and thereby providing the means to develop the survey.

The actual survey whose results are reported here would not have been possible without financial support from the Spencer Foundation and especially the National Endowment for the Humanities, an independent federal agency. We would like particularly to thank John Barcroft of the Spencer Foundation and Fred Miller, Marsha Semmel, Clay Lewis, and Sheldon Hackney of the NEH for their enthusiasm for our work as well as their understanding of the inevitable delays in completing this project. Funding for early COHMIA meetings in Bloomington, Indianapolis, Buffalo, and St. Paul, which led ultimately to the survey, was provided by the state humanities councils of Indiana, New York, and Minnesota as well as the Skaggs Foundation. And we received valuable administrative help at Indiana University from Bill Brescia, Jimmie Brescia, Nancy Croker, David Nordloh, and Barbara Tarrant. George Mason University, and particularly the successive chairs of the history department, Marion Deshmukh and Jack Censer, has also been generously supportive of Roy Rosenzweig's work on the project.

Our most constant and dedicated collaborator has been Andy Draheim. He took primary responsibility for working with the Center for Survey Research and in general for compiling and organizing the results of the survey. His good sense and tireless enthusiasm were simply indispensable to the completion of the project. Although Andy's formal title was "research assistant," he was much more that and took an active role in shaping the study, training dozens of interviewers, modifying programs, analyzing the data, and closely and perceptively commenting on successive drafts of the manuscript. In the earliest stages of the project, Dave Wilson provided important research and administrative help, and in the closing months, Patrick Ettinger took on the painstaking job of re-checking all of our quotes and descriptions of individual interviewees against the original data.

As the introduction makes clear, the actual questionnaire was developed through a process of piloting and pretesting that brought in many different voices, including two classes of talented and tireless graduate students at Arizona State University and the University of Toledo. Our thanks to Noel Stowe and Beth Luey at Arizona State and Diane F. Britton at Toledo for providing us with these opportunities to refine and run the crucial pilots of the survey. Dozens of others tried out versions of the questions with friends, students, and neighbors and generously sent in their results, including some seventy-five professionals who reported experience with these questions at institutions across the country. We are especially indebted to more than forty academic and public historians who responded to our plea for comments on a preliminary draft of the telephone questionnaire. We would also like to thank several people—including Rodolfo Acuña, Rina Benmayor, Elsa Barkeley Brown, Roberto Calderon, Jorge Chapa, Robin D. G. Kelley, Fred Hoxie, Faith Ruffins, Anna M. Santiago, John Kuo Wei Tchen, and David Weber—for advice on developing strategies for interviewing minority populations. Several Indiana University faculty members—especially John Bodnar, Michael Hogan, David Nordloh, and Phil Scarpino—not only helped to refine questions for the survey but also offered support and ideas for the work of COHMIA. Herb Thelen gave wise counsel throughout.

The most important advice we received on how to conduct the survey came, not surprisingly, from the staff at the Center for Survey Research at Indiana University, who actually carried out the survey. We want to thank Nancy Bannister, Christopher Botsko, Barbara Hopkins, Kevin Tharp, and especially the CSR's astute director, John Kennedy, for their incredible dedication, flexibility, and professionalism. Although we can't name all of them here, we are also deeply indebted to other members of the center staff, who patiently helped to put the data into usable form, and the more than sixty staff interviewers who made the hundreds of phone calls and carefully transcribed the responses for us to read. We were also fortunate to be able to turn repeatedly to Scott Keeter, former head of the Survey Research Laboratory at Virginia Commonwealth University (and Roy's neighbor), for sharp and sensible advice on matters of survey procedure and statistical analysis.

Many individuals collaborated by reading various drafts of the manuscript and responding to the data we collected and our interpretations of it. Particular chapters and sections were commented on by Rodolfo Acuña, Steve Brier, Peter Dimock, Gary Gerstle, Ron Grele, Arthur Hansen, Lu Ann Jones, Deborah Kaplan, Harvey Kaye, Scott Keeter, John Kennedy, Oscar Martinez, Ricardo Romo, and Esther Thelen. We wish we could individually thank all of the people who read and commented on the entire manuscript. But since we were fortunate to have so many generous and perceptive critics, we can only list them here: Bud Bynack, Ken Cmiel, Andy Draheim, Tom Engelhardt, Barbara Franco, John Gillis, David Glassberg, Mike Frisch, Jeannette Hopkins, Fred Hoxie, Robin D. G. Kelley, Warren Leon, Earl Lewis, Edward Linenthal, Robert Orsi, Nancy Grey Osterud, Marsha Semmel, and Linda Shopes. We received tremendous help from people who commented on oral presentations that we made about our results at such places as the annual meetings of the Japanese American Studies Association and the Oral History Association, the Smithsonian Institution, the universities of California-San Diego, Cambridge, Indiana, Toledo, Virginia, Wisconsin-Green Bay, and Witwatersrand, as well as the Autonomous University of Madrid and the University of Technology, Sydney. A long conversation between Dave Thelen and Alessandro Portelli was crucial in rethinking some key formulations. Finally, we want to express our warm thanks to Mike Frisch, who has been a friend and inspiration throughout the project—from the very first meetings in Indianapolis through two brilliantly perceptive readings of the entire manuscript.

After we had completed our next-to-final draft of the manuscript, we were fortunate to team up with an extraordinarily talented editor, M. Mark, for one last round of revisions. M.'s sharp insights, gentle cajoling, and fine editorial hand made this into a much sharper, smoother, and shorter book than it would have been otherwise. We thank her for both for her transformative influence on the book as well as for her willingness to join in a complex collaboration with two idiosyncratic authors.

The final stages of work on this project have been overseen by Columbia University Press. We would like to thank our editor Kate Wittenberg for her enthusiasm and support for this project and Leslie Kriesel for her careful final review of the manuscript.

Since this book emphasizes intimate pasts and intimate uses of the past, it is perhaps not surprising that our deepest debts in the making of this book have been personal ones to our spouses, Esther Thelen and Deborah Kaplan. We thank them for the intellectual and moral support that has repeatedly sustained us over the past four years.

THE PRESENCE OF THE PAST

"How Do Americans Understand Their Pasts?" Beginning an Inquiry, Spring 1989

On Monday morning, May 15, 1989, ten people crowded around the dining-room table at the Chateau Delaware, a nineteenth-century stone mansion in Indianapolis. The mansion—recently converted into a bed-and-breakfast—seemed an appropriate setting for a retreat devoted to mapping previously uncharted intersections between present and past. We looked out on a historic block—Benjamin Harrison's house was down Delaware Street—in a neighborhood just north of the city's thoroughly modern downtown. Next door, another mansion housed the Indiana Humanities Council.

The retreat itself was the brainchild of Allie Stuart, a program officer with the Council. A few months earlier, she had invited David Thelen to lunch at a Cajun cafe in Bloomington to talk about better ways of connecting academic historians with larger audiences. Dave had said that he knew several professionals at universities and museums who shared the same dream, and mused that it would be great to get them together. He remembers choking on his Diet Coke when Allie replied that the Indiana Humanities Council would provide the funding for such a conference if Dave would invite participants and report their ideas.

The defining moment of the weekend—and the birth of this book—occurred that first morning as we went around the table, sharing our concerns about the practice of professional history. Person after person described struggles to imagine or build alternatives that might break down barriers between professionals and wider audiences. As we talked, it became clear that we shared the conviction that professional historians were painfully unaware of how people outside their own circles understood and used the past. We discussed books we'd read and experiments we'd tried, and as these began to mount, we felt a sense of excitement—a sense that we, the individuals in that room, might actually be able to make a difference in narrowing the gap.

John Gillis, who was leading a project on the historical construction of identities at Rutgers University, said his research had led him to see the history that families create as a rich alternative to academic history. D. D. Hilke, director of audience research at the National Museum of American History, described her ethnographic studies of how museum visitors turned exhibits into things they recognized from their own experience. Philip Scarpino, John Bodnar, and Michael Frisch, leaders in the fields of oral history and public history, discussed oral historians' attempts to share authority—to create history jointly with the people they interviewed. The historians around the table reported on studies and theories from many fields that investigated the ways Americans use the past in their everyday lives, screening professional "texts" (museum exhibits, books, movies) through these everyday uses.

We spent the rest of the weekend trying to design ways of improving exchanges between professional and popular historians. Someone would grab a Magic Marker, write four or five themes on a piece of paper, and drape it over the back of a chair. Then someone else would impose a second dimension and turn the list into a grid. On grids and maps we constructed models that compared professional historymaking with that done by individuals in their daily lives, by television producers, by advertisers, by leaders of ethnic and religious groups, and by collectors.

How should we proceed? Each of us had brought along favorite ideas for projects, and we dreamed up more on the spot: ethnographic observation of people in natural settings; in-depth interviews with people who pursue history as a hobby; participant observation of the uses of history in family conversations; textual analyses of diaries or memoirs; experiments that ask people to visualize the past by having them draw a picture of what history looks like to them. While this group of humanists had ingrained skepticism about the scientific claims of survey research, some of us were enthusiastic about surveying a cross section of Americans. We believed that this would allow us to listen to people as they used the past in their daily lives, to map out patterns, and to define starting points for deeper investigations.

As we tried to define the questions to investigate, we used terms like "historical consciousness" and "historical memory." At one point somebody threw out the phrase "popular historymaking." Many of us liked its implication that Americans take an active role in using and understanding the past—that they're not just passive consumers of histories constructed by others.

The intensity and urgency of our conversation that weekend grew out of the conjunction of two historical circumstances. Writing a few months later in one of the dozens of internal documents generated by the group, Michael Frisch captured this intellectual and political moment: "The study and understanding of history occupies a paradoxical and problematic place in contemporary American culture. On the one hand, it is widely believed that we face a general crisis of historical amnesia; on the other hand, there is clearly enormous and growing public interest in history, manifest in museum attendance, historically oriented tourism, participation in festivals, and even the media-driven excesses of nostalgia and commemoration of recent historical periods."[1]

We met in an atmosphere of both crisis and excitement, Roy recalls, about the state of historymaking in America. In the late 1980s, much-publicized jeremiads warned ominously of historical amnesia and historical illiteracy suffocating the nation. Shortly before Dave began to plan the Indianapolis meeting, Lynne Cheney, then chairman of the National Endowment for the Humanities, had issued a pamphlet called *American Memory*, which began with the declaration: "A refusal to remember . . . is a primary characteristic of our nation."[2]

The historians gathered in Indianapolis thought that the real issue was not, as pundits were declaring, what Americans did not know about the past but what they *did* know and think. Incredibly, since many commentators had surveyed American ignorance, no one had actually investigated how Americans understood and used the past. And we believed that we needed to seek out and listen to the voices of the people who were being denounced for their ignorance.

Our motivations were more complex than a desire to offer a different perspective on what would become known as the culture wars and the history wars. We also approached the question of "how Americans understand the past" from the opposite direction—from excitement rather than worry, from our perception of deep public fascination with the past. Here, the historical context was not the conservative assault on historical illiteracy but the emergence, starting in the late 1960s, of what was called "public history" or "people's history."

Carried along by the social movements of the 1960s and 1970s, many advocates of people's history and public history saw the past as a source of empowerment and political mobilization. They wanted to democratize not just the content of history (adding the stories of African Americans, industrial workers, immigrants, women, and gays) but also its practice; they wanted to turn audiences into collaborators. In the 1970s and 1980s some of us had begun collaborating with new audiences through museums and state humanities councils, historical films, community oral history programs, and trade union historical classes. These successes inspired us at the Chateau Delaware.

But our failures also goaded us. While we and others of our generation had widened the topics, voices, methods, and viewpoints that scholars called "history"—indeed, this success had provoked the conservative counterattack—we had been less successful in turning audiences into partners. In a paper he presented that weekend, Dave argued that the major barrier to such collaboration came not from conservatives but from scholars who had failed to overcome habits of professionalization. Reporting responses from a thousand readers to a *Journal of American History* survey, he noted that an increasingly voluminous, fragmented, and specialized scholarship—though wonderfully rich and diverse—seemed "narrow, overspecialized, and boring" even to many *Journal* subscribers.[3]

As we contemplated reaching outside our professional circles, we realized how little we knew about the values and perspectives Americans were bringing from their personal experiences to these historical dialogues. To help create a history that would extend beyond the content and practice of elites, we needed to hear a much wider range of people tell us about how (or even whether) the past mattered to them.

Because many of us in Indianapolis had contributed to an emerging body of scholarship on popular historical consciousness and historical memory,[4] we were particularly aware of the limitations of this scholarship. It told much more about how the past had been popularly presented than about how it had been popularly understood. Historians had begun to look at the presentations of the past in textbooks, children's books, movies, museums, and magazines, but we often fell back on speculation when it came time to talk about what people made of those sources. We had been influenced by the movement to write "history from the bottom up," but we had done little to uncover popular historical consciousness at its most obvious source—the perspectives of a cross section of Americans.

By the late 1980s, scholars from many fields were decrying this omission and developing theories and methods to study popular reception, reader response, and visitor behavior. The studies in these new fields suggested that Americans engaged historical texts (and all cultural forms) in ways molded by their own personalities, experiences, and traditions and that their engagements were often quite different from what producers of those texts had hoped for.[5]

These overlapping practical, political, and scholarly agendas heated up our conversations in Indianapolis and propelled us forward. As we circulated position papers and met once again, we evolved a concrete plan and sketched out a number of ambitious projects.

One of them was a national survey.

Piloting the Survey, October 1990–January 1992

On October 19, 1990, we walked through the Smithsonian's National Museum of American History, acutely aware of the presence of the past. Time frames shifted and merged; the air seemed saturated with their fluidity. Hundreds of visitors streamed by exhibits of eighteenth-century chairs and nineteenth-century guns and twentieth-century cars, intently scrutinizing these artifacts or chatting with their companions about what they'd observed.

That afternoon four of us (D. D. Hilke, Roy Rosenzweig, Dave Thelen, and Lois Silverman, who had recently come to work at Indiana University on history projects) met in one of the museum's conference rooms to brainstorm about the popular historymakers outside the door. What did they make of what they were seeing? What questions would allow them, and Americans like them, to open up to us—to speak candidly about how they used and understood the past?

D. D. and Lois had both studied the responses of museum visitors; they pointed us in useful directions, helping to hone and refine questions for a survey of popular historymaking. By the end of the meeting, we'd come up with an eclectic list that covered both historical activities (How often do you visit history museums? Have you done any research—formal or informal—into your family's history?) and attitudes (What do you think of when you hear the word history/past/heritage/tradition? Where do you go for trustworthy information on the Civil War, the Vietnam War, and your family's history? Do you use a knowledge of the past in everyday life?). It was time to take the questions on the road for their first tryout.

In January 1991 fifteen graduate students in the Public History Program at Arizona State University joined Dave for a week-long course designed to test and refine the questions we had come up with. For him, Dave recalls, the challenge of turning vision into reality took concrete form in Tempe. The first morning began with some rough questions we hoped might lead people to talk about their uses of the past. Each afternoon students would conduct two- or three-hour-long open-ended interviews with people of all ages and educational backgrounds from the rich ethnic mix of people in Phoenix. (All together, they interviewed 135 people that week.) The next morning the class would compare results, trying to find wording that had elicited the richest responses. At the end of the week, students wrote essays about the questions that had worked best and the themes that had emerged during the interviews.

The conversations reported by these students convinced us that we needed to pay attention to how we introduced our topic. *History* is the word that scholars privilege to describe how they approach the past. But in Phoenix *history* conjured up something done by famous people that others studied in school; respondents said history was formal, analytical, official, or distant. Words like *heritage* and *tradition* conjured up warm and fuzzy feelings but not very rich experience or sharp observation. *The past* was the term that best invited people to talk about family, race, and nation, about where they had come from and what they had learned along the way. *Trust* was the concept that best captured how people viewed sources of information about the past. And the metaphor that best captured what mattered to them in the past could be elicited by the concept of *connection*. To which pasts did they feel most connected?

A few months later, graduate students at the University of Toledo took our questions into the field. These and other trials convinced us that it was time to carry out the project in a systematic, nationwide manner. But that required money—around $200,000. Our best bet, the National Endowment for the Humanities, turned us down initially. In the summer of 1993, we hatched a last-ditch funding scheme that sought money from a consortium of state humanities councils.

As we worked on that complicated series of proposals, we received unexpected good news: we had received a $25,000 chairman's discretionary grant from the Spencer Foundation and the NEH had reconsidered its rejection of our proposal. In the winter of 1993–94, we suddenly had money to carry out the survey we had conceived in Indianapolis three and a half years before.

Listening to Americans Talk About the Past: Bloomington, Indiana, March 1994

On March 7, 1994, we crowded around the desk in the office of John Kennedy, director of the Center for Survey Research at Indiana University, listening to amplified snatches of telephone conversations. With some trepidation, we had just begun a week of what survey professionals call pretesting. Having thought and talked about this survey for almost five years, we were finally getting a chance to try out our questions through random telephone calling. The pretesting might be less politely and more accurately called eavesdropping. John Kennedy would push a button, and his office would be filled with voices from an interview in progress. Next door, in a large room segmented into small cubicles, half a dozen Indiana University students talked on the telephone. As these young interviewers conversed, they stared at computer screens that generated questions for them to ask and space for them to type in answers. The process was mechanistic, but the conversations themselves were intensely human.

Person after person was willing—even eager—to talk. We felt a rush of excitement and relief. Anyone who has been interrupted at dinner by phone calls from salespeople and solicitors (and who in the 1990s has not?) knows the strong temptation to slam down the phone. But that week more than forty people spent half an hour talking with a stranger from Indiana. For many of them, the past was clearly part of the rhythm of everyday life. We listened as a government office clerk told an interviewer: "When you think about the past, you feel comfortable, like you belong, and that is the way I feel with my family."

We had feared that a telephone survey would evoke vague or abstract responses. But people took the past personally: many of their answers were vivid, candid, creative, passionate. We had fretted that people might not reveal their deepest feelings. On the contrary, emotions often ran high in the conversations we overheard. Several people shared intimate details about their past and their present. One woman described being sexually abused. Another started to cry when asked to talk about the person from the past—her mother—who had particularly affected her.

That week we were often moved by the powerful presence of the past. But we had work to do. We were trying to refine the survey—to decide which questions gave us the richest answers, to come up with final wording for those questions. We wanted to feel that we had taken full advantage of every phone call, that the interviewer had given the person at the other end of the telephone line the most compelling invitation to talk.

Every evening at ten or eleven o'clock, when the students had finished their interviews, they met with us to discuss which prompts and follow-ups had worked and which hadn't. We learned, for example, that we got next to nothing when we asked historians' favorite question—Why did you do something?—but we got wonderful answers when we asked how or when or with whom, when we asked respondents to elaborate on an experience. The interviewers were our collaborators. We'd all sit around a table and toss out alternative wordings. (We describe our methods in fuller detail in appendix 1.)

By the time the week was over, we had confirmed some of the hunches we had had at the Chateau Delaware—about both the depth and variety of popular historymaking and the value of surveying a cross section of Americans. We felt exhilarated, but also a little worried. Nothing in our professional training had prepared us to interpret what we were hearing. With the help of these terrific student interviewers, we were getting transcripts of rich conversations, but how would we find general patterns to make sense of these individual encounters?

Interpreting Patterns of Popular Historymaking: Arlington, Virginia, June 1994

On June 5, 1994, the past lay piled up on the porch of Roy's house in Arlington, Virginia. It lay on our laps in thick spiral-bound volumes and printouts of computer-generated tables as we tried to get a hold on what we had learned since March. How *do* Americans understand their pasts?

The data in front of us were somewhat overwhelming. Between March and June, John Kennedy's survey team had called almost all the 808 people who would make up the "national sample." The calls had taken about thirty minutes each. Interviewers had devoted about ten minutes of each call to asking closed-ended (and hence readily quantifiable) questions like: "During the past twelve months, have you read any books about the past?" They used the rest of the time for follow-up questions like "What were the reasons you looked into the history of your family or worked on your family tree?" In an innovation in standard survey practice, the interviewers had been allowed to use humor, interjections, and more probing questions ("Can you recall any of the history books you read?") to get people to open up. Typing as rapidly as possible, the interviewers transcribed respondents' answers. Those transcripts filled the formidable spiral volumes stacked before us.

Although the national survey was not quite done and we were still planning three "minority" samples that would eventually reach more than six hundred African Americans, Mexican Americans, and American Indians, we decided that this was a good moment to compare notes on what we had gathered so far and describe to each other the headlines that leaped out at us from the data.

From the start we saw that the interviews were filled with intimate talk about the past. Families and their stories dominated the numbers as well as the words. For the people we called, the past was pervasive, a natural part of everyday life, central to any effort to live in the present. By June, our quick impressions from listening to the pretest interviews could be confirmed by the statistical evidence. Looking at the tables, we found overwhelming evidence that Americans participated regularly in a wide range of past-related "activities," from taking photos to preserve memories, to watching historical films and television programs, to taking part in groups involved in preserving or presenting the past. We also found that people said they felt particularly connected to the past in a range of different settings, from museums and historical sites to gatherings with their families.

If the past was omnipresent in these interviews, "history" as it is usually defined in textbooks was not. This absence of conventional historical narratives and frameworks surprised us. Roy recalls that he had assumed we would hear people talking about how the defeat of the South in the Civil War, the struggle to settle Montana, or the victory of the auto workers in the 1937 sit-down strikes shaped their identities or their current political views. He had expected to gather stories about how grandparents had faced "No Irish Need Apply" signs or had been barred from neighborhoods because they were Jewish. But these stories weren't there. Neither were the narratives of American national progress—the landing of the Pilgrims, the winning of the American Revolution, the writing of the Constitution, the settling of the West—that have been told for generations in grade school classes and high school textbooks.

Dave remembers our excitement as we discovered that each of us had separately identified the same social traits as consistently important to respondents and others as strangely unimportant—strange because the absent traits were ones that scholars presumed to be essential in determining values and behavior. We had independently concluded that social class, regional identity, political conviction, and ethnicity among whites were much less important in shaping respondents' understanding of the past than race (particularly for blacks and Indians) and religion (particularly for evangelicals of all kinds).

Black respondents started out sounding like white respondents as they talked about the importance of the family. But most of them quickly moved beyond their families to talk of African Americans. In extending out from the family to broader historical narratives, black respondents shared a common set of references—slavery, the civil rights movement, and Martin Luther King Jr.—that we couldn't find in the interviews with European Americans. Black respondents not only constructed group narratives and drew on materials from the conventional canon of American history (like the story of slavery), they also presented stories that fit the standard narrative of group progress. A 42-year-old African American from Milwaukee said he was born in Mississippi, where "you always got to say yes ma'am and no ma'am," but that thanks to the civil rights movement, "we don't have to be on the back of the bus."

Sitting on the porch that afternoon, we got an inkling that Native Americans also tended to move from family stories to group stories and connect to larger national narratives. Asked why he rated the history of his "racial or ethnic group" as most important to him, one man said, "I'm an Indian. We got screwed out of everything that was ours, pushed aside." The national sample—which reached 76 African Americans, 33 Latinos, 20 American Indians, and 13 Asian Americans—did not include enough minority voices for us to be sure about these conclusions. But we couldn't ignore what we saw.

Since the transcripts were reported by case number and not by demographic characteristic, we had to refer to a separate record when we wanted to know about the social characteristics of a respondent. As we read transcripts without reference to demographic features, we thought we could almost always tell whether a respondent was black or Indian. Since we hadn't asked about religion, we both were struck by how important religion was for evangelicals in ordering their perspectives on family and nation alike. We, two secular scholars, were so puzzled by this finding that at dinner that night we kept talking about it with Deborah Kaplan,

Roy's very patient wife, who shared our attempts to understand the implications of a society in which the only things that seemed really to unite some blacks and some whites in their uses of the past were their commitments to family and evangelical religion.

Understanding How Americans Understand the Past, May 1995–June 1997

On May 16, 1995, six years after our meeting in Indianapolis, we sat around another dining-room table, this time at Roy's house in Arlington. We'd moved beyond "data" to our interpretation of the data, organized into rough drafts of chapters. Our training as historians did not equip us to handle the rich and messy responses we heard. (During the nine months of the survey, interviewers spent a thousand hours talking to 1,500 Americans. The transcripts of those conversations totaled about 850,000 words and the statistical summary of the answers that could be tabulated covered several hundred pages.) On many big questions we nodded in agreement, but on many specific issues we argued for different frameworks or interpretations.

We have come to understand that, given the intractable and unfamiliar material we're analyzing, different responses to the same information are inevitable. Our long conversations (and sometimes arguments) have led us to a joint interpretation of most of the data—but not all of it. Over the next two years we returned on many occasions to the interviews themselves, questioning and revising our interpretations. Our different interpretive preferences and styles—for example, Roy's tendency to comment on group distinctions and Dave's tendency to emphasize shared human qualities—inevitably shaped these chapters.

We concluded that we could best make our different emphases into strengths by writing separate chapters, so that each wrote about the material he most cared about. Roy drafted chapters 1, 5, 6, and appendix 1; Dave drafted chapters 2, 3, and 4. And we have written separate statements for the conclusion—not only because we sometimes disagree, but also because individual afterthoughts seem particularly appropriate to a book built on the experience and belief of individual Americans. We thought that this division of labor both solved the problem of getting the data reported in book form and conveyed that we agreed on the large patterns buried in these stories and disagreed more often on the weight or centrality to assign to those patterns.

Chapter 1 ("The Presence of the Past: Patterns of Popular History-making") provides an overview of what we heard from the 1,453 Americans who told us about the ubiquitous presence of the past in their everyday lives. More than one third had investigated the history of their family in the previous year; two fifths had worked on a hobby or collection related to the past. For most of the people who talked with us, the familial and intimate past, along with intimate uses of other pasts, matters most. They prefer the personal and firsthand because they feel at home with that past: they live with it, relive it, interpret and reinterpret it; they use it to define themselves, their place in their families, and their families' place in the world.

In chapter 2 ("Using the Past to Live in the Present") and chapter 3 ("Revisiting the Past to Shape the Future") we listen to Americans talk about their intimate uses of the past—about how they engage the past to live their lives. Individuals turn to their personal experiences to grapple with questions about where they come from and where they are heading, who they are and how they want to be remembered. Again and again, the Americans we interviewed said they want to make a difference, to take responsibility for themselves and others. And so they assemble their experiences into patterns, narratives that allow them to make sense of the past, set priorities, project what might happen next, and try to shape the future. By using these narratives to mark change and continuity, they chart the course of their lives.

The people who told us they want to get as close to experience as possible—to use the past on their own terms—also recognize the need to reach toward people who have lived in other times and other places. Chapter 4 (" 'Experience Is the Best Teacher': Participation, Mediation, Authority, Trust") follows Americans as they move beyond firsthand experience in search of sources with trustworthy perspectives on the past. Many respondents said they fear being manipulated by people who distort the past to meet their own needs—whether commercial greed, political ambition, or cultural prejudice. In their desire to strip away layers of mediation, respondents trust eyewitnesses more than television or movies. They feel connected to the past in museums because authentic artifacts seem to transport them straight back to the times when history was being made. They feel unconnected to the past in history classrooms because they don't recognize themselves in the version of the past presented there. When asked to describe studying history in school, they most often use the words *dull* and *irrelevant*.

The Americans we surveyed do not reject all aspects of national history; they simply reject nation-centered accounts they were forced to memorize and regurgitate in school. Chapter 5 ("Beyond the Intimate Past: Americans and Their Collective Pasts") explores the ways individuals reach into history by reaching out of their own lives. As they build bridges between personal pasts and larger historical stories, Americans—especially white Americans—tend to personalize the public past. African Americans, American Indians, and evangelical Christians sometimes construct a wider set of usable pasts, building ties to their communities as well as their families. Mexican Americans occupy a figurative—as well as geographical—borderland. Like white European Americans, they rely on family pasts as they work through multiple allegiances and sort out fundamental issues of identity, but they also draw on their ethnic and national roots. Unlike white European Americans, Mexican Americans tell a version of the traditional national narrative of progress: they talk about getting closer to owning a piece of the American dream.

In chapter 6 ("History in Black and Red") we hear another version of the national narrative—one with a bitter twist. In this counternarrative, the arrival of Columbus, the westward movement of European settlers, slavery and emancipation, wars and treaties at home and abroad add up to an American history in which blacks and Indians have been oppressed and betrayed by whites, who then depict their actions in movies and textbooks that lie about Indians and exclude African Americans. A collective voice comes easily to these two groups. African Americans speak of "our race," "our roots," "our people"; American Indians speak of "our history," "our heritage," "our culture," "our tribe." The "we" they invoke stands in sharp opposition to the triumphal American "we": the narrative of the American nation-state—the story often told by professional historians—is most alive for those who feel most alienated from it. This departure from conventional wisdom, like so many other insights that emerged during survey interviews, eloquently supports the hunch we discussed that weekend in Indianapolis: professional history practitioners have much to learn from listening to Americans talk about how they use and understand the past.

1. The Presence of the Past:

Patterns of Popular Historymaking

In April 1994, a young interviewer from Indiana University's Center for Survey Research called a 45-year-old man in Memphis, Tennessee. For the next thirty minutes the Memphis man, who owns a consulting company, eagerly described his encounters with the past. In the previous twelve months, he had seen "a lot of TV shows on history," read historical books, and visited at least one history museum. But he did more than passively absorb what others said about the past. One night, while he and his children were watching a TV program about black cowboys, "we got a picture of my great uncle who was a cowboy and, of course, I broke that out and showed it to them." As his children looked at the photograph, he told them what he had learned at family reunions from his mother, grandmother, and great-grandmother about their notable relative.

This man feels passionate about family history; he named "family genealogy" as one of his hobbies. He said he corresponds with a "European American" who has the same last name and wants to work with him on a joint family genealogy. And he makes sure his children get acquainted with his family's "rich history." He took them to a neighboring city so that they could see the headquarters of a major civil rights organization founded by his grandfather and housed in a building bearing his grandfather's name. They also visited another town in Tennessee, where "I can show them buildings that their grandfather had constructed." "In this society many blacks don't know their genealogy," he explained. "Therefore, so many of our kids don't grow up with a sense of self. . . . By knowing my genealogy I have known my family, and that has always made me want to leave something like they have left." He told the interviewer he was organizing his family reunion for the coming year.

In addition to family history, this man from Memphis wanted to learn more about African history. He cited the civil rights movement, in which he participated, as a historical event that affected him greatly and taught him to "treat everybody, regardless of race, creed, or color, equally." When he talked of his "love for history," he did not speak indiscriminately. Gathering with his family or celebrating a holiday made him feel connected to the past, but only certain museums—those devoted to civil rights or the Vietnam War—moved him. And studying history in school did not leave him feeling especially engaged with the past.

This man, an enthusiastic popular historymaker, was far from unique among the 808 randomly selected Americans and the additional 645 African Americans, American Indians, and Mexican Americans who talked with us about the past. A 36-year-old Georgia truck driver had not been to a history museum, read a history book, or done research on his family's history during the previous year. He said that studying history in school, visiting historic sites, reading about history, and watching films about the past meant little to him. But he does have a coin collection that he adds to as he drops in on coin shops along his trucking routes. As a third grader, he found an 1879 silver dollar and "gave it to my daddy." After his father's death, "the coin was given back to me," and he started his own collection. His favorite coins, he said, include buffalo nickels and flying eagle and Indian head pennies, which he may associate with his mother's Cherokee ancestry. This family-based sense of history probably explains why he told our interviewer that he feels strongly connected to the past when getting together with his family or celebrating holidays.

Our respondents found myriad ways to investigate and forge links with their familial or individual pasts. A 33-year-old psychologist from New Jersey frequently adds to a collection of cups and saucers that started when her grandmother tried to assemble a usable set of china in the rubble of Germany after World War II. "I like things with a tradition, a history," the psychologist said. "I like being able to know where my things come from. My husband and I talk about this all the time—we are the carriers of history in my family. We come from now relatively small families, and we carry the history along. Someone has to be the carrier of the history in every family."

Even more frequently, the people we interviewed carried family history along in diaries, family trees, photo albums, and especially in personal memories, which they shared at family reunions, over the dinner table, and around the Christmas tree. A 67-year-old West Virginia man, who grew up in an orphanage, explained the importance of his photo "portfolio full of the kids," which he often looks at. A 20-year-old Oklahoman noted that his family has just been updating "the book that's been passed down from generation to generation" and includes "all our relatives from the 1850s." Embracing new technology, the family has begun to "video my great-great-grandpa" telling his favorite stories, particularly one of a dramatic battle between Indians and settlers. Such attempts to preserve familial history sometimes reflect deeply felt obligations. Investigating his family history, a 30-year-old Long Island truck driver explained, is "a promise I made to my brother before he died; it's always on my mind."

Most Americans pursue the histories of their families; many also explore histories that extend beyond their families. A 73-year-old storekeeper from a small town in central Texas reported that she avidly reads anything she finds on Texas history. She is knowledgeable about local buildings, and says, "I like to pass this down to the younger generation." Another Texas woman in her seventies loves to read "pioneer stories about the settling of the West, the opening up of the Dakota territory, and the Yukon" as well as biographies of Winston Churchill and of Eleanor Roosevelt, whom she admires as a "forerunner . . . who pushed for women's equality."

Hobbyists ardently track the past beyond their family circles. A 20-year-old social work student from a medium-sized city in Oklahoma spends two hours a day working with an African dance group. Dance gives her a "better sense of where I come from." In high school, she complained, "they didn't teach anything" about African American or African culture. Her dancing and her study of the "history behind it" not only give her a sense of "something that was done by my ancestors" but also "can contribute to the African American community." Her interests in African and African American history go beyond dance, inflecting her reading (shortly before talking with us, she'd finished Chinua Achebe's *Things Fall Apart*) and her travel (she said she was planning a trip to Africa and had journeyed to Atlanta to visit Martin Luther King Jr.'s home).

A young mother from Kentucky feels a passionate commitment to the past that has led her in a very different direction. Like the Oklahoma student, she criticized the history she had been taught in high school but said she found deep meaning instead in Civil War reenactments: "I think it's important for people to remember to never forget. . . . We are from the South, and it is important to be proud of our history even if the people from the North think so or not." This Kentucky woman uses the past to think about the present, including current political issues like the display of the Confederate flag. She believes that "our history" is being stolen by the NAACP, which is trying to "take away our right to display our flag," as well as by the Klan and the skinheads who want to appropriate the Confederate flag "as a symbol of hatred." Americans, she said, fought the war over "states' rights" rather than slavery: "Many, many, many" of "our ancestors who fought in the Civil War . . . did not even own slaves." Civil War reenactment "preserv[es] our right to remember our history the way we want to do it . . . instead of the way some of the history books have portrayed it."

Americans, as these sketches show, make the past part of their everyday routines and turn to it as a way of grappling with profound questions about how to live. The people who talked with us did not view the past as distant, abstract, or insignificant. Quite the contrary: through their understanding of the past, this cross section of Americans addressed questions about relationships, identity, immortality, and agency. They also used the past for the business of everyday life—maintaining family and community ties and trying to deal with family health problems. For the young mother from Kentucky, learning about ancestors who fought in the Civil War helped her understand "where I come from." For the man from Memphis, the civil rights movement taught a basic moral lesson about racial equality. For the New Jersey psychologist and her husband, collecting old china perpetuated the memory of their family and themselves to pass down to future generations. For the Oklahoma student, hearing about the past from her mother and grandmother "makes me feel I have a lot of responsibility for what goes on in the world" and "helps me realize the things I need to do in the future."

This chapter provides an overview of what Americans told us about popular historymaking—especially about more formal activities, from watching historical films to investigating family history. The overview illuminates a conclusion that underlies the entire book: people pursue the past actively and make it part of everyday life. The stories of the 1,453 individual Americans we called and the statistical summaries of their responses impress us with the *presence* of the past—its ubiquity and its connection to current-day concerns—rather than its frequently bemoaned absence.

How, When, and Why Americans Pursue the Past: A Statistical Overview

The pundits who describe Americans as uninterested in history don't seem to be talking about the people we surveyed. Asked whether they had participated in past-related activities during the previous year, more than half said that they had looked at photos with family and friends, taken photos or videos to preserve memories, watched movies or TV programs about the past, attended a reunion, visited a history museum, or read a history book. Between one and two fifths told us that they had joined a historical group, written in a journal or diary, investigated their family's history, or participated in a hobby or worked on a collection related to the past (see table 1.1). Almost no one (only 7 of the 808 people interviewed in our national sample) reported that they did *none* of the ten activities we asked about.[1]

TABLE 1.1

Percentage of Americans surveyed who have done the following in the past 12 months:

Looked at photographs with family or friends	91%
Taken photographs or videos to preserve memories	83
Watched any movies or television programs about the past	81
Attended a family reunion or a reunion of some other group of people with whom you have a shared experience	64
Visited any history museums or historic sites	57
Read any books about the past	53
Participated in any hobbies or worked on any collections related to the past	39
Looked into the history of your family or worked on your family tree	36
Written in a journal or diary	29
Participated in a group devoted to studying, preserving, or presenting the past	20

Of course, these numbers don't tell the whole story. One of the seven people who answered "no" to all our questions about history-related activities, for example, was an 82-year-old widow in Texas who reported that she "never goes out now" except to bowl with other senior citizens on Wednesday afternoons. But she still spent much of her time thinking about the past. "I remember those people that lived around me," she explained to a youthful interviewer. "They were so nice, the people . . . around where I live."

To find out more than the simple frequency of activities, we asked our respondents to use a 10-point scale to describe the intensity of their engagement with the past. Most had no trouble assigning a number between 1 and 10 to describe how "connected to the past" they felt when they celebrated holidays, gathered with their families, studied history in school, read history books, visited history museums and historic sites, and watched historical films and television programs (see table 1.2). If we decide that a choice of 8, 9, or 10 indicates a close association with the past, then more than half our respondents felt very strongly connected to the past on holidays, at family gatherings, and in museums.

TABLE 1.2

How connected to the past do you feel (1-10 scale)?

		Percent choosing	
	Mean	8-10	1-3
Gathering with your family	7.9	67.7%	6.7%
Visiting a history museum or historic site	7.3	56.0	8.6
Celebrating a holiday	7.0	52.7	13.8
Reading a book about the past	6.5	39.5	12.0
Watching a movie or television program about the past	6.0	27.4	14.0
Studying history in school	5.7	27.8	20.8

A 32-year-old physical therapist reported feeling most connected to the past in the three contexts most often given by our respondents. Asked to explain why he felt connected to the past at holiday celebrations, he answered, "Usually when you celebrate holidays, you have your ancestors there—your grandmothers and great-grandmothers. They're bringing a part of their traditions and so forth into the celebration. " For him, all family events evoked the past: "Because when you gather with your family, everyone has stories about the way things used to be. It's always story time. We don't gather for that particular purpose, but we always end up telling stories, and it inevitably ends up being about what life was like when they were kids."

Although respondents described the past as being with them in many settings, they shared the sense that the familial and intimate past, along with intimate uses of other pasts, mattered most. More than two thirds said that they felt very strongly connected to the past when gathering with their families; more than half said the same about visiting museums and historic sites and celebrating holidays—activities they usually did with family members.[2] Only 16 people in the national sample gave gathering with their family the lowest possible "connectedness" score of 1.

Respondents felt most unconnected to the past when they encountered it in books, movies, or classrooms. They felt most connected when they encountered the past with the people who mattered the most to them, and they often pursued the past in ways that drew in family and friends. Five sixths of those surveyed took pictures to preserve memories of their experiences; more than nine tenths looked at photographs with family and friends; more than one third worked on their family trees or investigated the history of their families; almost two thirds attended reunions—three quarters of them family reunions.[3] More than half of the respondents who pursued hobbies or collections related to the past said that family members had initially interested them in that hobby or that the hobby preserved a family tradition. Typically, a 25-year-old student from Massachusetts described refinishing a small chest and dollhouse from her grandmother that she wants "to pass down as an heirloom . . . if I have a daughter someday."

Respondents put great trust in relatives. Asked to rank the trustworthiness of sources for information about the past, respondents gave a mean score of 8.0 to "personal accounts from your grandparents or other relatives"—compared, for example, to a 5.0 for movies and television programs. More than two thirds gave grandparents a rating of 8, 9, or 10; only about one third gave high school teachers such a high ranking (see table 1.3). Forty-six people (out of 808 in our national survey) described movies and television as "not at all" trustworthy (by giving them a score of 1); only seven said the same about accounts from grandparents and other relatives. People who talked with us preferred the personal and the firsthand, with

TABLE 1.3

Trustworthiness of Sources on 10-point scale:

	Mean	Percent choosing	
		8-10	1-3
Museums	8.4	79.9%	1.3%
Personal accounts from grandparents or other relatives	8.0	68.9	2.4
Conversation with someone who was there (witness)	7.8	64.4	2.8
College history professors	7.3	54.3	5.2
High school teachers	6.6	35.5	8.8
Nonfiction books	6.4	32.1	9.1
Movies and television programs	5.0	11.0	22.3

one exception: respondents ranked history museums even higher than personal accounts from relatives. But some of the reasoning behind their choices—museums appeared to contain authentic objects from the past, people visited museums with other family members—confirmed the same desire for unmediated experience, as we'll see in chapter 4.

Whatever questions we asked, respondents emphasized the importance they attached to the intimate past and intimate uses of the past. Asked to "name a person, either a historic figure or someone from your personal past, who has particularly affected you," 52 percent named family members—29 percent parents, 14 percent grandparents, 9 percent other family members—while 36 percent named public or historical figures. Reminded that the past includes "everything from the very recent past to the very distant past, from your personal and family past to the past of the United States and other nations," respondents were asked, "What event or period in the past has most affected you?" Again, the largest number (nearly two fifths) mentioned a purely personal event like the birth, death, marriage, or divorce of a loved one.

For many respondents the line blurred between "personal" and "national" pasts. Some turned national events into settings for personal stories. For example, more than a tenth reported a public event in which they participated (most often by fighting in a war); more than a quarter chose a public event that had personal significance. Rather than abstractly discussing the significance of World War II or the assassination of John F. Kennedy, they talked about how such an event had figured in their personal development or the setting in which they heard about it. Only one in five chose a public event without also indicating some personal association with that event.

We tried to get at how people thought about the past when we asked which past was most important to them: that of their family, their ethnic or racial group, their community, or the United States. Sixty-six percent named the past of their family. Twenty-two percent named the United States, 8 percent chose their racial or ethnic group, and 4 percent chose their community. Ethnic and racial groups varied in how they responded to this question, as we'll see in chapter 5. But every subgroup of the population—men and women; young and old; rich and poor; white, black, and Indian—listed family history first. To put the statistical findings of our study in a single sentence: Almost every American deeply engages the past, and the past that engages them most deeply is that of their family.

How Americans Create Their Own History

To get a fuller sense of how Americans use the past in their everyday lives, we need to look more closely at the ten past-related activities asked about. On the surface we might distinguish between the four activities that involve interpreting historical information constructed by others (watching films, reading books, visiting museums, looking at photos) and the six that require people to construct, record, or conserve their own version of the past (taking photos, sharing experiences at a reunion, investigating family history, working on hobbies or collections, writing in a journal or diary, taking part in a group interested in the past). But this distinction between "reading" and "writing" the past doesn't always hold. A college student dragged to a family reunion where he half-listens to relatives talk about experiences he views as distant and unimportant is passively consuming history constructed by others. A woman who visits a museum with her children and enthusiastically tells them about connections to their family is actively interpreting and constructing her own historical narrative.

Many respondents told us, for example, about films and books that sparked reminiscences or family discussions. A 39-year-old Alabama woman fondly recalled films on John and Jacqueline Kennedy because "when I see something like that it makes me relate to my childhood, what age I was, what I was doing at that time, what grade I was in, things that I liked to do at that time. I guess it brings back a lot of memories of being in the early sixties." A 46-year-old Arizona woman liked books on the Civil War because her "great-great-great-grandfather was a scoundrel" who was represented by Abraham Lincoln in "the first case he ever lost back in Illinois." A 30-year-old custodian from California remembered reading a biography of Martin Luther King Jr. because his mother had told him about living in the civil rights era "and the things [King] went through when she was growing up." A 27-year-old Rochester glass coater said family reunions linked him to the past because his relatives described the days when his southern sharecropper ancestors picked okra. He noted that the television series *Roots* made him feel equally connected to the past: "There are some things . . . depicted in the movie that my parents and grandparents have gone through—just working in the field most of their life."

If people engage, discuss, use, and interpret the past while watching movies and reading books, they grapple even more directly with the past when they investigate family history or do other things that require (rather than just permit) them to confront memories and artifacts. To borrow a set of categories familiar to professional historians, we can say that millions of Americans regularly document, preserve, research, narrate, discuss, and study the past.

The largest number of respondents talked about documenting the past. Almost one third wrote in diaries or journals. More than four fifths documented historical memories by taking photos or videos, and many shot their photos with a clear archival purpose. "A photograph helps stimulate the memory," said an Albuquerque contractor; it's also something "to show to other people and so that my son can see things that he won't remember and he'll be able to . . . know about us and our lives." Recalling a picture he took of his son wearing a towel "as though it were Batman's cape," the man explained, "he was in this one moment or one stage where Batman means everything to him and I wanted to be able to remember him. . . . It's hard to remember things. . . . If I don't write them down or take pictures, they fly out of my memory."

Many people who keep diaries and journals are attempting to preserve a family record for posterity. A 51-year-old Louisiana nurse said her diary contained "just everyday things—family get-togethers, things that happened at work, the weather . . . the birth of a niece, visiting with a brother from out of town . . . a wedding in the family." "I've done that for ever since I can remember," she explained. "As the years pass, you forget everyday events, but if you write them down you can recall them for yourself and you'll be able to pass this information down to your kids, nieces, and nephews."

Respondents not only discussed this impulse to document the past, they also talked about their efforts to preserve pieces of it. They said they turned photo albums and diaries into treasured artifacts passed from one generation to the next. A 30-year-old South Dakota woman described the "family book" and "family tree" that she was preparing "for my kids." One contained "pictures and paragraphs" of family members going back to the "third generation of grandparents"; the other compiled "stories" about what relatives "were like." Popular preservationists also collect objects that link them or their children to the past. A 42-year-old floral designer from Maryland, raised by her grandparents, explained that she collects kitchen items from the 1940s and 1950s because "it just brings back childhood memories. . . . They were things that my grandmother had too." A retired Missouri woman had recently "dug up some quilts" that belonged to her mother, who "was a very pioneer lady." She told the youthful questioner that she planned to turn them into bedspreads for her "boys" as "a memento from their grandmother."

Collections and hobbies often connect different generations. Many respondents talked about relatives who inspired them—a grandmother who started a South Carolina man on collecting 1930s glassware; another grandmother who started an Illinois woman on collecting old teapots; an uncle who started a Georgia man on collecting trains; a grandfather who started a New York man on collecting coins. A remarkable 39 percent of our respondents worked on a hobby or collection related to the past.

This energetic preservation of the past often requires research. The South Dakota woman who was assembling a "family book" questions relatives about "what they did and when they came over from different countries" and asks them to identify and talk about people in old photos she has gathered. Other respondents, particularly genealogists, told us they spend years searching through courthouses, cemeteries, microfilms, old newspapers, birth and death records, wills, and Civil War pension files. One third of the Americans we interviewed were involved in tracing their family's history—which suggests that more historical research is done on families in this country than on any other subject.

After researching and preserving the past, popular historymakers often create narratives in the form of photo albums, family trees, and family heirlooms. Even more often, they craft oral narratives that they pass on in casual dinner conversations, while watching television, or at reunions, family gatherings, and holiday celebrations. When we asked people why they felt connected to the past at family gatherings, they immediately (and often in great detail) described stories shared on such occasions—narratives of adversity, struggle, and accomplishment or narratives of adventure, nostalgia, and humor. A 47-year-old New Jersey police officer recounted "just reminiscing about the ol' days, talking about fathers and grandfathers and how it was way back when. . . . How you made the most out of very little."

Probably less than 10 percent of our respondents formally studied the past after they left school. One fifth of them belonged to groups related to the past, but fewer than half of these groups study, rather than preserve or present, the past. Evangelical Christians, African Americans, and American Indians, however, showed more interest in formally studying the past. Evangelical Christians said Bible study groups allowed them to examine the past and "the way [it] relates to now," in the words of a 32-year-old Kentucky woman. Several black Americans described informal

African American history study groups. A 45-year-old counselor from Cleveland explained that her group "doesn't necessarily have a name" but that it brings together people who "are studying African American history" to find out "the validity of the information we have been given." "For my race of people," she continued, "knowledge" is "the only [thing] that can turn [us] around." One quarter of the Sioux we interviewed (versus one fifth of the overall national sample) participated in groups that study, preserve, or present the past; almost all those groups—the Wounded Knee Pine Ridge Survivors Association, Lakota culture classes, and the Big Foot and Memorial Riders, for example—focus on Indian culture. Through the Grey Eagles Society, a member explained, "elderly tribal members . . . tell about history" and "try to preserve the culture."

Respondents described their activities but didn't necessarily say which of them required the most commitment, energy, and passion. They gave us clues, however, when they talked about a pursuit without any prompting. In our survey, the interviewers took down spontaneous comments. Activities that involved engaging and interpreting historical information constructed by others ("reading the past") provoked relatively few and relatively brief spontaneous comments; activities that required people to construct, record, or conserve their own history ("writing the past") evoked considerably more—almost twice as many—and considerably longer spontaneous responses, even though fewer people took part in those activities. Of the 653 people who reported watching a historical film or television program, only 11 wanted to immediately discuss what they had seen. Although just 290 reported looking into the history of their family, 61 quickly volunteered comments about their historical investigations. Before our interviewer asked about investigating family history, a 71-year-old Philadelphia woman said that she organized annual family reunions, researched the history of her family, and encouraged younger family members to carry the story farther back into the nineteenth century.[4]

Both broad social patterns and particular family histories suggest why some people passionately recover their family histories while others fanatically preserve objects like old kitchen utensils and still others avidly document the past through photos or diaries. Women and men, for example, tend to select different hobbies and collections—quilts and china versus trains and tools. And gifts from grandparents often launch lifelong collections. But some preferences in historical pursuits—what could be called "historical tastes"—are as difficult to explain as tastes in music, food, and clothes.

Such tastes emerged over and over in our interviews. "I like biographies," noted a Danville, Illinois, woman. An Indiana woman explained her fondness for westerns: "I just like the idea that they had to ride horses and go bareback and they had to hunt for deer and stuff." A 58-year-old Phoenix woman said, "I like tools, wooden spoons, things that can be used day-to-day" as well as "old cookbooks." Other respondents embraced general categories of historical activities. "I always loved to hear my mother tell me stories about the past," said a northern Virginia woman. "I'm a picture nut," reported a 56-year-old Illinois woman who described her particular interest in "family pictures." "My husband loves museums and history," explained a 30-year-old woman from Raleigh, North Carolina. "I like the old cemeteries," noted an Ohio woman, "because I work in a new cemetery and they have so many restrictions. . . . The old cemeteries don't have those restrictions, they have a lot of history in them. The old cemeteries have so many different sizes and types of stones, and you're not going to see that in these new cemeteries." The pursuit of the past is a national preoccupation, it seems, but one with many variations.

Who Pursues the Past?

Social and demographic variables sometimes predict behavior: in general, wealthy people play golf and working-class people go bowling; women sew and men build shelves. But not always. We spent considerable time with computers and statistical programs looking for variations in patterns of responses based on age, income, education, race, and gender. What we learned can be summarized very simply: participation in historical activities is not for the most part tied to particular social groups or backgrounds.[5]

Black and white Americans, for example, participate in pretty much the same set of historical activities over the course of a year.[6] So do Sioux and Mexican Americans.[7] These broad similarities should not mislead us into thinking that Mexican Americans, American Indians, and African Americans stand in precisely the same relationship to the past as white European Americans. African Americans and American Indians, for example, offered somewhat different answers from white Americans to our questions about connectedness to the past and trust of historical authorities. (See tables 2 and 3 in appendix 2.) In general, blacks and Indians seem more likely to distrust mainstream sources of historical authority. African Americans, for instance, trust historical information from schoolteachers and books less than white European Americans do. Moreover, although nonwhites center history on their families and pursue pretty much the same set of activities as whites, they take different meanings away from those experiences, as chapter 6 discusses in detail.

While sociodemographic variables like race, age, and income do not fundamentally explain whether people participate in historical activities, education and gender do have some effect on patterns of participation. For example, people with more education more often read historical books, write in journals and diaries, visit history museums, watch history films, and participate in historical groups.[8] Almost two thirds of the college graduates we interviewed had read a book about the past during the previous year, compared to fewer than one third of the people who had not graduated high school; more than one third of the college graduates had written in a journal or diary, compared to one sixth of the people who hadn't gone beyond high school. Perhaps not surprisingly, education can give people tools that make it easier to participate in historical activities and deal with institutions (like museums) or cultural objects (like books) that assume a certain amount of literacy and historical knowledge.

At the same time, the differences in levels of participation are often relatively small—35 percent of those with high school education or less participate in hobbies or collections related to the past, compared to 41 percent of those with a college degree. And Americans who don't have college degrees told us that they feel just as connected to the past as those with more education. Demographic variables explain even less about a sense of connectedness to the past than about the level of participation in historical activities.[9]

Our survey offers little support for the claim that an interest in the past or in formal history is the property of "elites." Income, for example, significantly affects participation in only one activity: taking photographs or videos, which requires money to purchase the equipment (see table 21, appendix 2). And even when education sharply inflects the pursuit of a particular activity, many people with limited education still participate. More than twice as many college graduates as non–high school graduates had read a history book or visited a history museum or historic site in the past year. Yet about one third of those without a high school degree had done both.

The possible associations between gender and historymaking present some of the most exciting themes for speculation and further research. Women reported higher levels of participation in seven of the ten histori-

cal activities we asked about; they also told us they felt more connected to
the past in two of the six settings we described. More women than men
took photos (84 percent of women compared with 82 percent of men),
wrote in journals (34 percent compared with 24 percent), attended family
reunions (68 percent compared with 59 percent), investigated their family's past (42 percent compared with 29 percent), and participated in
groups devoted to studying, preserving, or presenting the past (22 percent
compared with 18 percent). More women than men said they felt strongly
connected to the past at holiday celebrations (with a mean score of 7.6 for
women and 6.3 for men) and family gatherings (a mean score of 8.3 for
women and 7.4 for men).[10]

For women, as for men, the intimate and familial past matters most, but
for women it is even *more* important. When we asked people which of four
different "areas of the past"—that of your family, your racial or ethnic
group, the community in which you now live, or the United States—is
"most important to you," 73 percent of the women selected family history,
compared to 58 percent of the men. When we asked about a person from
the past who'd had an important effect on them, two fifths of male and
three fifths of female respondents chose a family member.[11] And women
preferred activities—investigating the lives of ancestors, writing in journals and diaries, attending reunions—concerned with family history.

In their answers to follow-up questions too, some women illustrated
how they pursued the past to maintain family ties or continuity. Not only
did more women than men report keeping journals, they apparently kept
them for different reasons. Of the twenty respondents who described a
diary or journal as a permanent family record, sixteen were women.[12]
Asked what sorts of things she wrote in her journal or diary, a female executive from Cleveland at first diminished the project: "To be honest with
you, they were just day-to-day things about interactions with family." But
then she added that she thought it gave her a "touch of immortality" to
leave a document in which "my children and grandchildren will be able to
read what I was thinking on that day."

An 80-year-old widow noted that her work on family history had been
sparked by her granddaughter: gathering "all the information before I
pass on" is "important so my granddaughter will know what has happened in the family on my side because her mother has also passed away
and I'm the only one left on my side." A 63-year-old retired woman from
Missouri said that her mother "was working on" a family history when
"she passed away last August." After some of the respondent's children

and cousins began asking questions about the family, she "took over what [my mother] had been doing." A 58-year-old manufacturer's representative from New York explained that she doesn't "make a study of" family history, but relatives always turn to her for information because "my mother was the record keeper and I have all her books." Family members, our respondents told us, often turn to women, especially older women, for information about the family's past. Of eighteen people who said that requests from other relatives sparked their investigations of family history, fourteen were women—all but two of them more than fifty years old.[13]

Though just as many men as women had hobbies or collections related to the past, women undertook them for quite distinct reasons. Thirty-six respondents described their hobbies or collections as ways to maintain family ties or traditions; thirty of them were women.[14] A Tampa woman reported that her husband collects fishing rods from the early 1900s, while she restores "granny's quilt" from the 1880s. "I want to give it to my daughter one day," she explained. A young mother in Baton Rouge uses her skill at calligraphy to create a "time capsule book" that she will give to her daughter when she turns sixteen.

Both men and women care about the past. Most of the men we interviewed care passionately about family history and feel strongly connected to the past at family gatherings. But the words *past* and *history* (understood as the world of presidents and treaties) may have gendered associations in American society. Men occupy most seats around Civil War roundtables, for example, and three times as many men as women join the History Book Club, which emphasizes military and political history.[15] By contrast, many Americans see the job of maintaining a sense of continuity with the past broadly defined as part of "women's work" within the family. Women often take responsibility for compiling and maintaining family stories and records; they feel comfortable in the more expansive, yet intimate, realm of the past.

But the statistical evidence is not clear cut and some of it can be used to point up other patterns. Men, for example, were more likely than women (by a 40 to 35 percent margin) to select personal instead of public events as the ones most important to them. Men and women felt equally disconnected from the past when they studied history in school. Both men and women were more likely to participate in activities to sustain their families than in more public and formal activities, more likely to attend a family reunion than to read a book about the past, and more likely to investigate the history of their families than to take part in a group devoted to studying or preserving the past. Both men and women felt more connected to the past when they gathered with their families than in any other setting. Chapters 2 and 3 explore how and why both men and women found intimate uses of personal pasts more meaningful than formal uses of national pasts.

When and How Americans Engage the Past: Formal and Informal, Unplanned and Passionate Encounters with the Past

Many of the Americans we interviewed "read" accounts of the past—especially in books or films—relatively casually. Although more than four fifths of them had seen a historical film or television program in the past year and more than half had read a history book, few had much to say about them. "I must have read something—right offhand I can't think of what it was," a Minnesota woman remarked. Indeed, only one third of the respondents mentioned specific film titles or TV shows, even when prompted to describe the "kinds of movies or television programs about the past you like."[16] These vague comments contrast sharply with their more detailed commentary on other historical activities. Not surprisingly, perhaps, films and books were two of the three experiences that summoned up the least sense of connection to the past.

The only activity that elicited even less of a sense of connection was the one most widely shared: studying history in school. (For a fuller description of these responses, see chapter 4.) While respondents spoke of films and books with indifference, they described studying history in vividly negative terms. When we asked some of them "to pick one word or phrase to describe your experiences with history classes in elementary or high school," almost three fifths chose such words as "irrelevant," "incomplete," "dry," or, most commonly, "boring." In the entire study, respondents almost never described encounters with the past as boring—except when they talked about school. "I hated it," a 60-year-old Yonkers, New York woman said when we asked why she had given studying history her lowest possible score on the connectedness scale.

Obviously, respondents didn't view their most pervasive and formal encounters with the past as the most profound. They often reserved their enthusiasm for unplanned or incidental encounters with the past. Most museum visits, by the evidence of this survey, occur during trips undertaken with some other goal—usually a vacation—in view. "We were on vacation . . . to Sea World and came back through Canton, Ohio, and stopped by the McKinley museum," explained a school custodian from a medium-sized city in Ohio. "I was passing through the town, Carthage, Missouri," recalled a home health aide who lived near Joplin, Missouri. "It was a museum of guns, of Winchester guns and the history of something . . . old guns, stuff from the world war. My husband wanted to go through it; so we did."[17]

Given these often incidental circumstances, it comes as a surprise to learn that visits to museums and historic sites made respondents feel extremely connected to the past. Part of the reason, it seems, is that Americans believe they uncover "real" or "true" history at museums and historic sites. Some sense of the power of encountering a "piece of the true cross"[18] can be glimpsed in the story of a Long Island truck driver who felt more connected to the past when visiting a historic site than when gathering with his family or watching a movie: "I was with a friend—we were stationed in Germany ten or fifteen years ago—and he had a very good knowledge of Roman history. We went out looking for old Roman walls. I figured they were going to be like brick and we wouldn't find them till I fell off them. They were hills! They were thirty feet high, and I suddenly realized they were these old defensive works still standing there after a thousand years." Museums and historic sites also worked a powerful magic because they evoked immediate personal and familial connections. Asked why she had recently visited the Cahokia Indian mounds near East St. Louis, an Indiana woman said, "I wanted my little girl to see something . . . I've seen when I was little."

For this woman and many other respondents, visits to historic sites and museums sparked an associative process of recalling and reminiscing about the past that connected them to their own history. Their visits—far from a passive viewing of a version of the past arranged by a museum professional—became a joint venture of constructing their own histories either mentally or in conversation with their friends and kin. Although respondents said movies and books occasionally stimulated associative reminiscing, they often portrayed museum visits—made in small groups, generally with members of their immediate family—as collective and collaborative.

Looking at old photos also inspired collective reminiscing. When we asked people the reasons or occasions for looking at photographs with family or friends, they described how holidays, family gatherings, birthdays, and funerals led to creating collaborative narratives about the past.

"On holidays," reported a young Minneapolis housewife, "you just all get together and start talking about what happened, a specific incident usually, and somebody says 'let me go get the album.'"

Family gatherings and reunions may not start out as deliberate efforts to investigate or examine the past, but they often turn into the equivalent of historical seminars. A 35-year-old female dispatcher from Tennessee described how the past saturates a setting not normally labeled "historical": "You are with family and friends and there is a lot of remembering. . . . The older people get together and talk about the past and they are just remembering things you did when you were a child. . . . There will be a lot of things that you have not talked about in a long time, that you do not necessarily have the time to think about in everyday life. Being with family, somebody will bring up something that leads to something else, and then it starts a conversation about something that happened twenty years ago."

We tried the patience of our interviewees by asking them to explain why family gatherings made them feel so connected to the past, since the answer seemed evident to them. A 44-year-old painter from a dairy-processing town in central Wisconsin explained why he felt more connected to the past in family gatherings than in any other setting: "These are people you have a lot in common with. I'm sure you never get together without bringing up the past; it's something that always pops up. It's your own personal past that you're talking about versus going to a museum, something more impersonal, not connected to you. Any time you gather for a wedding or a funeral—essentially the whole family is present—you bring up deceased relatives or probably happy occasions when we were all children; you remember something fond."

Exploring family history, like visiting a museum, could be casual. "I've discussed it, but I haven't really gone into detail," a Pennsylvania nurse explained somewhat apologetically. An Albuquerque man ascribed his interest in family history to "curiosity" and noted that he hadn't written anything down or looked at a genealogy and that his research consisted of "discussions I have with my family when I'm around them." But after a pause, he explained some deeper motivations: he wanted "to learn who my ancestors were because I feel as though I am a derivative of them and to find out a little more about who I am."

Respondents described how their investigations of history sometimes emerged serendipitously out of family gatherings; at other times they proceeded quite deliberately. Asked why she had looked into her family's past, a Mexican immigrant replied, "We were trying to make a booklet on our history to distribute to all the [150] members of the family" at the annual reunion. "I called some relatives and we decided it was time to make a family tree." Other respondents—particularly those few who described themselves as genealogists—turned investigating family history into a passionate and systematic pursuit. An Indiana factory worker reported that he had used local and national records as well as conversations with his grandparents to trace his family back to Scotland.

Hundreds of thousands of Americans who do not earn their living as history professionals dedicate considerable time, money, and even love to historical pursuits. They volunteer at local historical organizations, lead tours of historic houses, don uniforms for battle reenactments, repair old locomotives for the railway history society, subscribe to *American Heritage* and *American History Illustrated*, maintain the archives for their trade union or church, assemble libraries from the History Book Club, construct family genealogies, restore old houses, devise and play World War II board games, collect early twentieth-century circus memorabilia, and lobby to preserve art deco movie houses. These amateur historians might be considered a third group, distinct from the history professionals who pursue the past for a living and the popular historymakers who made up the bulk of our study.

We encountered many amateur historians. One fifth of those we interviewed reported that they took part in a group that studies, preserves, or presents the past. And two fifths said that they had a hobby or collection related to the past. Many more people watch movies or look at old photos, but hobbyists, collectors, and group members tend to devote considerably more time. (A railroad conductor from an Ohio manufacturing city reported that he spent about a hundred hours per year on his hobby of rebuilding antique farm machinery.) Projecting these results nationally shows that startlingly large numbers of people—76 million—undertake hobbies and collections related to the past.[19] Even if we decided that only one quarter of the people who said they had worked on a hobby or collection in the previous year were moderately serious about these pursuits, our survey would suggest that 20 million Americans pursue historical hobbies and collections.

Similar projections would put millions of Americans in past-related organizations. To be sure, many respondents defined past-connected groups more broadly than professional historians might: they frequently cited Bible study groups and environmental organizations (since they preserved the past of nature) along with more conventional historical and genealogical societies and hobbyist groups—from the Daughters of the American Revolution to the National Antique Fire Truck Association and the Plymouth Genealogical Society.[20]

These groups include some people—amateur historians—who give much of their free time to historical pursuits. We talked with a retired electrical engineer who had spent six years as a director and three years as president of his local historical society; he also volunteered at a nearby historical museum, working on "some antique horological materials . . . cataloging, repairing, and preparing exhibits." He attributed his original enthusiasm for old timepieces to a pocket watch that his grandfather had given him; then his annoyance at a local watchmaker led him to sign up for an evening course in watch repair. "As is my usual practice," he explained, "I got out lists of books on the subject . . . starting with my interest as a mechanic—that is, my interest in small mechanisms. It increased to an interest in the history of timepieces, both the technology, the philosophy, the social aspects, and so on. And so I became a member of the National Association of Watch and Clock Collectors, and it is through the local chapter that we're doing this work at the museum."

Hobbyists' passions are extraordinarily eclectic. We talked to collectors of old barn paintings, Christian art, needlework, quilts, stamps, coins, Australian money, World War II relics, photos, beer mirrors, tractors, motorcycles, cars, liberty bells, fire equipment, books, trains, china, watches, dolls, clocks, Victorian wreaths, arrowheads, folk art, carpentry tools, old newspaper clippings, early American glass, railroad schedules, bird plates, toby jugs, Indian artifacts, comic cards, old LPs, baseball cards, and Pete Rose items. We also encountered a smaller, but equally diverse, group of people who construct or reconstruct items with historic associations: old tractors and antique cars; needlework and dolls; wooden golf clubs and wooden airplanes; Native American baskets, beadwork, and ceramic sculptures.

These diverse collections and hobbies often inspired great dedication. No other questions (except perhaps those about family gatherings) received such lengthy answers and revealed such close links between historical pursuits and everyday life. A 38-year-old Oklahoma man, who collects motorcycles, could have been speaking for many when he answered our question about "some of the reasons" for his collection by saying: "It is my life." A number of hobbyists and genealogists were so avid in their pursuit of the past that our phone call interrupted them in what seems to be a constant preoccupation. A Florida man, asked about his interest in family history, replied: "Right now in front of me, I'm working on the saga of my great-uncle—he was in Corregidor Island in the Philippines. . . . I've got about 325 pages written about his experiences." When we asked another man about his hobbies and collections, he said: "I'm downstairs polishing antique fire extinguishers for a collection."[21]

Although some hobbyists operate alone, they often create nurturing subcommunities. An Ohio junior high school teacher who collects folk art (and whose husband collects Civil War objects) noted that they meet regularly with other local antique dealers and collectors. "It's a hobby," she observes, "but it's also like a counterculture of people . . . a different breed of people. It's just a very comfortable group of people. You never feel like you don't belong there."

Americans feel at home with the past; day to day, hour to hour, the past is present in their lives. Encountering the past, examining it, interpreting it, living and reliving it, they root themselves in families—biological or constructed—and root their families in the world. Maybe we shouldn't have been surprised that the Americans we called welcomed us so graciously into their lives, shared their memories and their passions, allowed us to be part of their present and their past—allowed us, in a sense, to join the family. Their openness made our survey an arena for cultural conversation, the sort of joint venture they told us they enjoyed. Respondents spent an average of thirty-nine minutes—thirty minutes in the national sample and fifty-one minutes in the minority sample—conversing with people they didn't know.[22] Twenty-one people stayed on the phone for more than two hours; hundreds more took out substantial time to speak with a stranger about their intimate uses of the past. How and why these uses of the past figured so strongly in the everyday lives of Americans is the subject of the next two chapters.

2. Using the Past to Live in the Present:

Relationships, Identity, Immortality

The Americans we talked with engaged the past to live their lives. As they thought about the kinds of people they wanted to be and the futures they wanted to carve for themselves, they turned to the past to frame their quests. In describing how intimate uses of the past mattered so much in every aspect of their lives, our respondents seemed to circle back to some basic understandings of "experience" as starting assumptions for their reflections.

A 50-year-old African American high school counselor from Alabama spoke for many of the people we interviewed when he described how a focus on experience grounded his reflections on the past:

> If you didn't live through certain things, you just go by what people say, what history says. If they lived through it they know what they are talking about. I lived through segregation. My grandchildren are learning about it in school. It's hard for me to know anything that I didn't come through. I didn't come through slavery times. But integration times I came through. When my kids read something they can say, "Is it true?" and I know because I was there.

In distinguishing between things that people had themselves "come through" and things they had learned about from others, this counselor explained an important difference between his approach to the past and what he understood as "history." Content—slavery or integration—mattered less than how people had participated in the experience. To experience something, dictionaries remind us, is to undergo or undertake it. The Latin origins of "experience" refer to knowledge acquired by actual trial or observation or test, by personal and practical engagement; participants acquire this knowledge firsthand. Historians, like lawyers and journalists, have long believed that participants make the best observers. (By contrast, the event, perhaps the most familiar unit of history, is defined in dictionaries as an occurrence that carries no particular relationship to the observer or participant.) Looking at experiences and not events as the basic units for engaging the past presented respondents with two exciting possibilities that history teachers and textbooks had usually ignored: that participants could change the thing they experienced or that the experience could change them. And it was to these possibilities that they often returned as they drew on the past to shape the course of their lives. By thinking about the past as a reservoir of experience they could use it in their own lives and understand it in the lives of others.

Experiences did not come to respondents with prefabricated lessons; their meanings had to be made. They presented paradoxes and contradictions. They had to be approached through each of the senses, poked and handled. They could be revisited and reinterpreted to address changing needs and desires. Respondents worked hard to make meanings: to recognize, recall, interrogate, and empathize.

The look and feel of an experience depends on its context and the perspective of the participant. "We may go to the same event," explained a black Baltimore retail manager, "but my travels through that event may be different. My experience in those events may differ. I create different speculations about events." Other people provided perspectives that helped respondents clarify their own observations. By recognizing and interpreting experiences—their own and others'—respondents drew the past toward the present as they drew themselves toward others.

Seeing themselves as agents who could change and be changed by experiences, and using the past most frequently and creatively to meet personal needs and sustain relationships, the people we spoke with often developed different ways of thinking about the significance of larger events than they had learned in history classes. Instead of beginning with larger circumstances and events like wars and depressions and tending to assume that individuals reflected and adapted to initiatives from institutions and cultures, our respondents saw themselves as independent actors with capacities to influence and be influenced by larger developments. Instead of seeing individuals as exemplifying larger trends—as typical industrial workers in the 1930s or housewives in the 1950s—our informants used the past to meet changing needs in their intimate relationships, and they saw themselves as capable of resisting, reflecting, or modifying pressures from the larger world. Our respondents used terms like "pride," "shame," "guilt," and "commitment" to talk about dreams, ambitions, and tragedies that have been better presented by poets and novelists than by historians because they are about basic human and individual dilemmas, often more moral than secular, that may transcend time, place, and circumstance.

Starting with these basic understandings, respondents turned the discovery, recognition, sharing, and reliving of experience into means of using the past. In the rest of this chapter we explore how they interpreted and revised what experiences meant to them in order to build and sustain relationships, to question and discover identity, and to create and pass on legacies of their own choosing. And in chapter 3 we explore how, facing the possibility of changing or being changed by an experience, they built narratives that enabled them to shape the courses of their own and others' lives.

"The past is your connection": Building Relationships

A 27-year-old woman from Westerville, Ohio, told us that the birth of her first child brought back "all the memories of what you did when you were a little monster." Having her own child, she felt closer to her parents, even concluding that "my parents aren't as bad as I always thought they were." Respondents said they tried to make sense of new experiences by scouring their pasts for patterns they could recognize. An African American daycare provider from Pennsylvania had discerned a pattern of "family life" from "growing up in a single-parent home." She expected that this pattern would "go on and on" and that her "daughter will most likely become a single parent herself."

Respondents felt more deeply connected to people who had come through experiences with them. At the same time, they reexamined conclusions they had drawn about those events. In order to look at the present in light of the past and the past in light of the present, they even reenacted moments from the past. As a Wyoming resident screened in a porch his late father had once worked on, he felt closer to his father because "you can see how he did things . . . what his brain was thinking when he was doing that . . . wondering . . . what was in his mind."

Accustomed to sharing her life with her brother, a 26-year-old black waitress in Detroit said she continued to write him daily letters, even though he had been murdered three years earlier: "We was really close," she explained. "I miss that part of him, talking to him, so I just write it. I know he won't be reading the letters, but I write some about me and my family every day." Asked for details, she said: "I have three kids, and with kids something's new every day. So I tell him about the kids, how they're doing in school, how his mother [is doing], and the things that are going on. He was in a little rap group, so I tell him how they're doing. 'Cause I miss him."

Respondents said they felt closest to the past when they gathered with their families. "It gives me enjoyment," reported a 64-year-old widow from Fort Lauderdale, "to see who looks like whom, and the habits of them. The grandchildren pick up habits of the grandparents." She began to visualize "who has the dimples, who has the blue eyes, who has the red hair. And dispositions." "What you see in [your relatives] reflects what you see in yourself," concluded a 34-year-old woman from Naples, New York. "When you're gathered with your family," said a woman from Newton Falls, Ohio, "you can't look at your brother without thinking what he looked like as a kid, about what it used to be like. . . . People grow into themselves. You can see a family with a problem, and depending how clear you are with yourself you can see where it comes from."

As individuals left their families behind and made new lives in new places, they found in the retelling of experiences the cement that kept the family together. "My family is spread out," said a firefighter from Columbus, Ohio, "so when you get together you talk about things that have happened in the past and memories. So that automatically becomes a focus, and the past is your connection really."

Like family members, acquaintances grew closer by revisiting the past. "The more you know about [a new acquaintance] the easier to bond and feel the relationship," explained a Florida fund-raiser. Many respondents felt closer to people as they explored one another's pasts and discovered shared experiences. A 43-year-old black computer programmer from Georgia recalled the discoveries that drew her to a co-worker:

> We talk about family. We came up in the same background pickin' cotton, doing a lot of farming and things like that. She is a for real down-to-earth person. She doesn't try to put on a show. I'm the same way. It's nice to work with somebody who can relate to the past, the early fifties, it's nice to talk

about the past. We can't cope. We wish things were like they were then. We try to raise our kids like we were raised.

A 66-year-old woman from Chesterfield, Missouri, recalled how shared experiences had created bonds with her father-in-law: "He and I had very similar growing-up experiences. We both grew up on very poor farms where we had food on the table and that was the extent of it. We both had brothers that were ne'er-to-do." A receptionist in Carmichael, California, knew how to deepen her friendships: "When a friend is upset or angry, knowing a little about their past helps [me] to relate to them."

What they learned about others could become part of their own history and even that of their children. A 51-year-old real estate agent from Hopewell, New Jersey, was interested in "the past of my husband's family" because "it's what his past was, combined with mine, which is going to be what the children's past is." "My future depends on my husband's history and his ancestors," reported a Michigan woman in her early thirties. "There could be a genetic trace from his family that could go on to our children."

"When you're with more distant relatives you talk about the past, but when you're with your immediate family you are reliving the past," said a writer from the Bronx in her forties. "Talk of old times, just people dead that aren't around any more, things that happen . . . talking to your kinfolk who were there when it happened kind of takes you back," observed an Oklahoman in his late thirties. By telling stories family members turned moments from the past into the intimate present. "Just talking about . . . the past things that happened in your life as an early person or their life as an early person . . . brings out the memories that you have stored away," observed a software developer from California. Storytellers brought dead loved ones back to life, kindling the pleasures and pains of intimacy. A woman from Baton Rouge, Louisiana, described a family gathering where an 87-year-old aunt and her sister "were telling us stories about our father when he was a child. . . . He died young. . . . That was definitely a connection with the past. It was pleasure but with pain, too, because of the loss."

"In the summertime, when everything's pretty and green" on South Dakota's Pine Ridge reservation, an Oglala Sioux office worker in her thirties looked forward to the annual powwow of extended families, which always "bring back memories when people would share, gather and share themselves. . . . The music, the singing makes me feel proud. You know that your grandparents have listened to the same music, that they've seen some of the same dances done." By reenacting the past respondents cut through the intervening years to revisit people and scenes, to rekindle the range of feelings that had accompanied the experience as well as connections that had accumulated between the earlier moment and the present. For a plumber from Buffalo, New York, family gatherings elicited "old memories, feelings, thoughts, personal situations, things growing up, you know, inadequacies, everything. They're just the general feeling that you have toward each person that triggers [recollections], and you know that they have as much a part of your feelings as you have of theirs." A 38-year-old piano teacher from Tennessee was reminded at gatherings of "things we've done together as a family—confrontations as well as pleasant times."

Family gatherings connected a student from Charlottesville, Virginia, to the past in "two ways. First, the retelling of stories or remembering different occasions that members in the family experienced either together or apart, and secondly, simply the fact that many people in the family are older [and] their conversation of experiences or the occasion for which we are gathered serves to kind of connect history to the present moment," as when they recalled how his grandfather had fled the Nazis in Czechoslovakia.

Many respondents particularly wanted to hear older people tell about their experiences. An African American janitor from Virginia described how at family reunions he would meet "older people that you haven't met for several years and sometimes you don't know they were alive. . . . You can sit down and talk to these old people and they tell you about things that happened in the past and I think it will help you if you take heed to it."

In their eagerness to be transported to the past by aging family members, some respondents even sounded a little desperate, almost as if their own connections with the past would die along with their elders. When an African American man from Atlanta learned that his only living relative was "gravely ill," he tried to find out all he could from her: "I was curious about what information she might be able to give me regarding my father . . . his profession, where he lived, some of his likes and dislikes. . . . I basically didn't know much about him and this was my only chance to find out more about him." Because she wanted to synthesize her family's past lives and its ongoing experiences, a secretary from Sparks, Nevada, encouraged her mother to enter recollections into a computer. As family members gathered, they would read what her mother had written and enter their own additions and recollections. A 49-year-old clerk from southern

California lamented, "There isn't much family left, and so it is important to me that when we can, we get together." After they learned that their father was in failing health, the family of a caregiver from North Dakota held its first reunion in fifteen years to make a final connection with him.

When respondents selected "gathering with your family" and "celebrating holidays" as the occasions that made them feel most connected to the past, they were often describing the same situations. For most of these Americans, holidays provided the time for families to relive and reinterpret the past. Celebrating holidays with her family reminded a 72-year-old widow from Louisiana of "where we come from and the resemblance in the children and the older folks. . . . In these little bitty fellas you can see some looks of your own children when they were little. The little 2-year-old reminds us of the 21-year-olds now . . . little quirks they do and they do a lot." "The purpose of the holidays is to remember," explained an 47-year-old broker from suburban New Jersey.

A woman from Muskogee, Oklahoma, celebrated Veterans Day because her brother had served in Vietnam, and a teacher from Woonsocket, Rhode Island, celebrated both Veterans and Decoration Day because her father had served in World War I. "Decoration Day has always meant a lot to me," said a 79-year-old woman from New Concord, Ohio, because "there is always a ceremony at the cemetery. When my husband was alive he made speeches at the ceremony. I can remember Decoration Day from way back when I was a child and we would always go to the cemetery and decorate the graves of our family members."

For a Mexican American woman from Earlimart, California, different holidays enveloped her in different families and their traditions. Easter and Christmas were "both very good for me," she said, because Easter was for "my dad's side of the family" while Christmas was for "my mom's side of the family." She added, "I go to their houses and I remember my childhood there." What mattered was the gathering of families, not the official content of each holiday. The fourth of July, observed an office manager from Oceanside, California, was an occasion to think "of my parents. . . . I think about my life and my family, and I do not think about history. . . . Christmas is supposed to be the birth of Christ, but I do not think of that. I think about getting together with my family. Everything that I remember about my past Christmas is about family."

"When you celebrate holidays you have your ancestors there. They're bringing a part of their traditions . . . into the celebration," said a physical therapist from Pasadena, California. "I like the way my family celebrates

Christmas. My relatives are from Germany, and it's the big tradition of putting up the tree the night before Christmas and telling the children that Santa Claus would come and bring presents." On Christmas morning "the kids come out and it's the first time that they've seen the tree. . . . Then we open gifts and have a turkey dinner and . . . the whole family usually goes for a walk." A 52-year-old black service technician from Washington said, "Christmas always gets me emotional because of what it represents. I went home for Christmas to be with my mother and father. I look more for Christmas also for my children, the joy of seeing their faces when they open toys. I guess even now, I think about going up in spirits [at Christmas]. Seeing my mother bake and things like that. I could listen to Christmas music all twelve months."

Christmas in the family of a police officer from Cliffside Park, New Jersey, was a time when family members "got a fire going" and then sang Christmas carols while someone played the piano. On the Pine Ridge Sioux reservation, Christmas was "the time of year we all come to my folks' home and all get together" for a religious ceremony in which each member of the family takes part. "The ceremony starts in the evening and lasts all night. Singing and praying, that's all it is, with instruments like the drum and some of the instruments we have." In the family of a machinist from central Texas, Christmas dinner was always a "big lasagna" prepared by his Italian-born grandmother. For a Mexican American teacher in her fifties from San Benito, Texas, tamale making was a holiday ritual:

> On Christmas, the tamale making, we always involve everyone, even the boys, and there is one aspect of tamale making where everyone participates in one way or another. You have to have your dough and then you have to have your meat prepared and it takes time to do that, and you have to have your corn husks prepared, it's going to be messy, then you have people spreading or wrapping them up with meat, and another person fixes them in a certain position, they have to be standing and turned around the right way, and then of course they're cooked, and ready to eat. This is unique in our family, but tamale making is cultural for our group, for this area. This has been done for many, many years. My grandmother, actually both my grandmothers, passed this tradition on to us, actually to my mother, and then to us.

The Americans we interviewed reenacted rituals with great precision at holiday time. A 39-year-old cook from Hewitt, Texas, reported that her family had set "family traditions" for celebrating holidays. On Veterans

Day "we barbecue. For Easter we all get together and go to the zoo. For Mom's Day we go out to Luby's." One family followed the same menu each Thanksgiving. Another attended the same rodeo each fourth of July. Still another water-skied on the same lake each Memorial Day.

Respondents lovingly and painstakingly relived the past through their rituals. A Cheyenne River Sioux respondent said that her family re-created traditional menus for holidays: "It's like 'my grandmother did it this way' and it never changes." An African American medical secretary from California traced her rituals for celebrating Christmas to "a tradition in our family that goes back to our great-grandfather." For a Jewish contractor from Albuquerque, religious holidays called forth "continuing traditions, doing the very things, saying the very words that I know my ancestors have done and said for countless generations."

The inventors of holidays hoped to sustain the memories of moments and lessons from the past as the original participants died and new generations took their place. In the same way, respondents told us, reenacting their rituals helped sustain the centrality of their families even as births, marriages, and deaths changed their compositions. By reenacting "traditions that have come through the family," explained a 74-year-old woman from Madison, Wisconsin, "we try to pass those along to the younger people in the family so the children have a sense of identity and roots. Otherwise they don't know who they are." By recalling and reliving experiences, the people we talked with did indeed develop "a sense of identity and roots." But those shared moments and their subsequent reenactments, those roots, contained troubling ambiguities and explosive conflicts that our respondents could not ignore as they tried to figure out who they were and wanted to be.

"Why I am like I am": The Quest for Identity

"To find out why I am like I am," a factory worker from Indiana talked with his grandparents, looked up published family genealogies, went through state and federal records, and consulted a computer database. He did not stop until "I basically found out about everything." As part of his quest "to find out what direction we were coming from and what direction we're heading," a commissary manager from Texas began to investigate his family tree.

When respondents explained why they wanted to find out more about their pasts, the most frequent reason they gave was their wish to explore where they and their families had come from and how they had become the kinds of people they were. To satisfy her "desire to know where my personality traits come from," a fund-raiser from St. Petersburg, Florida, worked her "way back in generations, talking with my great-grand-mother," poring over old photographs. Her findings reassured her: "It's nice to go back that far and see that . . . I have a solid family life in my his-tory . . . not any major divorces or mental type things . . . that [our family] kind of stick[s] together through thick and thin, [because of the] genuine love family has for each other." Wondering "where we came from," a 58-year-old flight engineer from Mississippi joined his brothers, sisters, and mother in a collective exploration of their family's past that reached "all the way down as far as we can go." By finding out where those who went before them had come from and what they had passed through, respon-dents hoped to discover secrets of their own identities. "I'm interested in knowing where I come from, what are our values, what drove my relatives in the past," explained a 29-year-old Mexican American manager from Brownsville, Texas.

Respondents looked for experiences that they could recognize as sources for their own traits or beliefs. They revisited those experiences for clues about what made them the way they were and how they fit as they did within families, among friends, and in a larger society where cultures sought to speak in their names. They found answers in intimate moments like making love and public moments like attending a wedding, active moments like tracing ancestors through genealogical records and passive moments like watching a television show.

Reaching back into the past to explore what they had learned from their parents and grandparents, turning over sources of pride and shame with people who mattered to them, respondents began from two different needs in the present. Not everyone wanted to find answers to mysteries that would help them figure out why they thought or acted as they did. Some of the Americans who talked with us recognized only too well the legacies they had inherited; those experiences continued to shape their core beings. They wondered how they could incorporate or move beyond those experiences to become the kinds of people they wanted to be. And they understood the value of actively exploring and questioning their pasts.

Many of them had questions about physical and mental health. "I come from an alcoholic home and some of those things are affecting me now," an administrative assistant from Wisconsin told an interviewer. A carpenter from Cincinnati launched his investigation of his family "to track down mental illness. It kind of runs in the family. It goes through the family up to my dad." "I just wanted to know the histories of my mother and father because I wanted to know their health history," said a 52-year-old African American beautician from Washington. "I have a son who has water on the brain. I wanted to know if this was related to someone down the past. I wanted to know if they had the same health problem." A 36-year-old customer service manager from suburban Virginia reported, "I have a very ill uncle that has a very rare heart disease. I'm trying to learn more about if this is something that has been passed down, is hereditary, or if it's just ill fate on his part, a fluke."

Others, like a woman in her twenties from Sheboygan Falls, Wisconsin, wanted "to see who all was in my family, people who I have never known before and to ask questions about them." The need to identify their ancestors was more urgent on South Dakota's Pine Ridge reservation, explained a Sioux member of the local school board: "The Oglala Sioux and all the other tribes were somehow interrelated. They need to know who their relatives are so they don't get into an interfamily relation, so they don't marry their cousins." Casual questions sent respondents scurrying to the past for answers. A medical clerk in Alabama wondered from whom her two children inherited their "very recessive things, blond hair, blue eyes, so we got kind of interested in . . . where some of those traits came from."

As they contemplated major changes in their lives, many respondents felt inspired to reexamine and sometimes refashion their identities. The decision to share their lives with others, most commonly by getting married, presented couples with the challenge of creating an identity flexible enough to incorporate their separate individual pasts and their new joint sense of themselves. A writer from Ponte Vedra Beach, Florida, said he was ready for the challenge: "Both of us have strong roots in our families, so we have the base for a strong life with each other. . . . Because of our interest in our families and how we got where we are today, it will assist us in where we're going." To make identities for themselves, many adopted children wanted to reconnect with their biological parents, to find out where they had come from. A 24-year-old adopted woman from Burlington, North Carolina, for example, decided to find out more about her ancestors when she discovered that her parents had been American Indians.

Many Americans found legacies in surprising places. A woman from Orlando, Florida in her thirties reported that she was "very protective over my son" because she had grown up in foster homes: "I was basically tossed around like a sack of potatoes. Some were mean. Some weren't. When I came out I was very insecure." So instead of using actual family experiences, she turned to television programs like *The Waltons* and *Little House on the Prairie* for models of the "closeness and bonding" she wanted to create with her son. Another Florida woman, forty years older, turned to *The Waltons* to describe where she had come from. The program "reminds me of my family. I was from a large family during the depression years. It fits. It's my era. That's just the way it was. Even the closeness. That's how I came up. . . . And we're still close." A Phoenix woman said she was "working with an organization to try to find" the children she had adopted but subsequently lost "through the welfare system." She told us that by rediscovering those children, she would be "establishing roots" to carry forward.

Most respondents began with their parents when they tried to forge a recognizable identity. Their parents had shaped their basic natures, they said, taught them who they were and how they should relate to others. A 24-year-old African American woman explained:

> I learned everything from my mother: how to carry myself like a lady, to treat people the way they wanted to be treated, to respect your elders, how important family is. That if you had something on your mind you should express yourself whether the other person would like it or not. Responsibility, now that I'm on my own. . . . She would sit my sister and me down and just have mother and daughter talks all the time. She would . . . tell us how much she loved us, expected from us, how to carry ourselves, what she liked and disliked from us. She would also stress our communication with our dad. Just because you don't feel comfortable talking with him he'd want to know. We just started talking with our father and our family is just really close now.

From her mother, a 25-year-old teacher's assistant who lives in Irvine, California "learned how to be a person. I learned how to be socially competent, read and write, I learned how to love, how to be strong." A 30-year-old black pharmacist from New Jersey "learned everything I know from my father: how to love myself, priorities, how to be a man. Respect, dignity, strength, discipline, you name it, all those good stuff folks are made of." A New York makeup artist in his thirties said his father taught him "how to treat people properly and how to be independent, how to be creative, how to be inspired, how to be quiet and listen to life, and how to keep searching and asking questions." Some people even remembered expressions that encapsulated their parents' legacies. A Mexican American teacher in San Benito, Texas, recalled his father's basic lesson in how to live and translated it for our interviewer: "By the stick that you measure others, so will you be measured. In other words, what you do to others, or the way you treat others, that is how you will be treated. But it sounds better in Spanish."

As they reflected on how their parents had shaped them, many respondents focused on the behaviors that had been encouraged and those that had been punished. "My father was so strict that we always had to be in the house when he got home. I can say now that it has affected me to the point where I was very shy. I couldn't be around very many people and feel at ease. I would feel very nervous because of the way I was brought up," a 51-year-old Mexican American home-care worker said. Respondents often traced their families' self-images to styles of discipline that extended back across generations. "I was brought up in a strict discipline house and feel I should be that way with my children . . . in order for them to develop into good upstanding adults. So understanding my roots, that this was the way my parents and their parents were brought up, I can understand why I had that in me," said a Latino in his forties from Brownsville, Texas. An African American secretary from Grambling, Louisiana, traced her troubled relationship with her father back to his father:

I made a point of finding out about the past of my dad. He did not have a good relationship with his dad. And it was the same with me. He molded his children based on how he was raised. My grandfather was a very strict disciplinarian. My grandfather made my daddy work in the fields and not allow him to go to school. The tradition continued through the family, each of the children following in the paths that my grandfather had set.

"I'm an overachiever," declared a customer support technician from Utah. "I get that from my father and grandfather."

A Latino man who has Indian ancestors reported:

My raising time . . . really affected me. I was raised in the wrong way and it has done me a lot of wrong. It's guided me to go through penitentiaries and jails. . . . I never had a father to tell me what's right and what's wrong. This made me choose the wrong road. I was also the *kaode* [youngest son in Indian family]. It means that you are a nobody in the family. . . . My mother got involved with this man, he was my father and my family didn't like him, and because of him I was the one who took the blame. I really hate to talk but it is really important to me.

A young West Indian woman from Brooklyn still lived with childhood nightmares: "My father was abusive, physically, mentally, sexually, to me. I think about it. My mother says get on with your life. But you can't tell me how to deal with that, unless you're there. It kind of messes you up. So I think that's why I'm so emotional. I think that maybe I'm hurt so inside that I react a little differently." A Seattle man was abused by his spiritual rather than biological father: "The most affected I have been by an individual," he said, was when "I was sexually abused by a priest." Years after the incident he sounded shaken: "If I only looked at it negatively, it would really bring me down, but if I look at the growth that you get from a situation like that, then that's positive."

Through good experiences and bad, moments of conflict and moments of harmony, bonds of deference and obligation, through feelings of closeness and distance from particular individuals, respondents made their families the starting places in their quests for identity. Within the peculiar familiarity of family life, where individuals observed others trying to become bright angels and overcome dark demons, families developed a sense of common destiny. Respondents not only identified this sense of shared destiny at the center of their identities but also saw it as a buffer against the world beyond the family. At home, family members learned and transmitted the values that set them apart and propelled them forward.

Our informants asserted that a family essence transcended individual ambitions and personalities, that an identity with traditions could override everything in its way. They called this essence "your family's philosophy," in the words of an African American woman from Yonkers, New York, or "the reasons that my family is the way that it is," in the words of a teacher from Bozeman, Montana. A woman from Garland, Texas, called it "the heritage of the family and the knowledge and understanding of our forefathers." As she was growing up, a woman from Augusta, Georgia, learned from her grandparents and parents the basic message: "Our family, we just don't do things like that."

A 43-year-old Mexican American counselor from Brownsville, Texas, recalled how members of the family repeated "old sayings that outside our circle of family no one understands." "It's just the day-to-day things that we've experienced together that make us unique," said an accounting assistant from Irvine, California. "I remember having to go to the store with my stepmother to buy underarm deodorant. . . . We laugh about awkward moments, about things that myself and another stranger could not

possibly share. My experiences make my family unique." "The together-
ness of the family that has held over through the years . . . the love and
respect that is shown for each other" was, for a manager from Santa Cruz,
California, "a great support to our life's struggle."

The combination of affection and obligation that family members felt
for each other provided a base from which respondents viewed the world
beyond. "Our family was closely knit," began a 65-year-old African
American woman from Hyattsville, Maryland who sought to sustain that
tradition of family closeness:

> My family was from North Carolina, and I would like my family here to be
> that close. I try to relate to them the things that were most important to me
> in my past, growing up. I have three girls, and I would like them to always
> try to help each other out and share with each other. We always shared in
> North Carolina. We had to share in order to make it.

A 69-year-old Oglala Sioux woman defined the basic expectations of
family responsibility simply: "Because they're my family I have to worry
about them." A black warehouse worker in St. Louis said, "The past of my
family is in a sense my identity. It lets you know where I came [from] and
who [is] from my family. The importance of knowing my family is my
identity. My family is my fall back if all else fails and you can't depend on
anyone else you can always depend on my family." A 28-year-old Utah
customer support technician observed, "All the other options will constantly change, but your family you are always connected with."

Even when they talked as if their families were harmoniously living out
a shared destiny, respondents reported challenges to the ideal of stable
family identity. The composition of families changed with each birth and
death, each marriage and divorce and estrangement. Individuals harbored
their own ambitions and wanted to do things their own ways. Bursts of
family cohesion alternated with seasons of suspicion and conflict.
Individuals felt tremendous pressure to reconcile their own needs and
deeds with the demand to uphold family honor. Indeed, the difficulty of
balancing experience with culture may be increasing. As other institutions
over the past two centuries have lost the capacity to reconcile differences
between the real and ideal in other arenas of life, John R. Gillis argues that
families have had to bear a growing burden to reconcile the idealized families that members are expected to "live *by*" with the real families that they
in fact "live *with*."[1]

"A family tree represents certain codes of conduct that people before you have laid down and you follow in their footsteps. The family history represents a whole book of knowledge for that person to live on so far as being a good person," said an African American mail carrier from Memphis. Trying to reconcile their current behavior with the family ideal, respondents often revisited the same formative experiences or the same elder exemplars of family continuity and identity. They wanted to create new narratives that could incorporate change while sustaining tradition, permitting individuals to be swept along by the shared identity that carried family members from past to future.

"My children are able to see the best of both worlds": Reaching from Family to the Outside World

Families looked inward, caring for their members, but they also looked outward, creating a borderland between individuals and the larger world outside. Individual respondents expected other family members to help them reach a world that presented opportunities for fulfilling hopes but also threats that could turn the brightest dreams into nightmares.

Respondents told us that national developments could be as transformative as intimate ones and that their families could help assess how larger developments might change them. They reported that family members sometimes argued about how outside events had transformed individuals beyond recognition. "What affected me the most" was the depression of the 1930s, declared an 85-year-old woman from Monticello, Iowa, but she said that members of her family who hadn't passed through the depression could not understand or accept how it had formed her values:

> I live differently than most. I try living a simple life. My children say, "Why don't you spend some of your money?" But I am going to try and stretch it. It is a matter of saving and being conservative and helping others that need help and things like that. I try and go and see several ladies in town and bring them little gifts. I think that my past has something to do with that, knowing all about hardships.

Passage through major cultural and political movements indeed changed the passenger. A 45-year-old technician from Colorado said that the 1960s was a "period in my life [that] was like the period in the history of this country. [It was] a pretty tumultuous time, and it had in a lot of ways a liberalizing effect on me." A 51-year-old woman from Cleveland also found the 1960s transformative:

> I was a brand-new adult, and that had the most important impact on who I became ultimately. I don't know if that impact was good or bad. There was a contradiction in how I was raised. My parents were older than the average parents. They reached adulthood in the early thirties. Vietnam was in progress as I reached adulthood. There were so many changes. The sixties were really something. It was like I was going in circles, as I didn't know how to act or what to do. The sixties to mid-seventies was a traumatic time for me. There were so many ideas. It was a period of consciousness raising for women, the sexual revolution, and you were trying to resolve things for personal harmony. The period was also a time of black consciousness raising. I was also in the middle of that.

From the larger society respondents picked up habits—like penny-pinching or rebelliousness—that troubled other members of their families. But the people we interviewed also saw their families as barriers against threats and temptations from outside. An Asian American man from Malden, Massachusetts put it succinctly: "When you're in your home you're safe." The barrier was built from the intensity and density of family members' attempts to meet each other's needs. Respondents said they brought experiences in their larger world back home and discussed them with those who mattered most. A 45-year-old computer programmer from Georgia told us that the candor of such conversations allowed him to reflect on how to incorporate new experiences. His marriage "provided me with, if you will, a mirror, so I could look at my behavior. I get gentle feedback, like if I'm being a jerk. It gives me a chance to assess my behavior and change if I decide that's appropriate." The family was a place to confront the dark sides people rarely wanted to show in public. Families protected intimacy from outside contamination; they guarded against revealing (and thereby letting outsiders engage) their most troubling and defining experiences.

The most powerful legacies that individuals brought from the larger society for families to engage—to include or exclude—were those of their cultures. Like families, cultures created narratives that described where their members had come from and were heading, what they had overcome and what they aspired to—all basic issues in defining identities. Cultures offered moral precepts about how to relate to others and how to raise children. Like families, cultures changed over time and presented ranges of experiences to identify with. Like families, cultures demanded that people identify more fully at some times than at others. Their leaders drew circles around poles of identity to keep members from straying and strangers from entering.

The people we talked with worked out creative ways of defining who they were as they embraced, remade, and ignored traditions they had more and less inherited from their cultures. Some families embedded their identities in their cultures. For other families, cultures offered competing identities that respondents resolved and dissolved in their intimate relationships. These identities were more complex for the many respondents who by blood or marriage were connected with multiple cultures; they were less relevant for respondents whose cultures had lost their defining edges by fading or blurring over time or for individuals who experienced their cultures in bits and pieces. While a majority of people from all racial groups told us that they were most interested in the pasts of their families, Native Americans, African Americans, and to a lesser extent Mexican Americans expressed more often than European Americans an interest in the pasts of their cultures, in narratives described in chapters 5 and 6. In the end, of course, respondents and their families from all backgrounds embraced and chose and blended, transformed and shunned, materials from their cultures in ways that best assisted them to define their origins and imagine their destinies.

At one extreme family flowed seamlessly into culture. Respondents created identities in which their cultures simply extended their families, in which older family members embedded stories of the family's origins in stories of the culture's past. A 44-year-old Sioux man from the Pine Ridge reservation talked about links between family and culture:

> We must have a starting point, and what better place to start than your own family, or your own grandmother. Lakota thought says if you look into the eyes of the seven generations before us and seven generations into the future, you realize the human factors that make us who we are. That connection is our family. If you understand your family history, you can then move on to the history of your ethnic group.

Many other Pine Ridge respondents elaborated. "In our culture," said a policeman, "family is the most important thing. . . . We have a strong family and before everything we do we think of how it will affect the family."

"Around here," a fireman reported, "your immediate and extended family, even as far as the fifth and sixth cousins, everybody treats you like brothers, sisters, moms and dads. That's how close Indians are." Grandmothers linked family to culture and enforced traditional standards of right and wrong: "The grandmother has the power," said a Sioux nurse. "She taught [grandchildren] when they were little about the things that you don't do in the culture. She has the controlling power if kids misbehave. They'll say 'you better behave or grandma will come after you' or 'we'll tell grandma.' "

At first glance, close connections between family and culture might seem inevitable on the Pine Ridge Sioux reservation, a place seemingly isolated by necessity and choice from broader currents in American life. Because Sioux identity was such an embracing reality in that place, individuals might appear to have grown up engulfed in a single heritage. But in fact Sioux culture was not a single living inheritance that all residents of Pine Ridge came by automatically. Many Pine Ridge residents were descended from and married to people of different tribes and races, though marriage to outsiders offended cultural nationalists of all persuasions, who warned that the offspring could not be true Sioux—or true anything else.

"Being a full-blood Indian and having a child from a white man was really looked down on. The child was shunned and not accepted," reported a teacher. Because Pine Ridge is a national center of movements for Indian rights and identity, residents faced competing leaders, rituals, and political movements, each of which claimed to be the true fulfillment of Sioux identity. The tension created by intermarriage between full- and half-bloods overlapped political conflicts between the tribal council and the American Indian Movement, according to a nurse on the reservation, as ethnicity became less a matter of natural biological descent than of political choice. Nationalists presented their programs as the true fulfillment of Sioux identity, but many Indians did not come by true "Sioux" ways automatically with their mothers' milk or their tribal membership.

Americans in all parts of the country made creative use of their pasts as they looked for recognizable themes in their own experiences and tried to practice cultures in their own ways. Respondents often described their embraces of cultures not as direct inheritances but as recovery of things they or their families had lost touch with—commitments to the future as much as expressions of the living past. "Basically in the urge to become Americanized a lot of the old family ways weren't really passed on in my family," lamented a Seattle systems analyst who felt deprived of the Ukrainian culture that he wished his immigrant forebears had passed intact to him. A teacher in her twenties told a similar story of lost and found identity. She explained why in her yearning to adopt an Indian identity she embraced her boyfriend's Lakota Sioux traditions instead of her mother's Chippewa ways:

> My mother thought it was more important that we be able to work in the white society and assimilate. She never taught us our language. Her mother never taught her. That would be Ojibway [the language of her Chippewa ancestors]. With our language [comes] our culture and our religion. . . . My boyfriend is Lakota, and I will learn his history, their religion, their traditional ways. When we have kids and get married, they will be Lakota. The religion, tradition, and culture would be Lakota.

Many respondents told stories about recovering cultural identities they had earlier lost touch with. A young Mexican American man in Coachella, California, was converted by his best friend, who "taught me to be a Mexican, not to be influenced by other people, mainly white people, not to let anybody bring you down. He explained how all this land was Mexican and that [the United States] has no right to it. He was very proud." A 54-year-old Mexican American woman from Whittier, California, may have been speaking autobiographically when she observed that "a lot of children have lost their heritage. If they don't learn it at home they don't learn it outside." As she grew older, she came to identify more strongly with her Mexican past: "I think I'm more proud of my heritage now. Growing up I didn't know how important it was because all I heard was negative in school." For many respondents cultural identity became more powerful over time.

When he learned that he might have Blackfoot ancestors, a 50-year-old black inhabitant of south central Los Angeles recognized how his newfound Indian roots might have shaped his present identity: "Indians are a very proud nation. They are very proud. I have that pride in my life." Until his discovery of Indian ancestry, he said, that pride had been in his blackness. A 25-year-old man from Pine Ridge explained how he connected with his French, German, and Native American heritages:

> I tend to be more interested in the people I'm descended from than in some absolute stranger that doesn't pertain to me in any way. Their lives have

something to do with my life. They've influenced someone who influenced someone who influenced someone who influenced me. A lot of my French ancestors were in this area, whereas most of my German history would be over in Germany or Russia. That part of the family was pretty fresh over here, whereas the [French and Indian] had been here a while.

Many respondents wanted or were expected to feel rich links to a cultural past that they had trouble recognizing in their own experience. Blacks reported particular difficulty in connecting African origins to their present lives. When conversation turned to ethnic heritage, a black Newark accountant wished that he could say more than " 'Well, I'm from the African continent,' and that's it. No point of origin. I think at times it sort of makes for a very shallow sort of feeling. Yes, it does, especially when all the other ethnic groups in this country know their point of origin." A 67-year-old black woman from Memphis also missed clear origins in Africa: "I don't know anything in the history of my family that comes from Africa. I know nothing about Africa."

While some respondents tried to incorporate an ancestral culture into their present identities, others faced a different challenge: How could they feel cultural pride when their families were shaped by more than one culture? They wanted to draw on all their cultural heritages as they formulated who they were. Much talk about multiculturalism assumes that individuals inherit single cultural identities, but for many people we talked with—as for a growing number of commentators—intermarriage made issues of identity matters of choice and invention, not inheritance and descent.[2]

When people brought two living cultures to the creation of a new family, they often had to face the prejudice of nationalists who doubted the loyalty of half-breeds, mulattos, and mestizos. Half-breeds could not belong in a world divided into racial and ethnic groups based on descent. A professional woman in her thirties from Prince George's County, Maryland, who identified herself as African American, described the bigotry: "My mother is white, my father is black, and we share the hard times that my mother had to go through having black children." She traced her own experience as the child of a biracial union farther back in her family: her grandmother was conceived when a slave master raped her great-grandmother.

A 20-year-old shift runner for a Detroit pizza parlor talked about living between races: "Some of my family is white and some black, and it's separating them," he began. It was hard for him to sit in schools where black teachers "want you to hate white people for what they did" in slavery. "It's confusing when you tell a kid to hate a race and that kid has that race in his family. It can really confuse that kid if you get a teacher like that." His mother faced ridicule when she went to school to pick up her black children—and he would "come home crying"—but his grandfather came to the rescue with the words: "You are who you are and you're the only one who's going to make it." He said that his grandfather helped him find an identity of his own—"to have it all together"—and "to never let anything get in my way. He also taught me to be proud for the person I am."

But how could individuals define identities for themselves in a larger world that seemed to see only cultures? Since prejudice was skin deep, people from mixed races never knew how they would be perceived. An Asian American from Malden, Massachusetts, who reported looking "Caucasian" but having an Asian last name, had learned that "If I'm speaking to another Caucasian face to face the fear of racism doesn't enter my mind, but when I'm sending out a resume and there is no face to go with my Asian name then I have a fear that potentially [the resume] will not be received favorably because the person might be prejudiced against Asians."

Though children of biracial families faced special prejudice, they said that they had also inherited a special advantage. Instead of choosing one culture, some respondents drew what they liked best from both. Many Mexican Americans felt they had come twice from bicultural families. First, said a 60-year-old woman from El Paso, "I come from Mexican parents so I am bicultural," part Spanish, part Indian. Second, in the United States, Mexican Americans often felt "betwixt and between" Mexican and American cultures, in George Sánchez's phrase, caught in a borderland made wider when they married Anglos.[3] By learning about both cultures, children of such unions would understand their parents better and have a wider selection of cultural heritages, explained a 24-year-old Brownsville, Texas, woman:

> My husband is an Anglo, and I am Mexican. I came from Mexican parents, I like my history, the history of Mexico. Our child may like both of them or neither of them. That's up to him or her. It is very beneficial for the child to learn both. She will know more about her father's history and her mother's history. She will learn both of them.

A Pine Ridge school counselor wanted to "look into mine and my husband's background, to find out for sure what ethnic background my children will be from, so they know where they came from and their history. They're going to be of mixed race, white and Indian, and I want them to know about both sides." Armed with that knowledge, she imagined, "they will hopefully be able to avoid some of the prejudice that I've grown up with." Even European American children often faced a choice of heritages. A 46-year-old accountant from Columbus, Ohio said the cultural "diversity of the family" left him with a choice: "Well, I kinda just ignored the southern part and I just identified with the northern branch instead."

"The main thing is trying to blend both sides, the Indian and the Anglo, and taking the best of each and applying it to yourself," argued a Pine Ridge bus driver. Proudly drawing on both of his heritages, another Oglala Sioux respondent, 55 years old, challenged religious leaders who spoke of "Catholicism and the Lakota being separate religions. I don't think that they are. I think I've been able to reconcile the Lakota religion with my Catholicism." A 31-year-old Mexican American bus driver from Montebello, California observed: "Although some people may find it different to have two backgrounds, I find it to be a plus. I have more to talk about." "I'm very family-oriented," said a 33-year-old woman who had come to Indianapolis from the Philippines:

> I have a family of my own, and I want to instill a sense of family values in them by being around their extended family. I wasn't born here in the U.S. I'm a transplant. My family immigrated here. Being around my family gives my children a different culture than what they're surrounded with. It gives them a broader base. They're able to see the best of both worlds.

Some respondents ignored cultures altogether and emphasized either the uniqueness of their individual pasts or the patterns they shared with all human beings. "People live their own lives. Everybody has their own history," said a 26-year-old African American pipe layer from Mobile. To a black retail manager from Baltimore, "the fact that I'm a different individual makes my past very different from everyone else's." At the other extreme, a black 33-year-old photographer from Memphis identified above all with his essential humanity: "We all are human. We all was born of a mother. We all have similarities. We all experience hurt, pain, financial burden, joy, disappointment." A dietary aide from Brooklyn, who claimed both black and Indian ancestors, had a ready answer for bigots: "I would tell them to live their lives like everyone else. We are all human. If you cut me the blood is the same color. I think all men are created equal. Everything else is ignorant."

"To leave a legacy": The Quest for Immortality

Like the search for identity, the need for immortality drove Americans into their pasts. They took steps to ensure that the past would not die with them, that they would live on in the memories of those they had touched in life. Particularly as they grew older, they burned with the wish to pass on everything—identity, example, experience, ideals, traditions, ethnicity, lessons, skills, wisdom, and above all love—so that the things they valued would survive. A retired aviator from Denton, Texas reported that the essence of adulthood was "trying to pass on your values to your children." A woman from Lynnwood, Washington became a political activist in her fifties because she was troubled by changes in the country and she wanted "to preserve it the best I can for my children and grandchildren."

"What I've tried to put into my kids," said a businessman from Conway, Arkansas, was "that words mean things. They need to remember when there were statesmen and not politicians, which is related to the values of knowing right from wrong." A Wisconsin widow in her eighties kept up her family tree "so I can leave it for my children so they know some things from the past, their heritage and such, where their grandparents came from and so forth. I just think they should know those things and some of the diseases that they died from." Like the Chinese American woman who gave her granddaughter a religious symbol that had been in the family for generations, they passed on physical mementos they hoped would sustain their memories in generations to come.

"Being close knit, we bring up past memories and teach our children and grandchildren and great-grandchildren what went on before they came so that they never forget the past," a man from Catskill, New York told us. "How children are reared and raised and why there are laws in the family and why they have to abide by this, that, and the other, so they don't act like free spirits and can't do what they please. So they can take and apply this in their lives as they grow older." Asked why she was assembling her family tree, a 70-year-old woman from Oklahoma City said she wanted "to leave a legacy to my children and grandchildren of their parents and grandparents. . . . I am getting older, and if I don't do this no one else will. I want them to know where they came from." A 78-year-old woman from Houston explained that she loved to talk with her grandchildren, to tell them about their parents "so that they will remember them.... We give them pictures, so that they can remember." "I like things with a tradition," a New Jersey psychologist said. "I like saying that was from my grandmother."

Among many Pine Ridge Sioux the desire to carry the family forward blended with the desire to perpetuate the culture. A professional in her thirties valued a Sioux ritual that advanced both her family and her culture in a single event. The event was "when I gave my oldest son his Indian name. It made me happy to have an older person give him his name and a feather and afterwards we celebrated by having a big feast for him and a powwow.... I want my sons to know more about their Indian heritage ... how to talk Indian, dancing and singing." A 60-year-old woman wanted her grandchildren "to know about the past and keep their culture as far as they can. Not to forget who they are. Keep up the tradition" of Sioux ways. Having been raised a Catholic and denied the right to learn his Lakota language, a 45-year-old Sioux man was thrilled to pass along a cultural legacy he had not been able to experience in his own childhood: "When I grew up I never got the chance to be proud of my culture. I don't want my children to miss out on that."

The Americans we talked with described the things they had experienced, the ways they had touched and been touched by passages through life. They alone had experienced these things and learned from them. They alone had the responsibility and the ability to pass them on, literally to provide continuity of experience from their own parents and grandparents to their own children and grandchildren. A 36-year-old Virginia suburbanite explained why she began to keep a journal:

I have just started to write to my daughter in it about things that I can remember now from when she was first born so that she can have something to look back on when she's my age or older and have answers to questions if I'm not around or if another family member isn't around that would know the answer to the question. I always loved to hear my mother tell me stories about the past, about when I was growing up, about when she was a young child, and those stories would be lost when my mother is gone or when I'm gone.

Within their families, respondents used experiences to address questions and meet needs at once unique and human—timeless quests for identity and immortality that have moved people through the ages. Families both connected individuals to the larger world and protected them from it, reaching toward and blending cultural traditions. Above all, the respondents to this survey drew our attention to the remarkably creative and diverse ways in which individuals and their families looked for, recognized, used, and revisited experiences to address concerns about where they came from and where they are heading, about who they are and how they will be remembered.

3. Using the Past to Shape the Future:

Building Narratives, Taking Responsibility

For the Americans we interviewed, the past exists not as a distant land but in the here and now. Many of our respondents, as we saw in chapter 2, turned to the past so that they could say with authority, "This is who I am today." They turned to the past to build relationships and communities, to make themselves at home in the present tense. And they turned to the past to envision tomorrow, to gather the legacies they wanted to leave behind. This chapter moves further inside the process of historymaking, as we listen to Americans describe the narratives they've built from past experiences to help them chart the courses of their individual and collective lives.

Again and again respondents said they wanted to make a difference; they wanted to take responsibility for themselves and others. With that goal in mind, they often revisited and interrogated their experience. They processed pieces of the past and arranged them into narratives that could be used to shape the present and imagine the future. These narratives varied from individual to individual, group to group, as chapters 5 and 6 will elaborate; but they shared an essential core. For all their idiosyncrasies, respondents seemed to be talking about variations on a common quest to uncover where they'd been and how they hoped to proceed.

"Kids, they don't have no worries": Letting Others Take Responsibility

Respondents told us that they did not inherit the ability to use the past; nor did that ability grow steadily as their bodies grew. Taking on new responsibilities—leaving home, getting married—required them to free themselves from other people's uses of the past and develop their own.

Asked "In what ways do you think differently about the past now than you did when you were younger?" many respondents depicted childhood as a time when parents and teachers provided the continuity that connected past to future while children lived in the present. As youngsters, they recalled, they had looked only forward, seeing their development as an unfolding linear product of individual effort, defined more by the calendar or their parents than by themselves. "When you are young, you don't do a whole lot of thinking. You want to get grown," said an African American woman from Decatur, Georgia. "You're pretty self-centered for a long time," began a woman from Lamar, Arkansas. She added that childhood was "pretty much geared toward Santa Claus, the Easter Bunny, what kind of car am I going to get." "When you're young you're thinking of the future all the time, the present and the future," recalled a widow in her late seventies from California. A 36-year-old Oglala Sioux man observed that children didn't need to become active users of the past: "Kids, they don't have no worries. They don't worry about nothing. But adults, they worry. Everything was happiness when I was a kid. We were living for the future. But as adults we were learning from the past for the future."

To be carefree was to be self-centered. Children could be self-centered, respondents said, because others took ultimate responsibility for where they lived and what they ate, for their health, education, and welfare. A 38-year-old cook from central Mississippi remembered that in childhood "I had people taking care of me and doing my thinking for me. It's not until you're in charge of somebody else that you think about the past. I have three boys now." "When I was younger, my mother and father did everything for me," said a 30-year-old Pine Ridge resident. "When you get older you have to work for it and earn it. When you're young you felt free, like there's no evil in the world. But when you get older you face reality and the fact that there is evil in the world." As "a kid you have no worries," recalled an African American manager of a home for the developmentally disabled. "A lot of stuff is camouflaged. Life seems great and parents were struggling and they hid that from you. It wasn't that they hid it, it was just that you didn't notice it. . . . I didn't have no clue. I was happy."

A 44-year-old secretary from Kansas said simply, "When I was younger I didn't care much about the past." As a boy, the manager of a truck fleet in Massachusetts thought history was "a lot of facts and dates and numbers, stuff . . . you have to learn to get your grades," but he later came to "realize how important this stuff was and have more insight." Children were spectators who watched others talk about pasts that felt remote.

Many respondents vividly remembered the moment they had suddenly discovered that they were using the past on their own terms. They traced this emerging independence to the transition between carefree childhood and responsible adulthood, which they located chronologically in late adolescence. For an Omaha man in his seventies the air force had bridged adolescence and adulthood: "I was a 19-year-old kid when I went in," he said, and four years later he was a flight commander carrying "ten people's lives in your hands every time you take off." "When you were younger you were immortal," said the owner of a Connecticut wire company in his late sixties. He added, "When you were seventeen and you were in the service it was always the other plane that was going to go down, the other person that was going to get killed. When you had your family you were very aware that you had to stay healthy and provide for them and their well-being."

As they took responsibility for others, respondents said, they were no longer willing to let parents or teachers present them with goals and with narratives about how to meet those goals. "Now that I'm older and able to judge for myself," said a Mexican American personnel employee from Los Angeles, "a lot of the past as taught to me by my parents I think differently about. The church and even family members were giving me their opinion. I'm an adult now and am able to define with my opinion." A Minneapolis electrician in his fifties remembered the surprise of learning from other family members that his parents were more complicated than he'd imagined. "Your aunts and uncles tell about your parents," he said, like the time "my mother was young, stealing watermelons out of the watermelon patch and losing her mother's butcher knife. My aunt told me this. My mother never would." As a youngster, a 46-year-old office cleaner from Michigan "trusted everybody and listened and thought what everybody told me was true. But now that I am older I realize that people say what others want to hear and make promises they can't keep."

"Life experience feeds introspection": Making Narratives to Monitor Change and Continuity

To reach the point where they could deeply engage the past while meeting responsibilities of everyday life, these Americans had to travel a long way from childhood's absorption in the present. "When you get older, you start opening your eyes and looking around, thinking, 'If this didn't happen in the past, maybe things would be different now,' " explained a 53-year-old Lakota Sioux woman from Pine Ridge. Many of them discovered that not only did the past shape the present, but passage through experiences in the past had shaped them as interpreters of the present. "When I was young I was just living in the present," began a Mexican American high school administrator from Texas. He said that he had come to "see that the past has made a lot of difference. There were a lot of things that helped me be whatever I am now." As they tried to become independent users of the past, respondents learned to probe how they themselves had changed or been changed by experiences they passed through. "Life experience feeds intro-spection," mused a retired man from Winston-Salem, North Carolina. As if to illustrate this maxim, a Wisconsin woman in her sixties told us that over time she had "lived through more history" and "when you see things firsthand, the history of it is a little easier to think about."

From her home in South Texas, a Mexican American school district employee in her late fifties turned to the past to understand how her family would be altered by an experience her son went through. "When we [Mexican Americans] were in school we had our own school on the other side of the track. We didn't mix with anybody until junior high. We weren't allowed to go swimming in the town swimming pool. I could go on and on with those kinds of things." But times changed. "I really thought [discrimination] was all over in 1976." But that year something shook her faith in progress: "My son was a senior in high school, and he asked a girl to the prom, and her parents would not let her go with him because he was Mexican American." This rejection was even more puz-zling because her son did not look like the kind of person Anglos discrim-inated against: "My son is blond-haired, blue-eyed." The prom rejection "upset me very much," she told our interviewer. "It just kind of brought it all back, and told me hey, it's not over, discrimination is not over, it's still around. It's very subtle."

She was troubled that she had failed to create an accurate narrative about discrimination from observing encounters between Mexican Americans and Anglos—in schools, at swimming pools, in their choices of partners for prom dates and marriage. And she grieved that by wrongly interpreting the extent of change and continuity, she had failed in one of the basic tasks of parenthood: preparing her children to fulfill their dreams. "I had not really said anything to my children because I thought [discrimination] was over and done with." After all, she later tried to reassure herself, "my kids have not really experienced the kind of discrimination that I did. They're all intermarried now, intermarried with Anglos." The clear difference in the experience of the two generations had given her hope for the future; she didn't want to alarm her children or dampen their dreams. "I didn't want to bring this to their attention." Wrestling with feelings of inadequacy both as an interpreter of experience and as a parent, she lamented, "I was naïve to think that it didn't exist."

Looking for patterns that could help to shape their lives, respondents discovered that experiences could be used in two ways. First, they were real occurrences, bedrock events experienced with powerful immediacy— and ambiguity. But experiences had a second use. They could be revisited, reenacted, and reinterpreted to meet changing needs in the present. "You don't recognize" the lessons at the time you first experience something, observed a hospital administrator from southern California. "You recognize them as you get older. As you get older you look back at the lessons you've learned." Only by revisiting moments from her past did she learn lessons like "sensitivity to other people."

Respondents interrogated the past as they addressed the present. The challenge of describing the course of discrimination against Mexican Americans was inseparable from the challenge of preparing children to make their way in the world. Faced by new challenges, many respondents tried to recall similar experiences in the past. A 20-year-old black woman from Detroit described what she'd learned about using the past: "I can see that things reoccur. I can actually recognize it. It probably helps me solve problems before they occur." "You have more perspective as you get older," said a medical technologist from Bern, New York. "You see more of an overall picture." By contrast, "when you're younger it's individual incidents" that stand out.

As respondents returned to experiences of the past to help them in the present, they reflected on how changes in their own lives could lead them to interpret the experiences differently. They questioned the narratives their elders had created for them. "You used to be presented biased things from teachers and parents, and when you're older you have more experience to make decisions and see through that," explained a Texas oil worker in his forties. "As your experience level rises in life you start to separate the wheat from the chaff." An Illinois electronic equipment salesman said the past became more important to him as he got older because he was "trying to understand how a person fits in the whole thing." "I feel more a sense of creating a past in my present. I see myself now becoming the wise old grandmother," explained a lawyer from northern Virginia. She could "see the cycles and circles more now than I did when I was younger and my place in them."

Using the past to serve interpretation in the present, respondents assembled isolated experiences into patterns. From these narratives they could project what might happen next, set priorities, take responsibility, and try to shape their futures. But these narratives differed from the plots of finished stories. Unlike classic narratives, these trajectories did not imply inevitable endings—only directions or paces in which things seemed to be moving. Respondents assumed that direction and pace could be changed either by the interpreters themselves or by obstacles or interventions. Indeed, people fashioned experiences into trajectories so that they could imagine how to sustain and change narratives.

To begin a story, many respondents compared past and present, looking for similarities and differences. "We sit around and talk about how it was when we grew up. We all have kids and talk of the differences between now and then," a black Detroit woman in her thirties observed. As children, they had assumed that the people and things around them would not change. They had concentrated on pursuing their individual lives. "I guess I thought that everything would stay the same," a New Jersey man in his fifties said of his childhood. A Pine Ridge Sioux woman in her early twenties told us, "I know now [that] everything changes, but [as a child] I don't think it ever crossed my mind." As they discovered change by comparing past with present, they also came to recognize and value continuity. A 67-year-old oil refinery salesman from Fort Worth, Texas explained the force of continuity with a metaphor: "Knowing the past gives continuity and meaning to life in the same sense that a river flows from its source to its ultimate goal. So life can be understood by looking at the past and seeing where it's leading a person." Some began trajectories of continuity at the source or origin; others, like a shipwright from Bremerton, Washington, began with the present and tried "to see the connection all the way back to creation."

A North Carolina carpenter wanted "to know how it was back then" in order to interpret "how much of it has changed over the years." By looking at longer-term patterns, respondents could find in each experience of the moment something that might either advance or retard a course of events. Since "history works in cycles and the more you can learn about the past the more you can predict your own future" and "it all comes around eventually in a big circle and we might be better prepared for what comes," a fund-raiser from St. Petersburg, Florida thought that figuring out those cycles would allow people to "alleviate any bad things that will happen."

The people we interviewed tended to group their narratives around recurring themes and issues. First, they looked for the direction of a pattern: where it had come from and seemed to be heading—whether their weight was going down or their grades were going up. They measured the pace of a development—of arguments in a marriage, alcohol consumption, or the waning of discrimination against Mexican Americans. They asked if events were moving too fast or too slow toward a hoped-for or dreaded outcome or away from a cherished or feared source. When they encountered a new development, they tried to assess whether it was for better or worse—and for whom. They noted obstacles that might divert a story from ending at the place they expected as well as things that might speed its arrival at the expected—or desired—outcome. And they often wondered how much longer a journey would take. A black Detroit auto worker in his forties said he could see progress: "The world is a lot better than when my father and grandfather were growing up." A 67-year-old black woman from Memphis agreed that race relations were moving in the right direction but expressed concern about the pace and amount of change: "We've come a long way. We're a lot freer, but we still have a long ways to go."

In their narratives many respondents framed assessments of change and continuity as stories of whether "things are better now or worse now," as a Nevada motorcycle shop owner put it. They compared new developments with more familiar landmarks. Two African American women defined increase in crime as the source of the greatest deterioration in their lives and slavery as the benchmark for comparison. A 27-year-old nursing assistant in Shreveport, Louisiana, said she felt much more "unsafe" than she had as a child—"you can't even walk out the door"—but added that the assessment of whether crime was a greater threat than slavery "depends on who you're talking to. I guess, according to the older people—I wasn't a slave, and they were—" slavery was worse." "I have fear of going out to my car," a 36-year-old woman from St. Louis told us, but in contrast to the Louisiana woman, she said crime had become so bad that she would prefer slavery:

> If I had a choice of living in slavery or living now I think I would have picked slavery. Because then there wasn't as much killing. Then you had

your own little place and if anything happened it wasn't enough to kill me. Then it was the white man doing it to you. Back then it wasn't enough to die over. Now it's everybody killing everybody.

While some respondents told stories of progress or decline, others drew trajectories in which things simultaneously got better in some ways and worse in others. A 49-year-old writer from the Bronx said she had changed her overall assessment of the progress of civilization: "In the past I would say look how far we've come. Now I think people are just as barbaric as in the past. We've only advanced technologically, and that's destroying the world." Even when they kept sharp focus on one development, many saw both good and bad long-term consequences. A 66-year-old woman from Panhandle, Texas talked about the transformation wrought by television: "When I was in school I didn't have television and you couldn't watch things as they were happening." But back then, she said, "You had to use your imagination." A Columbus, Ohio firefighter in his forties believed that "a generation lost trust in the Establishment" after the assassination of John F. Kennedy. He added, "I don't know if that is a good thing or a bad thing to learn." A black woman in Roxbury, Massachusetts concluded that "it was easier in some ways in the past, harder in some ways. Young people nowadays have to worry about getting killed, and back then they didn't." On the other hand, "if you get sick now you go to the hospital and they have medicines for you. Back then they might not have had the medicine."

"I learned different ways of viewing situations": Changing Perspectives

Narrators told stories not only about change in the wider world but also about how the past had colored their own perspectives and affected their own capacity to influence the course of events. They understood that experiences would be interpreted differently by different people and differently by the same person as needs and circumstances shifted; many respondents observed that their narratives changed as they did. Going to college "changed my way of thinking and the way I view experiences around me. I learned different ways of viewing situations," reported a 39-year-old teacher from Pomona, California. A Pennsylvania laboratory technician in her twenties explained how college changed the values she had learned from her parents:

I learned about women getting self-respect for themselves. I feel that I have grown because I have learned about life. I was very homophobic when I [entered college]. I had a thing about this. There was a percent of the gay population that did not feel that they had to hedge things. And I learned that it should not matter who you love. It should not matter what sex or color they are. Because my parents instilled certain values in me, I had to distance myself from that in order to learn. I feel that I have grown tremendously from those kinds of experiences. My parents were ignorant. They do not understand. They have not learned how to deal with that because they did not go to college.

Some respondents traced formative influences to events in the larger society. A retired public relations consultant from California said World War II "took me out of western Kentucky and made me aware of the world as a whole. It gave me the opportunity to see things and experience them. . . . It allowed me to get into foreign countries and . . . gave me an understanding and a feeling for other peoples." But the war also wounded him; he could not forget the "shootings and the killings." The life of a Kansas man was "upgraded significantly" by World War II; because of his service in the war, he was able to go to college and improve his job prospects.

Intimate relationships changed the perspectives of other people we talked with. For a veterinarian's assistant from California the divorce of her parents when she was nine "was very confusing. . . . It has its effects . . . . throughout your life. . . . You went and took a different road in your life." A Wisconsin woman in her sixties believed her marriage "pretty much defined who I am . . . where I live, and what my family is. I married a farmer, and moved out of the city and onto a farm, and [he] made a Dane out of me."

Many people told us that they had difficulty changing the perspectives they had learned in childhood. A Pennsylvania service technician in his forties learned from his parents "not to have any self-esteem" and "how to relate to people in a dysfunctional way. I learned twisted belief systems. I learned a way of thinking that is destructive and unhealthy in my adult life. It was my parents, the way they related to each other . . . that taught me all these things. I believed that was the way things were until I became an adult and realized that I was not functioning well." A route salesperson for a California potato chip company described a family struggle:

It's important to know where my family came from. . . . There are bad and good cycles started. The women started a cycle of getting married and having children very young. This started with my great-grandmother. From her down to me, including my son. I was married at 16, and had a son at 17, and I was married for five years. . . . I left [my husband] when he was abusive with me. I could not stand for him abusing my child. [My son] remembers defending me when he was three years old. He stood up against his father. He said, "Don't hurt my mommy." . . . My son has suffered greatly. He's having trouble breaking the cycle. . . . He calls me and says: "Why do I have the urge to do things that Dad did to you" and he goes "What can I do to stop this?" The last thing he wants to be is that way.

When they looked out from the family at society, many people said they sometimes felt puzzled about how their personal lives would intersect with cultural and political trajectories. They wondered how families could steer themselves in one direction when the larger society moved in a different direction. "Family values are important," maintained a black construction worker from Chicago. In talking about "the way things are going right now," he said that he was troubled by "the way things are going with *society*, not personally." A high school food service manager from Texas wanted the younger generation to learn about both continuity ("things that their grandma and grandpa did and things that they did also") and change ("the world is changing so much"). Continuity consisted of the recognizable small things that family members did, while change came from "the world." A New Jersey probation officer relished family gatherings where he could see and hear continuity across four generations. In his account as well, change originated outside the family:

A lot of the conversations [we]re about the . . . differences between the past and now, the present, and with the four generations each generation experienced things at a different time. Things that happened to my great-grandmother were totally different than things that happened to my sister or aunt.

War introduced the most common threat to family continuity from the outside world. Thinking of relatives killed and mangled in the Vietnam War, a Missouri home health administrator wondered "Why should we fight and kill each other?" In a split second, change from the outside world could sever generations of family continuity. A 33-year-old plumbing saleswoman from southeastern Michigan said that as she watched the Gulf

War of 1991 on television, "it scared me because I didn't know what to expect. I thought of my kid being in the war, which he is too young for right now. . . . it is just something I've never experienced before. . . . You don't take life for granted because something always can happen."

Since they were constantly watching for progress and decline, reexamining experiences to remake trajectories, respondents developed sophisticated monitoring techniques. They wanted to place the latest event in a pattern to see whether it would continue or disrupt familiar narratives, whether it posed a threat or an opportunity. To this end, they took photos or videos to record events and preserve memories and they scrutinized photographs for clues about the course and pace of change; they marked things in the present so that they could later be used to chart change and continuity. With cameras and video recorders, 83 percent of our respondents recorded visual images for observing development, and 91 percent said they looked at those images with family and friends. "He goes through stages so quickly," said an Albuquerque contractor, explaining why he took pictures of his son. He wanted to be able to refer back to each stage in his son's development.

A nurse from West Monroe, Louisiana recalled, "My husband and son were sitting in lounge chairs that were right next to each other. They were almost like shadows, just sitting the same way. Their feet were positioned the same. I just saw them there and went and picked up the camera and snapped it." A Pennsylvania sales manager said, "Skiing is a very important thing with the family. Everybody skis together." When his grandson went to Vermont to ski for the first time, they carried a video camera to record the occasion: "We wanted his great-grandmother to see him. We wanted him to be able to look back on it in years to come."

Looking at photographs gave respondents the chance to reflect on how their lives added up: the moments of pleasure and pain from which they told and retold the stories of their lives. A West Virginian in his sixties said photographs were crucial to what "I believe about life." "You're living a life, writing a book in memory," he explained, and "anytime you want to look back," photograph albums provide "the things you go back to, playing golf, fishing, playing. It's the book of life. You write it. You look back. Some things are funny. Some are sad." A woman from Augusta, Georgia in her seventies reported that "my grandchildren like to see pictures" of the family, beginning with their great-grandparents. "Our own children like to look back when they were little," she added, "and their children like very much to see when [their parents] were little."

Our informants found many ways to record and monitor their lives. Some marked their children's heights on an inconspicuous door or wall. Almost a third, 29 percent, wrote in diaries and journals. A 34-year-old Minneapolis woman began to enter accounts of "my daily activities and what I perceived as meaningful events or occurrences" when she was 14 or 15, and "I enjoy reading back to see where I was, if I have moved along any." A woman from West Bend, Wisconsin kept a journal because "my therapist says that I should use it as a tool to measure my progress. It helps me to write things down in order to sort them out better." A Mexican American secretary from Los Angeles in his twenties kept a journal in which he wrote about "problems that I've been having" with his family and his girlfriend. "Writing in a journal helps me to think of a solution and how to deal with it," he said.

About once a week a 25-year-old receptionist in Carmichael, California "just picked up a pen and starting writing all the things I have been feeling" into a journal—"intimate feelings and emotions regarding family and friends." Years ago, after a car accident, a 25-year-old Pine Ridge Sioux woman began to have experiences whose immediacy she did not want to lose: "A lot of spiritual things happened to me at the time. I had dreams and visions. Just to remember them I wrote them down and that's what started me writing the diary." A 73-year-old Mexican American woman from California wrote down "things that have upset me, things that have made me happy"; she could then "go back and read it a few days later" to monitor her own development as an interpreter as well as the narratives she told about her life. A teenaged student from New Port Richey, Florida kept a journal in order to monitor his running: "It tells about how far I've gone, how I felt when I ran, and how it was outside . . . what to watch for and how you'll progress."

For others, journals provided a more painful way of measuring change and continuity. An Illinois woman in her thirties kept a journal that was "personal, our marriage and alcoholism and how we are trying to survive things." Having "just split from my husband," a New Jersey woman wrote about her relationship with her husband and "my relationship with God and that type of thing." She said that in the future she wanted to assess the development of those relationships. A Pine Ridge Sioux woman in her fifties talked about dealing with her husband's abuse and her failed marriage:

What I've had to do was to go back for ten years of my life and the experiences of my life that I had with my husband and write that down. What I'm doing is purifying my soul and my spirit from the traumatic marriage that I was involved in. And I'm doing this in order to get on with my life in a more positive manner.

Fitting experience into trajectories that offered familiarity and context and coherence, the Americans we interviewed took responsibility for their lives. They revisited experiences from many perspectives and reinterpreted them to meet changing needs. By making—and remaking—narratives that shaped choices for the future, they learned to move through time on their own terms.

"Sometimes you grow up real fast": Taking Responsibility for the Future

"When you get older . . . you don't just assume that everything is fine and is just going to be happy. You try to control things more," explained a woman in her fifties from Winston-Salem, North Carolina. Many respondents examined the narratives they were fashioning to identify where they wanted to assume greater responsibility. They sought to move beyond a childhood pattern that veered between dependence on and defiance of parents, a rhythm of exaggerated extremes in which parents ultimately made the rules. "I want to know, I want to be prepared, to know what I am to be responsible for," mused a 35-year-old Albuquerque contractor as he pondered his responsibility not only for those around him but also for cruelty inflicted by his ancestors in the generations before his birth. A 19-year-old Mexican American man from Coachella, California faced the future determined "to change what's bad and leave what's good."

As they tried to transcend childhood extremes of helplessness and omnipotence, many of the people we interviewed said they revisited experiences and imagined how they might intervene in trajectories they had created. Which family members, friends, experts, or people with similar experiences could help them? What combination of commitment, faith, hard work, luck, and skills would allow them to change the course of events? These respondents said they wanted to know how to act in the future, how to identify and maintain continuities that were important to them, how to change patterns they did not like. They turned to their narratives of the past to find patterns of change and continuity from which they could predict or at least imagine how to intervene. Change could introduce joy and empowerment or tragedy and destruction. Respondents

extracted contradictory lessons, grappled with different possible outcomes, and faced choices among conflicting priorities. As they did so, several informants reported that people, sometimes including themselves in
the past, had failed to make or recognize accurate trajectories, moments
when they should have assumed responsibility, or failed to make a difference—in fact had made things worse—when they had intervened. But the
challenge, many people told us, still provided the most intense, difficult,
and important ways that they used the past.

By creating narratives from experiences that could yield many meanings and revising them to meet changing needs—to imagine how they
wanted those narratives to end—the people we talked with tried to understand how they could make a difference. When should they decide that
something was beyond reach, and when should they try to intervene? A St.
Louisan in his seventies concluded, "The only thing I can do is change
myself. I can't change other people. I'm more laid back now. I don't get
uptight about some situations that aren't important to some things I do. . .
. I can't worry about what I can't control."

Some found the strength to change the courses of their lives by looking
to people who had successfully solved the same problems. A Pine Ridge
woman in her thirties told us she was inspired by a mentor to stop drinking; she proudly added, "I've been eleven years sober." Others said that by
sharing what it felt like to be addicted to drugs or alcohol, they could help
both themselves and others. "I'm a recovered alcoholic, and it helps me to
stay sober working with other alcoholics," explained a 58-year-old man
from Buffalo, New York. "I like to use my past to help people when they
get in trouble." He answered calls from those struggling with alcohol
nearly every night, sometimes five or seven calls a night.

Respondents thought about events in the larger society as well as those
in their intimate lives when they weighed how they might make a difference. The successful landing of a man on the moon "simply expanded my
view of what is possible," reported a Texan in his thirties, while it proved
to a North Carolina inventor that "man can accomplish a great deal if they
put enough effort behind it." A Pennsylvania woman in her sixties said the
need during World War II to sacrifice family members on the battlefield
and familiar foods and comforts at home taught her that "you can do anything. . . . You could complain [about] the ration coupons but still you do
it. It didn't kill you to do without sugar . . . because you were trying and
stretching your own abilities, trying to accomplish something that had to
be finished."

The protest movements of the 1960s taught a Pennsylvania professor that "institutions *can* change"; the same events taught a Florida mail carrier that "it doesn't matter what you say or do. Things just keep on rolling. For all the protest, for all the indignation that there was during the sixties and early seventies . . . nothing really became of it after everybody grew out of their age of rebellion." One respondent learned from protesting the Vietnam War "that the will of the few can override the will of the many." Another learned that "people can really effect change . . . the will of the people in the U.S. can eventually make a difference as to the politics and actions of its government." Different answers to the same question: What difference can I make?

"The past kinda floods into you": Making Family Narratives

The people we interviewed said they often had to distinguish between long-term obligations and immediate gratification, the claims of family and those of self. Facing complex realities—family myths, denials of abuse, alcoholism, breakdowns, and divorce, as well as moments of achievement and delight—these respondents agonized over whether and how to intervene in family relationships. Interventions meant to sustain or challenge the family's continuity were sometimes met with support, sometimes with hostility.

As they contemplated new responsibilities, many people told us, they heard the echoes of earlier struggles between self and family. On the one hand, they grew up hearing that they should pursue their individual ambitions. A black nurse in Upper Marlboro, Maryland reported that her father had encouraged her "to perform to my fullest potential and never let anyone discourage me." "When you want something, just kinda do the best you can to get it and never quit," an 18-year-old Mexican American in Texas learned from his father. A nurse's assistant from Pennsylvania reported that her grandmother "always instilled in us that if you want something you have to work for it. You can't have it handed to you."

Yet they also heard over and over about their responsibility to sustain the family at any cost. Few received as vivid a lesson as a 50-year-old black painter from Washington:

> The family structure must be strong. I must keep the family as strong as possible. My father gave everything just to keep the family strong, constantly told me about people before him who made the family strong, told

me how strong they were. It made me strong by knowing that people before me carried the responsibility and made me know I had to carry mine.

"I have to be in a position where my past is a good past . . . keeping my standards up, my family up," reported an African American mail carrier from Memphis. While younger family members were permitted to worry about "a new car, new clothes," and other personal desires, family members who had reached their forties had to "worry about trying to do things right," to care for others. Many of them said they had learned to put family obligations ahead of individual pleasures, to subordinate their selfish and immediate needs to the long-term good of the whole family.

Respondents vividly recalled tensions between self and family at times that seemed, in retrospect, to be turning points. A number of them remembered the conflicting pulls of self-fulfillment and family responsibility when they moved away from home. A Latino receptionist from California returned home for the first time in six years for a family gathering: "Going home I feel a part of the family again but at the same time I feel a bit of an outcast. . . . I feel very connected at times with the family and also very distant." A businessman in his thirties who moved to California from Michigan, where his whole family lived, reported that he tried to reconnect with his past by visiting often: "When I go back there I feel very connected. I'm the black sheep of the family. They're probably unhappy that I'm not as close as my brothers and sisters are. I'm sure my ma's unhappy I'm not there. But they also love [me] to visit." Some of the people we interviewed said they took action because they had to ensure the family's survival. A widow from East Falmouth, Massachusetts explained, "I'm bringing up my grandchildren. [Their] mother and father were drinking and doing drugs, so they were taken away and given to me because they had nowhere else to go."

Many people told us that marriage had been a turning point that brought dramatic new responsibility. Suddenly, they had to "learn to coexist with another person, being able to learn trust and cooperation, and to make a family of your own," explained a Nebraska woman in her twenties. Describing himself as "pretty selfish and self-oriented" as a teenager, a Pennsylvania machinist reported that he learned from marriage "how to share and love more." When he got married, a retail manager from Hinsdale, Illinois felt he was "moving out from underneath Mom and Dad . . . taking on a new life." A truck driver in his twenties from Pine Ridge reported that marriage "changed the way I've lived. I became more responsible and started a new era of my life. My thinking has changed from thinking of just one to thinking of two and thinking ahead where I was pretty carefree before."

The birth of a child was another major turning point. A West Virginia woman recalled her children's births as "rude awakening to real responsibility." A Georgia computer programmer said parenthood "revealed to me things about myself which I didn't like and things about myself that I did not know I was capable of, specifically not making yourself the first priority. . . . It's tremendous responsibility, and on the other hand it's a tremendous gift." "Learning to care for someone else" was the lesson taught a woman from Toledo, Ohio who tried from the start to create a past for her children: "I want my children to remember me with fond memories. I want them to look back to their childhood fondly. . . . When they look back at a ball game that they hit a home run at, I want them to know that I was there." The birth of a child gave a marketing manager from Marietta, Georgia "a real feeling of being an adult. . . . I didn't feel like an adult before. It is just that now I have someone dependent on me, that I am responsible for making sure she gets everything that she needs." A 34-year-old Mexican American woman from El Paso reported that the birth of her children "taught me responsibility. It makes you look at things totally different." She said that new family obligations had caused her to become "more involved in politics and realize how conservative I was."

Our informants talked about many turning points in the trajectories of their lives. "Sometimes you grow up real fast," reported a woman from Elma, Washington, who said the sudden illness of both parents when she was a child forced her to care for her brother, take a job, and make meals while attending school. "Having one of your children sick . . . that'll be with you for life. That's all we care about is them," reported a man in his forties from Clifton, Texas. "I was afraid we was going to lose him," a woman from Amsterdam, Missouri told an interviewer as she remembered her newborn son hovering between death and life. A 30-year-old Pine Ridge resident described what he had learned from his son's illness: "I was so into my work up until five years ago, till one of my boys got sick, was in the hospital. I just got to sit back and think, 'I'm not really in control here. There's really a much more powerful person and that'd be my God.'"

In the face of sudden tragedy, respondents frequently cross-examined the priorities they had set for their lives. "When you go through crises you find out what's really important in life," explained a California man in his fifties. The death of a friend jolted a California software developer in his forties to place less value on "what appears to be important in our day-to-day lives, such as work, financial success, and possessions" and instead to recommit himself to "what is really much more important, like the interpersonal relationships one has with other human beings." After the deaths of his uncle and niece, a Pine Ridge police officer in his twenties learned "to stop and smell the roses. Before I was carefree. Now I look at things with a wider view. It made me more of a father than I was before. Before, I thought the kids should be raised by the mother, but now I am more a part of raising them."

Death taught many respondents that they should nurture the relationships they valued. "You thought they were going to be there" forever, a woman from Chesterfield, Missouri said of her parents. Only after they died did she realize "how much they really did for me." The death of her aunt taught an Oregon woman in her twenties "not to take my family for granted . . . because they might not always be there. It's very important to tell people you love [that] you love them."

Facing the ultimate discontinuity, many people told us that they rededicated themselves to continuity. After her brothers died, a 44-year-old manager of an Oregon fast-food restaurant committed herself to "try to do everything you can and try to love everybody [in your family] that you can *now*." "You never know when it is your time to go," a 38-year-old woman from St. Joseph, Missouri concluded after the deaths of her mother and grandfather. She determined "to be closer to my family, to not fight with them, and to love them and show them love." A fitness trainer in her twenties from Upper Darby, Pennsylvania learned from her grandmother's death that

> things never stay the same. Things always change. . . . When somebody dies you can completely close yourself off to the world around you and never get close to anyone else again. . . . That's building walls and not living. And that's pretty basically what I did. . . . I finally learned . . . that we are all going to die and . . . so appreciate the time you have to get close to as many people as you can.

The death of his daughter brought an Oregon Latino face-to-face with the eternal truth that "the time on this earth is short," and so "I am concentrating more on family."

When they wanted to try to assume greater responsibility for sustaining their families, respondents often had to revisit earlier conflicts and find ways to resume the broken narrative so that it could end in continuity, not conflict. "When you get to be middle-aged the past kinda floods into you," said a Wisconsin musician in his forties. He believed "it's kind of a mid-life crisis thing. . . . You see your parents aging and you really start concentrating. You feel the need to mend fences with parents and resolve differences" that may have festered for decades. When he began to appreciate continuity, a Philadelphia restaurant owner in his fifties reinterpreted the conflicts of his youth and concluded that his father had, after all, wanted the same things he wanted:

> For the longest time when I was young I thought that [my father] was the enemy. Then one day when I was about 27, 28 years old I woke up and realized that he is not the enemy but my friend, and all the things that he was telling me were only things that would be beneficial to me in the long run. I hope some day my kids will say the same thing about me.

Life and death—these were the stakes respondents kept in view as they revisited the past to set priorities in their everyday lives. The sudden death of a friend her own age taught a 23-year-old Mexican American woman from Texas "not to take life for granted. It can be taken away from you quickly. We raise our kids to be carefree. I got kind of a rude awakening. I thought being young we were untouchable." Over and over, our respondents told us, they examined priorities and remade trajectories in order to try to pay more attention to what they now saw as the fundamental themes in their life stories.

"I wish I knew then what I do now": Taking Responsibility for the Past

Before they could shape their futures, respondents said, they had to take responsibility for what they had or should have done in the past. When they spoke of "learning from the mistakes of the past"—and many did—they meant that they regretted not only the things they had done or said but also priorities they had set and narratives they had made to guide them from past to future. A number of them said they had vowed to change their life stories, or at least their behavior, and transform themselves into better people in the process of changing the directions of their lives.

Inspired by remorse or guilt or just plain curiosity, they began by reliving or revisiting experiences—events, decisions—and trying to imagine how they might have created different outcomes if they had acted differently. They revisited experiences that in retrospect appeared to be turning points (such as a particular moment of making love or trying drugs) and reexamined resulting narratives (such as a pregnancy or a pattern of drug addiction) as they contemplated how they might change or sustain the directions of their lives. In their mind's eyes they fixed moments from the past or themes in their relationships, sometimes obsessively, almost always with intensity.

By revisiting earlier experiences they imagined how differently they might have shaped them or been shaped by them. What signals had they missed? A South Carolina man uttered the frequent lament: "I wish I knew then what I do now." With knowledge acquired since, they could now see clearly that earlier actions or decisions had been mistakes. They had acquired skills as interpreters. "I'm more experienced," declared a housekeeper in her seventies from Philadelphia. "A lot of things I wouldn't do today that I guess I did in the past." Many respondents said they saw the past more clearly with the benefit of trajectories they had subsequently drawn. "If I could live it all over it would be a completely different everything," declared a woman from St. Joseph, Missouri. "I would have tried to have been a better daughter and a better student for . . . my mother's sake."

Seeing larger patterns now in what they had experienced at the time as discrete episodes, many wished that they had sought counsel from people who could have helped them change course. A woman in her eighties said she regretted her failure "to find a better way to stop what happened" when her husband acted in ways that meant "we couldn't be man and wife any more." She added, "I didn't know how to go about getting help. . . . I thought I was the only one that it happened to in my family." The burden of recognizing and modifying the trajectory of her husband's behavior was too much for her to handle by herself.

Respondents often tried to reconstruct the sequences of individual events, each harmless or insignificant enough, that led to the sources of their regret; they wanted to figure out at what points they should have spotted danger. From these sequences they hoped in the future to recognize—and prevent—similar tragedies. "You have to look at the steps that led to this happening and then avoid these steps," argued a firefighter from Columbus, Ohio. "The hard thing about history," he observed, is that "you can't always recognize the steps being the same, because they are always slightly different but intrinsically the same." When "I find things that are emotionally upsetting," reported a 52-year-old woman from Newton Falls, Ohio, "I find usually there is a pattern in the past which when healed allows me to move forward."

"Our generation should realize the mistakes that have been made in the past and try not to do those again," declared a 63-year-old woman from Pleasant Hill, Missouri, with Vietnam as her object lesson. Another respondent concluded that knowledge of the Third Reich, Vietnam, and other events can "teach us not to repeat the mistakes of the past." Seeing people around them follow patterns they disliked, many respondents vowed that they would take different paths. A number of them decided they didn't want to live as their parents had. A 33-year-old Mexican American hotel administrator in Texas "learn[ed] from the mistakes my dad made in life. . . . An example would be his treatment of women. My dad was very possessive, in control, wanting to control a wife. I believe in equal control over family matters."

Recalling his parents' fights, a 25-year-old Mexican American construction worker from Houston vowed, "If I ever get married, I would never do the same things they did. I try to get away from the way they did and do it the right way. I see life in a different perspective, a lot different from my mother and father. I see life not as bad or as a struggle. I see life as very wonderful, very beautiful." A customer service manager from Virginia in her mid-thirties said that "it may help me to better myself" to study her family's past and "identify traits that I may have that are traits in other family members. Maybe a path that a family member might have taken, if I see myself going down that same path I can alter it. We can learn by other people's mistakes. . . . I see how some people in my close family handle their temper that I have inherited. It's just like a mirror image and saying, 'My God, that's me!' I just don't want to be like that."

Learning from mistakes was often painful. At age 17 an Illinois woman had experienced her pregnancy as a disaster. In retrospect, however, she concluded that it had turned out "for the best" because she learned that "when bad things happen it doesn't mean the world is over. It made me stronger." She had, she said, learned to value long-term commitment more than instant pleasure and spoke of "the importance of marriage before sex." A German-born construction worker in his sixties reported from Florida, "I like the American way of life. . . . Let's live today and the hell with tomorrow. I was making money and blowing it at the same time." He expected "things would continue on for a few more years and then I could retire and that would be it." But then the construction boom busted and he

lost his job. "My world collapsed." His marriage broke up; he became sui-
cidal. From this tragic turn of events he learned that "you should allow for
bad times" and save resources to sustain the household. But he confessed,
"If you want to learn the truth, I didn't learn anything. . . . I am a construction worker and make money and still blow it when I get it." In
telling about his unsuccessful attempt to change the direction of his life,
this worker sounded like many informants who, in reporting their regrets
and failures, talked about great difficulties that had discouraged them
from trying to intervene and made it difficult to succeed when they did try.
And yet the failures and regrets of their pasts also inspired them to try to
change course and furnished their best resources for hoping to succeed
where earlier they had failed.

Respondents told us the key to taking responsibility for the future lay in
deciding to take responsibility for how they had acted in the past. Only by
acknowledging what they now felt about their pasts—the grief or loss or
shame or regret or guilt—could they incorporate those experiences into
new narratives. To relive moments or patterns he wanted to avoid in the
future, a store owner from Tampa kept what he called "my book of sins,
things that I would do differently if I had the opportunity. . . . It's basically
related to interpersonal relations." As they tried to change course in the
future, respondents felt the need to apologize and forgive each other for
things that had kept them apart in the past. A woman from Jersey Shore,
Pennsylvania recalled that after her grandmother had surgery a decade
earlier she had played with the invalid's walker; the woman said she still
wished she had apologized: "She died the next day, and I thought it was
my fault. I was being really bad that day, and I never got the chance to say
'I'm sorry.' "

"The children often do pay for the sins of their fathers," a contractor
from Albuquerque reported. He told us that he felt responsible for things
he had not himself done:

> Where my ancestors have treated people improperly I expect to have to
> make amends. . . . My grandparents . . . have hurt people [by their racism]
> and those hurt people and the children of those hurt people probably do
> carry some sort of a grudge and as a beneficiary of past injustice I can be
> held responsible to be a benefactor in some way to those harms.

When she revisited experiences she regretted from the past, a 30-year-old
Mexican American postal worker in San Jose not only acknowledged mis-

takes to herself but also filed them away as lessons for her children. She didn't want them to yield to temptation and act as she had: "You learn from your mistakes after you've done them. You carry it on to your children, telling them what's right and wrong. . . . When they get older, [able] to understand, that's when I'll want to tell them things I've learned from my mistakes."

As they tried to take responsibility for the past and chart trajectories for the future, respondents said they began to have a new sense of themselves as agents with the desire and capacity to change patterns they had fallen into. Instead of following what they now saw as their usual habit of drifting from day to day along a course of least resistance, perhaps sheltered by parents or stronger personalities, many of them told us with pride of those memorable and perhaps rare occasions when they had found within themselves the resources for becoming active people who could take responsibility in new ways. They often framed the decision to intervene as a choice between drift and mastery that resolved into a choice between immediate and long-term priorities, between concern with self and concern for others. Many of the people we talked with said that the commitment to chart a new course transformed them into "better" or "new" or "different" people, even "born again."

These respondents said that attempting to change their lives took will, strength, hope, and confidence. To stop drifting along with short-term temptations, they needed to commit themselves to a course regardless of diversions and obstacles. From his parents' divorce the owner of a motorcycle shop in Las Vegas learned that couples should not have children until they "make sure there is commitment on both sides" to sustain the relationship—that "you're not going to be together for just" a short time. "Don't get married unless you're sure," a California veterinarian's assistant decided after his parents' divorce. To help her children commit themselves to sustaining core values in her world, a Nevada radiology supervisor took her son to see movies about the Holocaust like *Schindler's List*: "I want to make sure he understands . . . to make sure nothing like that ever happens again."

Many people told us that newfound commitments to change were not simple choices or acts of will but the result of struggle and conversion. Trying to change the courses of their lives meant acknowledging that the habits they had fallen into were wrong in ways they called ignorant, harmful, dysfunctional, sinful. A 46-year-old Mexican-born teacher from Texas gave an extraordinary account of the his conversion from drift to mastery, a year-long transformative struggle:

When I was around 15 years of age I made a decision that I would not attend church anymore. I basically did what everybody was doing in the world, like doing drugs, sexual promiscuity, basically became an alcoholic. . . . I was the kind of person that drank all night and came home at 2, 3 A.M.

One day I was in my favorite beer joint drinking with my buddies. I heard a voice that spoke to me like an echo with lightning and thunder. The voice asked basically: "What are you doing here?" I thought that it was a friend talking to me, and I turned around to shake hands and there was no one behind me. So I sat there and thought about what I had heard. The voice spoke to me again and told me to get up and go home. "You are not like these people that are here with you." I answered: "What do you mean I am not like them? They gamble. I gamble. They drink. I drink. They do drugs. I do drugs. They commit adultery. I commit adultery. So I am just like them." I arrived home at 8 P.M. that evening. My wife greeted me at the door with surprise. I told her that I was not feeling good, which was a lie. I did not want to tell her what had happened.

After this for some unknown reason, now I know the reason, my children started asking me to take them to church. . . . I would always promise that I would but every Sunday I would wake up with such a hangover that all I wanted to do was sleep in later.

It was about this time that I began to experience attacks from the devil. [He would] walk inside my house and torment me. I would have fights with the devil, spiritual battles that seemed so real that you basically had physical evidence of such fights. One day my older son, he was about 10 years old, came to me and told me for Christmas he did not want any gift. All he wanted was for me to take him to church, which basically made me feel very bad and very sad. I considered myself to be a good person, a good father, and I basically said to myself: "How can you deny your children something good like going to church?"

In this one-year period, one of the things I was also doing, I would be very nervous, fidgety. Basically I was getting the urge to go drinking at noon. I began to cry out to God about my desire. I was asking God to make me a better person and a better father.

Respondents often used religious language: they equated drift with temptation and sin, with losing the way, and conversion with finding a new way, becoming a new person, being born again. To change the courses of their lives was to ask forgiveness for directions they had taken in the past. Once they had converted from living from day to day, these respondents told us, the historical horizon stretched from the beginning of time to the end of eternity. Religion offered rules to guide them as they moved through life. Reading the Bible led a 52-year-old black service technician from Washington to "think about my life before I was saved. I think of how grateful I am to be able to repent and be redeemed. It makes me think about my life before I gave it to Christ and received new life." Almost with a shudder he told an interviewer, "If it weren't for Christ I might not be here now."

A woman from Greenbrier, Arkansas talked about her faith in the resurrection of Jesus—"knowing that he would have died for me even if I was the only person in the world"—and added:

> I have been born again. . . . I remember my life before I met Christ and now the difference is just like dark to daylight. All of a sudden I had love in my heart for everybody, even for my enemies. . . . My husband drank and did things that weren't nice, but now it didn't matter because I had God. It gave me strength and hope. I didn't have anything to live for. I had suicidal tendencies because of the things that went on around me, and I couldn't see hope in the world or anyone around me. But then the Lord gave me . . . he was a problem solver. . . . He also gave me a reason to live. . . . He gave me this in the midst of turmoil.

A 37-year-old painter from Baton Rouge, Louisiana found in Jesus a way to sustain continuity in his life: "If you live your life according to his teachings then you will be a winner in the end. They have helped me straighten out my life, stop smoking marijuana, and pretty much just straightening out my life." A Michigan homemaker explained that Jesus "has taught me how to live my life in every area. It helps me because it gives me direction." A 21-year-old Mexican American woman said her faith in Jesus taught her "how to become a better person, to have faith, to care for others, to love."

Many Indians embraced religious teachings and practices for the spiritual strength to change trajectories. When a 32-year-old Sioux woman from South Dakota wanted to overcome her "problem with alcohol," she turned to her father-in-law, a medicine man, who taught her to cure herself the Lakota way by entering a sweat lodge for four days of fasting, praying, and smoking a peace pipe. In the sweat lodge they communicated with the spirits of earlier generations that taught the importance of sustaining continuity in the face of the transitory problems of everyday life. A 31-year-old Pine Ridge Sioux woman reported that the spiritual struggle she underwent in a sweat lodge kept the father of her children out of jail: "I went on a vision quest. I sat in a sweat lodge for a whole day with a peace pipe and when I came out I felt it worked. A week later when he went to court he was freed." Another Sioux, this one a 38-year-old woman, described sweat lodges as places where families cleansed themselves as they prayed for members whose lives were heading in the wrong direction.

"Coming from a stage of chronic alcoholism," a 31-year-old black welder from North Carolina said, he used Alcoholics Anonymous meetings "as a crutch to remind myself of the past." Her father's death after decades of closet alcoholism "started my healing process," said a 45-year-old black woman from Cleveland who recognized that "I followed that pattern and married an alcoholic." With her father's death "I saw a pattern I had created for myself, and I made a decision to change. When I made that decision things in my life started to change."

Knowing at first hand the difficulty of changing directions, a 28-year-old man from Brooklyn said he hoped to inspire others by talking about how he got past a life that centered on selling and using drugs. "Being a young black male in sobriety," he wanted "to share a few things with people using drugs today." He had learned from experience "not to use drugs never again in my life, no kind." He wanted to become an example to others of how they could change the trajectories of their lives and become better people. "One time in my life I was an addict. I was pushing youth drugs. It caused me to have a lot of bad experiences. It was a fault in my life that was uncontrollable. Knowing now how I was back then, I am a better person than I was back then."

With dedication—and often with pain—people told us how they revisited and reinterpreted the past, trying to make a difference in their own lives and those of others. Again and again, they described how they worked to take responsibility for the future and the past, to change their behavior, and to become different people in the process.

Participation, Mediation, Authority, Trust

"I've personally always wanted to go to Africa" in order to study "my own culture," reported a 51-year-old black woman from Cleveland. So she signed up for a tour of museums and villages of Ghana that was organized by a community recreation center. She traveled through centuries and across continents to visit dungeons along the Ghanaian coast, where slaves were held before they were forced onto the slave ships for the infamous middle passage that transported Africans to America. And she imagined her way back into their experience:

> I was overcome with self-pity when I was standing on this hill and the coconut trees and the ocean were so pretty and you could look over into the village. It was as if my ancestors were all of a sudden ripped from this place that was so beautiful and they were put in these dungeons and they were never going to see the villages again. That blew my mind, the dungeon. When I was in the dungeon, it wasn't so bad, but when I got back outside that had the most significant contrast, the beauty of the scenery and the starkness of the dungeon. That was the emotional state that I was in when I was there.

Listening to her great-grandmother talk about living on the Kansas frontier in boxcar houses with dirt floors, a 22-year-old woman from Missouri told us, "makes me feel like I was there, the way she tells the stories." Ken Burns's televised Civil War documentary "made you feel like you were there experiencing it also," said a Mexican American respondent.

For this viewer Burns brought the Civil War to life by having actors read "letters participants wrote that told about their experiences. They weren't sanitized at all."

Since the past contained resources for defining identity and imagining possibilities, for spotting possible danger and possible support, for sustaining continuity or introducing change, many respondents tried to broaden the pasts they could use beyond what they had experienced for themselves. They wanted to reach toward people who had lived at other times and places. They visited historic sites and talked with grandparents. They watched movies and read books. They studied history in formal classes. And they tried to adapt what they knew from their uses of firsthand and intimate experience to the challenge of using more distant pasts.

The people we interviewed wanted to approach the broader past on their own terms. Only by getting close to experience could they see the ambiguities, multiple perspectives, and transformative potential they had learned to expect in their intimate worlds. The key to using the past fully and freely to meet needs in the present, they learned, lay in the sources through which they retrieved it. But as they moved beyond firsthand experience, many people told us that they faced a basic problem: sources for wider pasts had come into existence to advance their creators' agendas. Some versions of the past were presented to win elections, to increase television ratings, to sell books, or to teach patriotism. Others were intended to deepen relationships or win arguments.

Since these sources mediated between past and present, respondents had to assess patterns of mediation between what they wanted to know about from the past and why they wanted to know about it in the present. When they encountered history in school or on their television sets, they had to develop methods for evaluating what they were presented, for taming the sources. They tended to worry as much about how and why a source was mediating between them and a moment in the past as about whether the account was accurate. They could make more sense of an account when they recognized its author or when they had experienced contexts like those in which it had been created. The people we interviewed were searching for sources with perspectives on the past they could trust, and their searches employed a range of skills: interrogation and cross-examination; reaching out with empathy; forming and testing hypotheses and prejudices.

Many people we talked with carefully distinguished among individual accounts. They trusted one eyewitness more than another, one television program more than another. But they also distinguished among categories of sources. Eyewitnesses were different from textbooks, Hollywood movies from family stories. When we asked them to rank the overall trustworthiness of seven different "places where people get information about the past," respondents illustrated their preference for approaching experiences on their own terms. They declared their preferences when they answered interviewers' directions to assign a number on a scale from 1 to 10, "where 1 means not at all trustworthy and 10 means very trustworthy," to the following kinds of sources:[1]

TABLE 4.1

Trustworthiness of Sources on 10-point scale:

	Mean	Percent 8-10	Choosing 1-3
Museums	8.4	79.9%	1.3%
Personal accounts from grandparents or other relatives	8.0	68.9	2.4
Conversation with someone who was there (witness)	7.8	64.4	2.8
College history professors	7.3	54.3	5.2
High school teachers	6.6	35.5	8.8
Nonfiction books	6.4	32.1	9.1
Movies and television programs	5.0	11.0	22.3

Respondents brought different tastes to the historical texts they engaged. Some individuals preferred to stimulate their dramatic imaginations with films, while others wanted to strengthen their personal relationships by talking with family members. In contrast to the larger pattern, a few respondents found movies trustworthy and eyewitnesses untrustworthy. While the pattern of greater trust in firsthand sources and lesser trust in impersonal sources held up across demographic groups, there were still some variations that readers can explore in appendix 1 and the tables we've posted on the Web. By tests of statistical association women generally trusted all sources more than did men. People with more schooling were more likely to trust books and less likely to trust television programs than people with less schooling. And the Oglala Sioux distrusted movies and television programs more than any other demographic group distrusted any single category.

Many of our informants drew on a wide range of sources and used sources of one type to cross-examine those of another. What mattered, they said, was how well a given source held up against their other knowledge. A 33-year-old Mexican American plumber from San Antonio said he trusted exhibits at the Texas Institute of Culture because "usually the Institute pretty much tells the same things" he heard from "old folks I have spoken with." To a 20-year-old woman from McAllen, Texas, a Houston art museum's exhibition of portraits from the First and Second World Wars "seemed real" because "it related very well with books that I had read about the wars." A 42-year-old Mexican American man from Asherton, Texas believed that the movie *Bonnie and Clyde* "was completely flawed" based on his "reading from other sources." A 25-year-old Pine Ridge Sioux resident came to trust his high school history teacher because "he would teach something and I would look it up or I would come across it later and it would be true. He had said the exact same thing." A 38-year-old Pine Ridge Sioux woman came to distrust what she had learned: "What I was being told in school is so different than what I have found out since."

As they talked about why they trusted or distrusted sources, many respondents displayed the same creativity they brought to the challenge of using sources to connect past with present. Their attitudes toward mediation contained some surprises. We conclude this chapter with the remarkable finding that respondents consistently felt deeply connected to the past when they visited history museums and historic sites and notably disconnected from the past when they studied history in school.

"When you're living with it, it gets more to your head": Family Members and Eyewitnesses as Sources

"Experience is the best teacher," explained a 24-year-old African American woman from Detroit. "It's important because you're there. You can hear what people say and see it for yourself and experience it. You know for yourself." Respondents said that the real advantage to experiencing something at first hand was not so much knowing its details—who said or did what—but sensing the multiple meanings and possibilities evident only to participants. "When you're living it, it gets more into your head," observed a 52-year-old Mexican American housekeeper from Texas.

The people we interviewed trusted eyewitnesses more than other sources because witnesses could use the rich variety of their experiences in interpreting what they'd come through. "I believe you can get more from someone who was at a certain event—a sense of what they were feeling as things were happening," reported a Mexican American commodity trader from Los Angeles. In contrast to "just facts in a book," the chance to hear a personal account from an eyewitness "gives you a whole different insight, more on a personal level . . . something you can feel. . . . It just sticks with you longer," said a 39-year-old woman from Orange Park, Florida. A few people said that by traveling through space they could travel in time and observe at first hand what they had earlier heard from others. A 50-year-old African American woman from Los Angeles "never knew" what to make of stories she had heard about how southern whites treated blacks "until my father took me back South . . . and I had to go to the black section instead of the white section even though I am light-skinned."

When they talked about large events like war, depression, or natural disaster, people tended to start with individual experience. A 70-year-old man from Tulsa said that for him World War II was defined by his naval service in the South Pacific: "It's just an experience you really can't explain unless you've been through it. It's just such a big thing and you feel like such a small part of it, but it took all to be victorious." The meaning of the large lay in the stories of the small. A Mexican American respondent valued his parents' account of "a very personal aspect" of a 1933 hurricane: "The way they told it you felt that you were there. . . . It was just their expressions in telling it and the experiences they had during that time, and how frightened they were. It was something that was not announced. It just happened and to them, and to them it was happening." Another Mexican American respondent trusted his cousins' accounts of Vietnam because "they could tell me firsthand information about what they went through—like the adventures, not really about government, but about how life was there."

Many of the people we interviewed said they wanted to get close enough to others' experiences to know how participants had shaped and been shaped by events as large as wars. "I had read books" about World War II, began an African American woman from Dallas, but "my father was in World War II . . . and the way he told it really gave me some insight into the way things happened. It really brings it closer to home." A technician from Utah in his late twenties felt drawn to the Second World War by his grandfather's stories of flying planes that bombed German cities. A physical therapist from Pasadena saw the bombing of German cities from another perspective: she talked about her mother's stories of trying to survive in Germany with Allied bombs falling all around her.

Respondents understood that experiences could evoke a range of reactions. A 50-year-old black woman from Decatur, Georgia, who remembered a time "when you had to go through different doors and sit in the back of the bus," said she had learned through her experiences with racial segregation "that everyone doesn't think like I was thinking." "I listen to the stories about Wounded Knee from several people that were here then and you get a different twist from every one of them," observed a 48-year-old Oglala Sioux man. "No two people who saw the same accident have the same story," an 85-year-old widow from Iowa observed. "Different people remember things differently. Two people can see the same thing and describe it totally differently," said a 34-year-old driver from Indiana.

To grasp a full range of perspectives, many respondents sought sources who could take them as close as possible to an experience. A 44-year-old mediator from Oshkosh, Wisconsin wanted to hear directly from participants because "they can give me their actual account rather than hand-me-down information." "I always find things more reliable coming out of the mouth of somebody who saw it with their own eyes [rather] than somebody who heard it second or third or fourth or fifth hand and then try to report it based on what they have heard," said a Virginia woman, whose conclusion came from her occupation as a lawyer. She added, "It is a fairly well-accepted premise in our society that the most reliable is eyewitness testimony."

Because they felt wary of changes brought about by the passage of time and the intervention of new agendas, respondents were more likely to trust an account from someone who hadn't "had time to embroider it, like with fiction," in the words of a man in his seventies from Tenn Colony, Texas. A contractor from Wauconda, Illinois worried that sources might have been "influenced by outside influences . . . so they could tell you something that is swayed and they could believe it but it may not be true"—like schoolchildren who "give back" whatever teachers want to hear "in order to get the grade." "As things get passed down I think they tend to get blown out of proportion," said an administrative assistant from West Bend, Wisconsin. "Over time stories change," explained a mental retardation worker in Philadelphia.

Even when time and bias did not distort accounts, people told us, eyewitnesses varied dramatically in their knowledge, perspective, and capacities for recall. "If they were there, I would assume that they would know what they were talking about," began a Pine Ridge woman, who stated the presumption of most respondents. "But," she added, "that would depend on who you're talking to." "Some people stretch the truth," said a 33-year-old salesman from Blissfield, Michigan. Other respondents said witnesses sometimes exaggerated their own importance or refined their stories for greater impact.

Since witnesses couldn't always be trusted, many respondents wanted to interrogate them. A 41-year-old Mexican American from Los Angeles trusted his friends' accounts of Vietnam because "you can talk with them. You can ask your own questions." A Mexican American woman from Los Angeles talked about the necessity of asking questions: "You're there to ask them about the event so they can elaborate on the event . . . and [you can] judge whether they're lying or not." A 24-year-old Indiana woman said she could "probably tell by a person's body language if they are telling you the truth." A 51-year-old Mexican American woman from San Antonio observed that "with the person that was there, I find it a bit easier to communicate because you can see their reaction to whatever you're talking about—their body language. You can always pick up things from body language. I would just find it more interesting, I guess, because I'd be able to talk one-on-one." "You can sort of weed out what's true by a person's gestures," said a 36-year-old Sioux school counselor.

Noting that she could not ask questions of a book, an African American nurse's aide from Detroit preferred sources she could "talk to . . . and really dig [in and see] if they are sincere or not." "When you watch TV you're just an object watching—you're not able to be a participant," explained a nurse from Albany; she was more likely to trust an account from a person she could engage so that "I would be able to rebuke it or argue with it."

Most respondents placed their greatest trust not in people with the clearest accounts but in those they knew best. They tended to value personal accounts by family members above those by professional historians because, as a 60-year-old clerk from Texas reported, "You can trust your family more than other people." A 21-year-old black woman from Brooklyn said, "People I don't know—a professor, a movie—could be telling me any old thing, but grandparents get my complete trust." "Sharing the same background and goals and experience, I would put much more stock" in stories by family members than those by "a total stranger," declared an African American automobile salesman from Missouri. A 33-year-old Pine Ridge Sioux respondent trusted stories told by his relatives because "I know what kind of people they are, whereas if I heard something from someone else I would have some doubt."

Many people said they could assess a family member's interpretation of experience because they could see what the experience had meant to the narrator when it originally happened. They evaluated the story based on their knowledge of the storyteller. "I can . . . see exaggerations because I know them. I know how they are talking [and] speaking from experience so I can adjust" for the storyteller, explained a shipwright from Bremerton, Washington. A 30-year-old fund-raiser from Florida trusted her grandfather because "I can see the emotion in his face as he talks. . . . It's a genuine emotion. He gets involved in the story when he's talking about it and it's more believable because I know he's not an actor and not trying to sway me to believe one way or the other."

Some respondents said they trusted relatives' stories because they were told for the purpose of sustaining the family, not for advancing a selfish agenda. Storytellers wanted to meet the needs of listeners. While it was important that older family members "were there when these things happened," it was more important in conversations about an earlier experience that "the trust warms the person that you love . . . and then you can be sure that the other person trusts you," in the words of a Mexican American clerk from Cameron County, Texas. A Mexican American clerk from Hidalgo County said that the important thing about stories from older relatives was not their content but their purpose: they were told "for our knowledge." The historymaking that mattered most to our respondents emerged as a byproduct of intimate relationships or as a way to strengthen them. An African American woman from Decatur, Georgia said she had a responsibility to pass along to her grandchildren "what they need to know" from the family's experience. "You can trust your relatives more than somebody else, mainly because they lead you," a 27-year-old Mexican American from Mercedes, Texas believed.

Since family members were drawing on the past to help each other shape their identities, many respondents simply did not expect to find deliberate distortion in their stories. They trusted accounts by family members because "I don't feel my parents would lie to me about anything," in the words of a 44-year-old black delicatessen manager from Salt Lake City, or because "my children don't lie to me," in the words of a 67-year-old widow from West Virginia. An African American woman from Philadelphia believed that family members "would not embellish for the sake of trying to impress me." "They would be less likely to stretch the truth with me," said a 49-year-old clerk from California. They did not necessarily believe everything older family members told them. Some people told us of exaggerated stories about hardships faced or achievements won by earlier family members, but family myths (and the skepticism that sometimes greeted their retelling) became part of family heritages because their distortions were harmless, meant not to mislead or manipulate people but to convey pride and love across generations in ways that listeners could decide exactly how to weigh.

Respondents often selected their grandparents as the sources they trusted most when they tried to draw on pasts beyond their own firsthand experience. A 37-year-old black government worker from Maryland described her grandmother's authority:

> When you are face to face with someone who has been there and is telling the story just from the gestures, from the emotion, just the aura that they give off, you know they are telling the truth. Grandmothers have the wisdom of all. They have hindsight. They can tell immediately if a person is of great character or not. All through your life when you come to a fork in the road you can hear your grandmother's voice saying, "I told you this would happen."

"Wisdom" came with a lifetime of experience and reflection, which was shared with younger people to help them develop their own perspectives for interpreting new experience and reading new sources.

Yet the authority of older family members had limits. "It depends on if you're talking about the past of the whole U.S. or about our family past," observed a 27-year-old Pine Ridge woman. She trusted older family members for stories "mostly about our culture and things that happened to the Indians a long time ago and also our family." While grandparents "know about the history just around the reservation," said a 46-year-old Pine Ridge resident, "professors know more about other things like facts. They read more." For breadth and diversity, many people told our interviewers, they had to reach beyond pasts their grandparents had experienced.

"They slant the picture deliberately": Mediation of Experience
Through Mass Media and Books

Television, movies, and books offered respondents the most accessible wide-ranging pasts to reach into. And yet on our scale for ranking the trustworthiness of sources, television programs and movies (5.0) and nonfiction books (6.4) were ranked lowest. In explaining why they distrusted movies and television, many respondents talked about their hatred and fear of being manipulated by people who distort the past to meet their own needs. The desire to make money, they told us, was by far the most pervasive reason for distorting the past. "Sometimes people do things just for money. They say things just for money," observed a 61-year-old bank manager from Pennsylvania.

Television and movies provided the most blatant arenas for distorting the past because they appealed to low common denominators that could assemble the largest possible audience. In contrast to intense engagements with firsthand experience, many respondents told us, in the words of a carpenter from Bainbridge, Georgia, that when "the profit margin" takes over "they will pretty much say anything to get you to watch the program and it loses what it's all about. They are a little more quick to lie to you." Since "historical accuracy is not the primary goal of movies and TV," a 31-year-old teacher from Montclair, New Jersey maintained that "in order to enhance the dramatic power of the film, I'm sure facts were altered and deleted, important facts were left out. . . . Films and TV glorify incidents in the past and de-emphasize the negative effects of those events." "It's all for entertainment . . . to get the ratings to make money . . . whatever sells. If they feel the program is losing its ratings they'll use a certain sensationalism," concluded a 53-year-old real estate lender from Los Angeles.

"Movies and TV are made for entertainment and for the major part they skip actual history," said a widow from Greenville, Texas. A 43-year-old parts manager from Dallas who had majored in history explained why producers often distort the past: "Facts about history are . . . frankly boring. TV and movies tend to embellish everything and tend to make it more than it really is." Moviemakers "have a tendency to make things fancy" (in the words of an 79-year-old Minnesota widow) or "to jazz it up" (in the words of a 36-year old carpenter from Washington State) or "to overdramatize and fictionalize history to make the movie more appealing and profitable" (in the words of a 26-year-old office manager from California). In short, television and movies "are embroidered to suit the producer and designed to make money. They are going to have enticing things in them which probably don't have anything to do with the truth at all," observed a 78-year-old woman from Houston.

Some people reported that it was hard to separate distortions introduced by commercial greed from those caused by cultural prejudices. Pine Ridge residents, for example, thoroughly distrusted movies. "The

Hollywood image of the Indians is generally for historical entertainment rather than historical accuracy," said a 55-year-old Oglala Sioux respondent. "I grew up with movies that were sometimes funny and sometimes very dumb. Recently it has gone in the opposite direction. Moviemakers are more sympathetic but still equally inaccurate with their representation" of Indians. John Wayne movies typified the distortion for a 40-year-old Pine Ridge man: "He's always the hero. He shoots one bullet and ten Indians fall." This distrust of movies showed up in our other samples as well. A 59-year-old Mexican American school district employee from Texas recalled that her father had dismissed many Hollywood productions with: "That's not the way it was. That's a gringo story."

Many of the people who talked with us worried that books were also distorted for purposes of commerce and entertainment. One respondent observed that "some people write books and they don't write it for the historical part of it. They write it for themselves and to make money. That's what book writing is about." "They may take some things out of context and dress it up . . . to make money," explained a 70-year-old man from Winter Haven, Florida. "Some of the newer books they put in whatever will sell the books," explained a 61-year-old man from St. Louis.

Money wasn't the only problem. Many respondents expressed concern that other agendas, particularly political ones, caused distorted views of the past—distortions some defined as propaganda. Since "the media, overall, including motion pictures and TV are biased in favor of being too liberal," reported a 75-year-old man from New Jersey, "they slant the picture deliberately." At an opposite ideological pole, a 19-year-old Filipino-Chinese woman from San Diego said, "The media are fascist liars. I don't trust anything about the media whatsoever." Authors, likewise, advanced ideological purposes in their books. "The history books have been historically not true," declared a 46-year-old African American recreation professional from Detroit, because they have been written by "persons who have had the upper hand."

Instead of abandoning books and popular entertainment as sources, many respondents said they'd found ways to screen distortions introduced by commerce, entertainment, ideology, and prejudice. They chose both individual texts and genres of sources to meet changing tastes and needs and then engaged those sources on their own terms. People repeatedly told our interviewers that every book or movie was different. Respondents often balked at giving a single numerical trustworthiness score to the whole category of "books" or "television programs." Asked to rate the trustworthiness of genres, many echoed the Albuquerque contractor who observed, "They run the range from 1 to 10."

Some people said they sought depictions of the past that seemed carefully researched and tempered by judicious evaluation of conflicting interpretations. Many believed that public television, for example, was less distorted by commerce and profit than commercial television. "Certain sources of television are better than others," began an 80-year-old from Montverde, Florida. "The publicly funded sources are more reliable. The others can be fiction stories that they love to naturally modify to make it more interesting. The public stations are as accurate as I can imagine." Defining the difference as "documentary versus entertainment," a salesman from Lakewood, New York gave PBS a trustworthiness score of 9 and commercial television "as low as 4." A 70-year-old engineer from New Albany, Indiana trusted public broadcasting because "they deal very factually" with history; on commercial television, he said, "pecuniary matters come into play."

Whatever the medium, respondents tended to look for presentations of the past that were grounded in primary sources. A 27-year-old Pine Ridge man singled out as reliable a book that grew from "the personal accounts of the people who were there. They used everybody's opinion of what had happened and what they felt about it. . . . It's not just some person's opinion of what went on." A Pine Ridge teacher's aide admired "all the research that was done" in a book: "I could look in the back and see where they got all their information." Trying to screen out mediation, a firefighter from Sebring, Florida explained that he liked the "first-person accounts" in a television program on Stalin: "I would much rather that it [come] from someone who was actually involved in the event either in their words or writing than from so-called experts."

Some respondents looked for depictions of the past that encompassed their own history. "Because I was half German," a 20-year-old from Marina, California reported reading many books on the Third Reich. Others chose books and movies that fed their hobbies. A 33-year-old government employee from Frankfort, Kentucky was an amateur astronomer who enjoyed reading books about the history of astronomy.

Many people looked for windows on pasts that permitted them to escape the present or transported them to other worlds. "I like movies like *JFK* and *Malcolm X*" better than books, said a 19-year-old Mexican American woman from Texas, because "when you read a book you can't picture it and you can't see what is happening, but when you see it in a film you get more emotional about it." A 32-year-old African American man from San Antonio enjoyed movies about the West and the Bible because of "the special effects" and "the way they were dressed . . . back then." A 23-year-old dishwasher from Zanesville, Ohio liked movies about "the old days of King Arthur" because he was "fascinated with the old types of armor." In using movies to be transported to a different time or to encounter a famous person or event from the past, they were not mainly looking for the current state of historical knowledge about that subject, because they did not believe this was the strength of movies.

A retired teacher from Round Lake, Illinois said that during the previous six months she'd read "about a book a day"—mostly "historical romances," which she called "sort of escapist." A 22-year-old Pine Ridge man praised a book "that makes you feel like you're connected to the Old West. It made me feel like there's a place like that around somewhere that I have to find, where you can go to hunt, and just feel free to do anything you want."

Respondents said they controlled their own access to wider pasts by selecting where they wanted to go and how they wanted to get there. A widow from Huntsville, Alabama commented, "There are very few programs that I let my TV watch." They also chose the contexts in which they engaged those texts. Respondents sought opinions from friends, co-workers, and family members. A 25-year-old x-ray technician from New Jersey decided to watch *Dr. Quinn Medicine Woman* after one of her teachers said it was a good presentation of medicine from the past. A 48-year-old truck driver from North Dakota reported that a movie "sticks in your mind" after it has been discussed with friends. A 68-year-old businessman from Waterbury, Connecticut said, "There were other people at the office who all commented on the same things" in a television program. "It wasn't just my opinion."

As they did with conversation about firsthand experience, many respondents used texts from wider pasts to draw closer to the people around them. A 65-year-old woman from Lock Haven, Pennsylvania said she was fascinated by the history of World War II, in which her husband had served. They were both "very interested," she reported, in television programs on the topic. Others likewise told us that they turned to people they trusted to help them screen and cross-examine texts about other times and places. They enlisted family and friends in testing, elaborating, rejecting, and affirming—in making those accounts their own, or dismissing them.

"They see things from every point of view": College Professors as Sources

"You shouldn't believe everything you hear," said a carpenter from Washington State. "You should research it for yourself." By researching a topic, respondents told us, they could approach it in their own way. They could ask their own questions and seek out appropriate sources. They could decide how much research would satisfy their curiosity or their audience.

The people we interviewed trusted sources informed by independent original research. With a composite trustworthiness score of 7.3, college history professors averaged closer to eyewitnesses (7.8) than to books (6.4) or movies and television programs (5.0). Many people told us that they valued the dedication and study associated with scholarship much more than the agendas of commerce and entertainment they associated with movies and books.

Respondents believed that scholars investigated the past, as they themselves did, to create their own truths and meet their own needs. "I feel like when I study something I can give out information that is more correct than if I hadn't studied it," said a 63-year-old North Carolina woman in explaining why accounts by professors would be "more trustworthy because they have studied it." Unlike the "hype" created by television producers because "they just want to get the ratings," college professors "have to study the field . . . have to delve into the information more," reported a 28-year-old teacher from Bozeman, Montana. Unlike schoolteachers, college professors had "freedom of choice" to investigate and conclude what they wanted, said a 51-year-old sales manager from the Philadelphia suburbs.

Many respondents assumed that college professors sought to get as close as they could to actual experiences in the past. Scholars went to primary sources so they could engage things directly without intervention and possible distortion from people who had agendas of their own. Scholars approached their topics "not only secondhand through books," said a 26-year-old stage manager from Atlanta, but also "through original papers, facts, and artifacts that not everyone gets to look at." They could take their research "from many sources and may even take it from firsthand sources," explained a 31-year-old model maker from Ohio. In contrast to high school teachers, college professors were able to "specialize and most of them have done intensive research in their areas," noted a Jamaican-born history teacher from Brooklyn.

Better yet, "some may have even experienced some of what they're teaching," said a 35-year-old woman from Lubbock, Texas. "Ideally," observed a 70-year-old sales engineer from Indiana, professors "have done all possible to visit or experience those areas and those communities . . . [about] which they teach. For instance, if they are teaching Middle Eastern history, they have been to Egypt, have been to Turkey, and . . . those experiences, powerfully presented, excite the student." A 23-year-old Pine Ridge woman trusted the history professor who taught her course on minorities because he had participated in marches with Indians and blacks. "He was there so it made you feel like you were there."

Since they believed that experiences were subject to many interpretations, respondents assumed that scholars would consider many perspectives. In fact, they trusted scholars precisely because they assumed that academic training centered on learning how to evaluate different perspectives. A 19-year-old African American from New York explained why he respected scholars who had done original research: "They get to see things from every point of view before they pick one." A Pine Ridge truck driver trusted professors because unlike most people, who "would only see one view, a college professor should cover all views and see it from all angles." By going to original sources, scholars could assess and perhaps reconcile contradictory accounts. "They have a more rounded view [because] they probably take into account more people's stories," said a dietitian from Youngstown, Ohio in her twenties. A Maryland telecommunications company manager in his forties reported that his professors stressed the value of original research: "In most of my courses . . . there's conflict of information. And when we have an opinion that conflicts . . . they make us research and come back and present our opinion."

Respondents thought that procedures by which scholars evaluated each other's stories were similar to the processes by which they themselves questioned and adapted their own stories when they encountered opposing or alternative accounts. A 38-year-old systems analyst from Seattle explained: scholars "usually had to publish something that's been under the scrutiny of the academic community. They have to defend what they say. [When] you come up with something and publish it, it has to be defended." "College professors have a professional pride to examine and sort through information and determine truth from fiction or truth from nonverifiable data," said a 41-year-old telecommunications professional from Santa Barbara. An engineer from Beaverton, Oregon put it another way: "It is in their best interest to make sure what we have learned is accurate. They have staked their reputation on the proper understanding of their expertise."

College history professors, like older family members, introduced young people to the past while helping them to develop as individuals. A 24-year-old man from Manhattan, Kansas believed that "college professors are a better source than books" because "there's more interaction from my point of view between myself and a college professor." To a 31-year-old Jamaican-born cook from New Jersey, college professors are "like a guiding light to tell you what's right from what's wrong." A 59-year-old truck driver from central Texas said of one professor: "I would trust him with my life." In contrast to movies or books, which respondents could not question, students "might question or even cross a teacher," a 72-year-old Philadelphian observed. Thinking of college professors' responsibility for the next generation in the same way that he envisioned the responsibility of grandparents, a 28-year-old songwriter, singer, and record producer from Los Angeles believed "that's a personal agenda with the college professor, that's about an education legacy, that drives a responsibility that in my opinion is of a higher order than what drives Hollywood."

Some of the people we interviewed expressed a less positive view of college professors. They accused scholars of failing to recognize the feel of the real world, indeed in some cases of writing abstractions for other scholars rather than talking about everyday experience in everyday language. "I think a historian tries to read into it while a person tells you what it was like. I am more interested in the emotion of it. History is too cold, too analytical," said a firefighter from Sebring, Florida. A salesman from Lockport, Illinois trusted family members more than professors because family members "would only tell me about things they experienced as opposed to history professors who've never experienced anything—just out of books, and it gets diluted along the way." "I've had some professors tell me some impossible things to support some grand theories," complained an African American social worker from Delaware. Professors "have a tendency . . . to change things around to suit their purposes," observed a Minneapolis furniture store owner. Professors too had ideologies that distorted their stories. "They tend to be very opinionated," said a 30-year-old truck driver from Islip, New York. "Their view is the only view."

Because they believed that the best engagements with the past encouraged them to become autonomous, respondents gave low marks to professors who failed to respond to their needs and help them develop on their own. Trusting family members because they told about the past to help people they loved to develop, some people complained about professors who seemed uninterested in the individual development of their students. From conversations with young people, a 70-year-old man from Winter Haven, Florida had come to fear that professors were not fulfilling their responsibility to help individual students: "Nowadays the professor goes in and gives a lecture and if you don't get it, that is too bad. You are just more or less a number. They get you in a big lecture hall and give you a test and could care less if you pass or not. The professor doesn't have much to do with you."

"You can come to some conclusions on your own": The Remarkable Story of Museums

Americans put more trust in history museums and historic sites than in any other sources for exploring the past. Over half the respondents assigned museums a score of 9 or 10 on the 10-point trustworthiness scale. At first glance museums might seem the sort of remote, impersonal authority that Americans distrust, but in fact many respondents felt that the best of each of the other sources could be found in museums and sites. They gave visitors a sense of immediacy—of personal participation—that respondents associated with eyewitnesses; they evoked the intimacy of family gatherings; and they encouraged an interaction with primary sources that reminded respondents of independent research.

The people who talked with us trusted history museums and historic sites because they transported visitors straight back to the times when people had used the artifacts on display or occupied the places where "history" had been made. Visiting the Alamo "makes me feel like I was there" at the fateful siege and battle back in 1836, said a Mexican American secretary from Laredo. A 34-year-old black postal worker from Detroit liked to visit the Henry Ford Museum because he was "able to sit in one of the early-model cars that were made, to walk down brick paved roads and go into the old general store and walk into a log cabin." When she looked at exhibitions of life in New Mexico 150 years ago, a Mexican American woman from El Paso noted, "You just can't help but go back to those days, feeling like you're there. I imagine how it was."

Approaching artifacts and sites on their own terms, visitors could cut through all the intervening stories, step around all the agendas that had been advanced in the meantime, and feel that they were experiencing a moment from the past almost as it had originally been experienced—and with none of the overwhelming distortions that they associated with movies and television, the other purveyors of immediacy. A 60-year-old man from Downers Grove, Illinois valued museums because visitors could observe the artifacts and "come to some conclusions on your own instead of listening to someone else's tainted conclusions." A 44-year-old painter from Wisconsin trusted museums because by displaying objects "for everybody to see," the museum "isn't trying to present you with any points of view. . . . You need to draw your own conclusions." Many respondents felt there was nothing between them and the reality of the past. A 35-year-old Pine Ridge man knew that he was seeing the real thing at the Dinosaur Museum: "The bones are right there. The bones don't lie."

"When you sit and look at an object," observed a 52-year-old woman from Newton Falls, Ohio, "your own senses come into play." "Seeing is believing," said an advertising agent from Palm Desert, California. In visiting "the long grave where they put all the bodies" after the Wounded Knee Massacre of 1890, a Sioux personnel adviser felt that "just by looking at the grave you know all those people are in there. I mean it's more real." From "the feel of the ground and the wind and how cold it was" at the site of the Wounded Knee Massacre, a Sioux truck driver in his twenties "could put myself back there and not feel how they felt but get an idea of how they felt. It is where a lot of my ancestors were killed." "I pass Wounded Knee, the massacre site, every day on my way to Pine Ridge," said a special education coordinator:

> You have to create a picture to really get involved. You can almost hear the voices. You can almost see the events taking place. You can't help but wonder how cold was it or how many people actually were alive, how hurt were they. Or I would put myself into it by asking myself what could I have done if I were there. Those kinds of questions come into your mind.

Thinking her way back to the time when the strange-looking cannon at the fort she was visiting might have been fired, a 56-year-old woman from St. Augustine, Florida "wondered how it did anything." Artifacts brought respondents closer to experiences from the past than even eyewitnesses could. Museum visitors could form their own questions by imagining that they were reexperiencing for themselves—without mediation—moments from the past.

Many respondents said they sought out museums that presented artifacts or themes from their own lives. A 45-year-old Memphis man who described himself as an "active participant" in the civil rights movement felt particularly drawn to the Civil Rights Museum. A 68-year-old woman from Erie, Pennsylvania spotted "something we used to have at home" when she saw an old butter churn in a museum. Some respondents felt more connected to museums because they knew the people who had donated the artifacts. A Pine Ridge police officer liked to visit a small fur trade museum in Nebraska because "they had my great-great-grandfather's belongings there. They had one of his shirts and some smaller articles." "Getting to know people in town who had artifacts" in the local Indian museum "made it more personal to me," said a 40-year-old woman from Muskogee, Oklahoma.

Some people told us that trips to museums and sites allowed them to deepen relationships with people who mattered in their lives. They went to museums when friends or family came to town or when they went on vacations. "My friend came to visit me and this is the first time she had ever been in this part of the country," began a 43-year-old Pine Ridge woman, who believed that their friendship would deepen if her guest could see Badlands National Park and the Wounded Knee Massacre site, which were such defining features of the Oglala Sioux past. In recalling a visit with a friend to ancient Roman walls when he was stationed in Germany, a 30-year-old truck driver from Long Island remembered the experience as a funny moment in a relationship with the friend: "We went out looking for old Roman walls. I figured they were going to be like brick and we wouldn't find them until I fell off them. They were hills! They were thirty feet high and I suddenly realized they were these old defensive works still standing there after a thousand years."

Standing with others before the site of a slave prison in Ghana or an Indian massacre in South Dakota, bursting into laughter as they stumbled over Roman walls they had been hunting for, the people we interviewed made their visits to sites part of relationships that had begun long before and would continue long afterward. During such visits, engagements with the past resembled the intimacy of family gatherings. Some respondents saw other familial links: they said guides and other staffers were eager to meet their individual needs, as they expected grandparents (and professors) to do. The staff wanted to help them connect the museum's materials to their own experiences. "I liked how they treated me and conducted themselves," explained an African American custodian from Lynwood, California.

Museums also brought to mind the independent research and peer evaluation respondents admired in professional historical scholarship. But unlike authors of books, museums arrived at their interpretations only after experts pooled their independent research. Reasoning from her own experience as an interior decorator ("I had to come up with things that would be acceptable to half a dozen different people"), a 78-year-old woman from Houston trusted what she saw in museums because "it has been researched by more than one person. You are going to have a compilation of a lot of people. . . . They all discuss things and arrive at one version that they wish to promote to the public." "There's a new story every week about who was the first Pony Express rider," a 62-year-old man from St. Joseph, Missouri observed; he trusted the local Pony Express museum to evaluate the validity of these claims. "Museums are developed as a collaboration of many people and many resources," began a 37-year-old police officer from southern California, who added, "Information from a single source may not be as accurate, with the exception of those who have personally experienced" an event.

In distinguishing between museums and sites they trusted and those they did not, the people we surveyed reiterated what they trusted and distrusted in all sources. A 33-year-old man from Ponte Vedra Beach, Florida dismissed the Ripley's Believe-It-or-Not Museum as "pure entertainment." A counselor from Pine Ridge dismissed a museum on the reservation for its commercialism. A 32-year-old accounting assistant from Irvine, California said she would trust a museum if "it was backed by a society like a historical society" but not if it was "a ploy to get money." Visitors bristled when museums seemed not to respect the original experience they were presenting. A 40-year-old Pine Ridge woman walked into a museum and "saw a lot of artifacts that belonged to our people or to our tribe. Seeing those pipes there made me feel sad because they aren't supposed to be displayed that way because they're sacred." And they distrusted museums that interposed their ideas between visitors and artifacts. A 50-year-old woman from Colorado Springs assigned a 10 to museums that were "preserving artifacts from western or pioneer days," but, "since I come from a Christian standpoint, I cannot believe their credibility" when they present fossils or other artifacts that seem to confirm the theory of evolution.

"It was just a giant data dump": The Sad Story of History in Schools

Respondents described diverse, sometimes contradictory, and often negative reactions to their most common formal encounters with the past—as students of history in school. They trusted history teachers (6.6 on the 10-point scale) slightly more than books (6.4) and considerably more than television programs (5.0). Despite their admiration for individual teachers, however, most had little good to say about the actual classroom experience of studying history. Asked to assign a number between 1 and 10 that indicated how connected they felt to the past in each of seven situations, respondents ranked "studying history in school" dead last, with a average score of 5.7. While 49 percent of those we surveyed assigned a mark of 9 or 10 to describe how connected they felt with the past when they gathered with their families, only 12 percent assigned a 9 or 10 to describe how connected they felt with the past in school.

The source of alienation appeared to lie in the structure and content of classes, not in the individuals paid to teach. Some respondents said they respected high school history teachers for their dedication to studying the past and their knowledge about using materials from the past. "They know more about history than the average person," explained a Louisiana woman in her early thirties. Since teachers could not speak "off the top of their head," they "have to research it or should have researched it," added a saleswoman from Mt. Kisco, New York. "If a topic or an issue interests them . . . they'd be more likely to research it, whereas the other person might just stick with the first article they found on it," a 29-year-old mechanic from Scofield, Wisconsin believed.

Some valued teachers because, like older family members, they supplemented books with firsthand experience. A 40-year-old African American from Park Forest, Illinois recalled that her teacher had participated in the civil rights movement "and he knew what was true because he had been there and talked with those people." Like older relatives, teachers "have lived through things . . . more than I have been through," reported an 18-year-old Hispanic from Houston. Unlike popular entertainment, which "tends to glamorize things," a secretary from Portsmouth, Ohio believed that teachers "really try to teach the truth." In contrast to books and television programs that distorted the past, a 40-year-old trucking company manager from Beverly, Massachusetts "just saw [his high school history teachers] as very honest people."

"I wouldn't have a personal feeling" for books or television or movies because "I don't know the individual" author or producer, began a mechanical engineer from Royal Oak, Michigan, but "with a teacher you'd at least have some personality. It'd be a one-to-one relationship versus a removed, unknown person writing the book." Since "kids need someone to look up to," explained a 39-year-old property manager from Pocatello, Idaho, "most of them will look up to teachers as someone who is truthful and honest." "Teachers were more like a family in school," recalled a 48-year-old New Jersey police dispatcher. "When you did wrong you got punished. There was respect." A 30-year-old black woman from Los Angeles "really applauded" her high school history teacher for the way he responded to students' curiosity about the Vietnam War: "He had friends who were in it, and he brought them in to talk with us. He really cared what we thought, what our feelings were on the subject." A 19-year-old Virginian had "a lot of confidence" in a particular teacher because "he's the only one that took time to make sure that we understand what's going on."

People told our interviewers that they particularly admired teachers who helped them to revisit and investigate the past for themselves. They recalled history class projects in which students became active participants. A North Carolina marketing director in his mid-twenties recalled a teacher who "got us very involved" because she "took us on various trips and [we] got hands-on" history: "She took us to old colonial-type towns, the Capitol, White House, Indian reservations, museums, she took us everywhere." A Baton Rouge woman recalled how a teacher "made world history come alive. He had the ability to make the war stories live. This is where the Allied forces were, and this is where the Germans were, and he would have you sitting on the edge of your seats wondering what would happen next." They liked teachers who made them participants instead of spectators. "I had teachers that . . . would just get us more involved. They got us to do projects more than just sitting in front of the TV, and I learned from that," reported a New Jersey technician.

"You would have thought he had been there himself," a Florida Baptist preacher in his sixties said of a teacher. "Whenever he was lecturing he would really get involved—like when Washington was crossing the Potomac you could almost picture him being there." A Texan in his sixties remembered that his high school history teacher "made the kids feel like they were reliving history. They all loved it." "I loved history," recalled a 79-year-old Minnesota widow because "it made me feel very much like I was there." A Puerto Rican woman from the Bronx recalled the "realism" of a class project on an incident in Puerto Rican history: "Everybody had different information about it, and everyone was giving different things about the same thing, so it made it very exciting." An African American from Detroit hoped that celebrating Martin Luther King Jr.'s birthday as a holiday would teach "our young people more about the black Americans that contributed to society and not just leave it in the past."

Although teachers could sometimes make classrooms resemble settings where people liked to engage the past, most respondents said that history classes seemed to be shaped by remote bureaucrats, to cover subjects remote from their interests, and to feature memorization and regurgitation of senseless details. Asked for a single word to define their experience with history in school, they most frequently answered with "boring" and "irrelevant."[2]

People told us that they felt excluded from actively engaging the past—either as empathetic reliving or critical interrogation—because what happened in class was determined by outsiders, by school boards and school administrators. Respondents often pictured themselves as conscripts or even prisoners and their teachers as drill sergeants or wardens who simply did as they were told. "A lot of schools are forced to follow certain procedures, taken from certain books," observed a man from Palmyra, Wisconsin. His imagery was echoed by a man from Conway, Arkansas who talked of "force-fed subjects." Teachers "only teach what's in the book," observed an 88-year-old widow from Pennsylvania.

Respondents could seldom recognize themselves or their experiences in the content of history classes. For one thing, they thought that the history they heard about in the classroom was too neat and rosy, stories of times of personal and national glory they could not relate to. The content "seemed so fake . . . it does not give you an anchor, or anything to relate to," said a 21-year-old woman from Brigantine, New Jersey who disliked the "picture-perfect view of history" she received. "They all taught that the U.S. is the good guy," recalled a 24-year-old Latino shop owner from San Diego who dismissed high school history as "propaganda." A 58-year-old woman thought "they want to give you the very best of something" while leaving "the skeletons in the closet." "They wipe . . . anything that would portray the government or military or politics in a bad light," complained a 38-year-old Oklahoman. And a 39-year-old woman from Framingham, Massachusetts protested her "extremely biased" history class, which was "a narrow, white middle-class version of U.S. history."

As students, most respondents had not been able to see what history had to do with them. A widow from Morro Bay, California didn't think that high school history "had much bearing on my life." Like her, many of the people who talked with us had to look outside school to find themselves in "history." A Pine Ridge janitor in his twenties learned about his Native American heritage from parents, grandparents, and powwows because his American history teacher "was really racist, didn't really like Indians at all." Facing an unrecognizable history in this class, he got the only D in his high school career. A 46-year-old Sioux woman knew that what her teacher and textbook in Oakland, California were telling her about Indians "wasn't really what was going on. I would take the books to my grandmother and she would say: 'That's not how it was.'" Even when they encountered sympathetic treatments of events like the Battle of Little Big Horn, as a 21-year-old Sioux man did, they could not locate themselves: "If I asked any questions about ancestors who may have died that had to do with my personal life, they'd just forget about it and go back to the main program" in the text.

The curriculum shut students out. "It was just a giant data dump that we were supposed to memorize . . . just numbers and names and to this day I still can't remember them," declared a 36-year-old financial analyst from Palo Alto, California. And the pedagogy was as bad. "The teacher would [call] out a certain date and then we would have to stand at attention and say what the date was. I hated it," said a 64-year-old Floridian. "It was very cut and dried," remembered a St. Petersburg, Florida woman in her fifties. Like students, teachers seemed slaves to the books they had memorized. "They still teach the same information they learned twenty years ago," said a 31-year-old black teacher from Shreveport, Louisiana. "I remember one of my history teachers who was so old and had been a teacher for so long that you could tell that she had memorized what she said," reported a 54-year-old self-employed Mexican American from Whittier, California. History was details to be "learned."

Teachers, we were often told, made engagement with history an alien experience in which students were never treated as individuals. A clerk from Elma, Washington said that history classrooms were places for "shuffling papers like shuffling kids. . . . I don't think the teachers give a hoot. . . . I would like to see them care more about the kids, and not just their paychecks." "I have dyslexia and dysgraphia," explained a 23-year-old dishwasher from Ohio, "and the teachers never really cared, never wanted to help. The history teachers that we have in this town really don't care about the students. They just want their money." "It seems like they're doing it because they have to. . . . Today the teachers are not interested in the students," said a 52-year-old woman from Honaker, Washington.

Many respondents thought of teachers as disciplinarians dedicated to making students conform. A 50-year-old from Mobile, Alabama had the most vivid complaint: "My teacher was 70 years old and she carried a blackjack." Part of teachers' failure to engage students lay in their inability or unwillingness to hear perspectives different from their own. They tolerated no noise and no disagreement, creating an environment vastly different from the world of everyday historymaking, with its give and take and noisy exchanges. "If you have more than one side of the whole story you get a better perspective on what happened," explained a black 20-year-old student from Norman, Oklahoma, who said her high school teachers had taught from "textbooks that show one side of the situation." "Teachers want you to believe what they say and nothing else" was the lesson a 46-year-old African American from Providence, Rhode Island carried away from school.

Some teachers replied to students' questions not with answers but with authority. "When I would question it in school, I would be kind of looked down upon or told to be quiet and don't bring up such things. They would say I would be disrupting class," recalled a 38-year-old Pine Ridge woman. An 18-year-old Indian woman from Minneapolis recalled that she had grown so frustrated when school authorities suspended her from a class in which she had questioned the teacher that she dropped out of school. "I believe the teachers are afraid of different cultures and different groups," a 25-year-old American Indian factory worker from Indiana had learned. In real life, experience came in many perspectives, but in history classrooms it came in one and only one.

After listening to 1,500 Americans, we understand how a generation has grown up to say that something is "history" when it is dead and gone, irrelevant, beyond any use in the present. That is how many of the people we interviewed described their classroom encounters with the past. While some of them praised individual teachers, their stories only underscored how deeply respondents felt alienated from the structure and content of history classes. Those with positive experiences—and even though the overall average was low, one eighth of respondents did assign history classes a "connectedness" score of 9 or 10—told us that what they liked most about their experiences with classroom history was the mirror opposite of what a majority had disliked: that they could explore the past on their own. The sources that respondents trusted most, unlike schools, helped them to think their way into the past for themselves. The people we interviewed hated some kinds of mediation—commercialism, for example—wherever they found it, because they wanted to get as close as possible to experience. In this desire they illustrated the essence of popular historical methodology: the stripping away of mediation so that individuals can use the past to meet their urgent needs.

5. Beyond the Intimate Past:

Americans and Their Collective Pasts

Talk of intimate pasts animated most of the conversations we had with Americans, as chapters 2 and 3 make clear. But people don't live in worlds populated solely by family and friends. The Americans we interviewed also talked about connecting with pasts outside their intimate worlds. Many told us they wanted to participate in the larger past, to experience it, to reach into history by reaching outward from their own lives. They wanted to personalize the public past. This chapter explores the terrain that lies between individual uses of the past and the collective and national themes most of us studied in school. The stories our respondents told—and how they told them—suggest some of the different ways popular and professional historymakers think themselves into the larger past.

To learn about the bridges people constructed between their personal pasts and larger historical stories, we asked respondents to name an event from the past that had affected them. Among public historical events, the most frequent choice was World War II—selected by 26 of the 358 respondents who answered the question.[1] Though some of them spoke about the futility of war or man's inhumanity to man, a much larger group—almost half of those who cited World War II—reflected on the war in more personal terms. A 71-year-old Philadelphia woman said she learned self-reliance from the war: "My husband was in that. It was a lot of heartache with both of us being young and him being away in his early twenties. I learned how to be independent and how to take care of myself." What they didn't talk about was the narrative most familiar to us from high school history books and popular culture: the war as a story of victory over fascism or as a key moment in a patriotic narrative of the nation-state.

Respondents rarely mentioned the triumphal national narrative favored by those who write textbooks or advocate history as a means of teaching patriotism and civics. Instead, like the Philadelphia woman, they placed national events within their familial stories or made national personages into familiar figures in personal narratives. Or they talked about national events as disconnected incidents not linked to a larger narrative, and about national figures and events in distant and attenuated terms, rather than the rich terms they used for describing moments in their personal and family histories. Or they did all of these. Our respondents did not reject or ignore national history; they simply rejected the textbook narratives of national greatness that they had been forced to passively consume and regurgitate in school.

Conservatives may be alarmed at how rarely our respondents referred to patriotic narratives. Liberals and leftists (especially historians) may be unsettled by another of our survey findings: when Americans think and talk about the past, many of them avoid collective frameworks like ethnicity, class, region, and gender—categories close to the hearts of professional history practitioners.[2] Some of our respondents did reach more directly for pasts beyond the world of their family and friends. Religious communities and religious narratives, for example, turned out to be a powerful way of understanding and using the past. And respondents also offered larger narratives of change and continuity about crime, discipline, and popular culture. But these popular historical narratives veered off in different directions from the textbook narratives of linear progress associated with capital "H" history. Americans engaged larger pasts on their own terms.

Several subgroups put distinctive spins on the process of making connections beyond the intimate past. Most white Americans kept their historical narratives focused on the family; when they discussed public events, they usually personalized them. African Americans, American Indians, and evangelical Christians drew upon and constructed a much wider set of usable pasts, building ties to their communities as well as their families. African Americans and American Indians were also more likely to create narratives of group progress, while white Americans tended to talk about decline. In this chapter we look at the ways Americans—particularly white Americans—use larger historical narratives; chapter 6 will look more closely at the ways African Americans and American Indians have constructed a collective past. Mexican Americans, with whom we end this chapter, occupy a figurative borderland—white European Americans on one side, American Indians and African Americans on the other. Mexican Americans share some modes and assumptions of each of the other groups, but translate them into a rich and vigorous historical narrative that is distinctly their own.

"It's tough to get together": White Americans and Their Collective Pasts

As they revisited the past to make a difference in the present, our respondents relied more on the histories of their families than those of their communities. Very few white Americans, for example, rooted their basic identities in sets of historical associations with particular places: they tended not to connect the past of their communities with their current lives.[3] Nor did these respondents make use of the language of class. When they talked about "the union," they were generally referring to the North in the Civil War and not the workers' side in unionization battles. When they talked of "class," they generally meant "history class."[4]

We might speculate that at an earlier time Americans would have found stories, figures, and events drawn from local, regional, labor, or ethnic histories more powerful resources for helping them make sense of the present. That possibility is reinforced by our feeling that in some interviews we were overhearing fading—or what might be called "residual"— uses of collective pasts.[5] In the late nineteenth century, for example, many Americans might have developed narratives rooted in the regional histories of the North and the South to establish who they were, what kind of behavior was proper, and where they and the nation were going. In our survey, such regional stories had only a faded resonance.

Two women we interviewed talked about the notorious Confederate prison at Andersonville, Georgia, where 13,000 Union prisoners died. A 65-year-old Tallahassee, Florida woman recalled a visit there: "We saw a prison and all of the graves where those people died in that prison." Without any indication of which side "those people" might have been on, without any hint of regional shame (or justification), she noted that the visit had made her "feel real bad." For this woman, it seems, the Andersonville story was a fragment of the past—a moral tale that floated free of larger narratives about slavery and freedom or states' rights and national union.

An 87-year-old Indianapolis woman put Andersonville in a broader and more traditional context. She was old enough to remember her grandfather, a "good storyteller" who lived to be 92 and told her about his own imprisonment at Andersonville. He even wrote a book about his prison experiences: "He didn't want us to forget." As part of her "inheritance" from her grandfather, and as a tribute to him, she joined the Daughters of the Union, an organization of Civil War descendants. She also participated in a Springfield, Illinois celebration of Lincoln's birthday, contributed to Lincoln Memorial University in Tennessee, and helped to furnish flags for the graves of Civil War soldiers. Perhaps because she realized that the Civil War no longer had the same meaning for young people as it did in her own youth, she explained to her interviewer that Confederates were "the Union's enemy." For her, Andersonville was a turning point in a narrative that stretched from the Civil War through her most recent contribution to Lincoln Memorial University. It was an inheritance that could not be escaped.

Like this woman, respondents who defined themselves in relation to ethnic traditions seemed to come out of earlier eras, to reflect fading or residual cultures.[6] A 72-year-old Philadelphia woman, who is treasurer of a local Italian-American society and who speaks and reads Italian, reported that her society has been "losing members." "We're all senior citizens. It's tough to get together and quite a few have not been able to attend meetings." Although studies such as ours cannot measure change over time, it does appear that people's views of their ethnic backgrounds have shifted. Many respondents said they used ethnic history to sort out familial or personal identity; not many spoke of creating a collective identity.[7] Few respondents talked with depth or intensity about the past of their ethnic groups; those who did tended to channel that larger passion into intimate settings.[8]

A 23-year-old veterinarian's assistant from California wanted to "know more about my background, Indian American or German or exactly what I am" as a way of "getting a better idea of myself." For her and many like her, ethnic family history seemed to be a series of disconnected fragments rather than a continuous history looming over actions in the present. Only twenty-five European Americans in our national sample (4 percent) rated the history of their ethnic or racial group as the most important area of the past. And only a handful of those revealed a strong collective ethnic identity rooted in the history of their group. Some historians might have expected stories about how my "Italian grandfather built the New York subways." We heard none.

Some respondents—mainly immigrants or the children of immigrants—expressed a broader sense of ethnic identity. An Irish-born carpenter from Fishkill, New York spoke lyrically about how "our ethnic group is founded on mythological forebears in which was encoded norms of human behavior that are still inspirational and edifying. We trace our origin and uniqueness back to those mythological forebears who provided a cohesiveness to a group and identity. . . . That is still relevant today. That is still the core of our beliefs, and these patterns of conduct are ingrained in the imagination, and they shape imagination and consequently human conduct and morality." He added that his interviewer ought to get a copy of William Butler Yeats and read it that very night. Such exuberant ethnic identity was rare in conversations with white respondents. A Nebraska mother in her mid-twenties told us that her ethnic background was important, but her exposure to that background seemed confined to a family reunion where "we got to meet a Swedish relative with our name . . . and we got to try some Swedish cooking and also got to see some pictures of their country."

A number of respondents who talked about their ethnic heritage were partners in mixed marriages, or products of them. Learning their ethnic history was a way of trying to work out their own identity—sorting through the pieces of many traditions—as well as a way of building relationships to others from different backgrounds. A 45-year-old Alabama medical clerk, whose family "came from Russia, Poland, France, and Germany," thought her ethnic heritage was particularly important because "it makes you realize where you came from goes back into the history of your family, and you pass it forward to your children." Sometimes intermarriage led partners to choose one ethnic background for the family. A 63-year-old Wisconsin woman of Irish-American lineage said her husband had "made a Dane out of me." She had even become vice-president of a local society "dedicated to preserving Danish heritage."

Still, in the midst of these fading uses of the past, we glimpsed patterns that seemed to be newly emerging. Gay respondents, for example, talked about creating a shared identity with other members of their community. An incipient historical consciousness was evident during interviews with people who found in their connection to a gay past a vital resource for understanding who they were and whether they could make a difference in the world. When we asked a 21-year-old Ohio student to name an area of the past besides family, nation, ethnic group, or community that was very important to him, he replied: "The struggle of gay rights."

A 33-year-old Texas student complained that our question about the relative importance of family, ethnic or racial group, community, and nation was much too constraining: "My answer to that question," he said, "would be the area in which the past is most important to me is the past of my community or sexual orientation, which is the gay and lesbian community." From this "incredibly rich" and "incredibly undervalued" history, as well as the stories of the civil rights movement with which he associated the struggle for gay liberation, he had learned not only a sense of his own self-worth but also "the power of change and progressive thinking."

This student, who found "the past of my community" "almost completely absent from mainstream history . . . as it is taught in the schools," is one of many contemporary Americans mobilizing a sense of the gay past to grapple with personal issues of morality and agency as well as to foster group identity and community. Such efforts show how new historical narratives can take root outside traditional networks.[9] Some Americans feel oppressed by the traditional family, or excluded from it. They're looking beyond blood and kinship—learning to redefine "family" in an expansive and socially powerful way.

"The Bible is the only book that I have read concerning the past": Religious Communities and the Collective Past

Most Americans said that an intimate past populated by friends and loved ones offered them the most useful tools for grappling with fundamental questions and building close relationships, but a significant minority chose another path. These respondents found larger communities in church and larger historical narratives in religious views of the past. Though we did not ask explicitly about religion, many respondents forced us to see its crucial role in determining how people think about and use the past. Asked whether "knowing about the past of any other area or group" beyond family, community, nation, or ethnic or racial group was "very important," almost 60 percent said yes. One fifth spoke about the importance of religion and the church—more than any other choice.[10]

This interest in religious history both drew upon and reinforced a sense of collective identity. A 65-year-old black woman from Detroit explained that because "I'm strong in the church," she was deeply interested in its history. For a 74-year-old Massachusetts woman who had been attending Bible study classes for years, the important thing was a sense of community. "The church is like a second home," she said. A Louisiana woman worked to bring together everyone who had ever been part of her church for a "homecoming" so that "the newcomers can see what happened in the past with the church." A 63-year-old North Carolina woman, who called her twice-yearly gatherings with other Jehovah's Witnesses "sort of like a big family" reunion, reported that she devoted "quite a bit" of time to studying "the past history of the Jehovah's Witnesses."

Learning about the pasts of particular denominations and congregations helped respondents locate themselves in historical trajectories and narratives that went beyond their families. Just as an interest in family history strengthened a sense of identity, for many respondents the statement "I am a Christian" provided the starting and ending point of investigations into religious history. The religious past also answered fundamental questions about morality. A retired Wyoming man explained that he frequently studied "the past of biblical characters" because of "what they have to show—what they show us, what we can learn from their past mistakes, also their right decisions."

Religion most dramatically shaped the historical interests and perspectives of evangelicals—outward-looking Christians who see the Bible as the word of God and publicly testify to their belief in Jesus. The historical vision of evangelical Christians is extraordinarily consistent and powerful. Few other Americans have such a vivid sense of how a specific set of past events guides their behavior in the present. Although we did not do a separate sample of people who identified themselves as evangelical Christians, the survey turned up compelling evidence of the centrality of evangelical religion to many Americans.[11] In effect, these respondents used their interviews as opportunities to testify about their commitment to Christ.

The presence of an evangelical view of the past became clear as we aggregated the survey responses. The Bible was named more often than any other work as the historical book respondents had recently read. Bible study groups were the second most common type of historical organization they had joined. Christ was the third most common public figure mentioned when we asked about a person from the past who had affected them. The birth or death of Christ was the seventh most common public event given in response to our question about a past event that had profound impact. Reading these answers, we could identify a distinct group of respondents—about 5 percent of the national sample—for whom a Christian identity both shaped and was shaped by a particular understanding of the past.[12]

During some interviews a religious consciousness of the past determined almost every answer. A 30-year-old Michigan homemaker told an interviewer that biblical films interested her most; "the Bible is the only book that I have read concerning the past"; "the past of the life of Jesus . . . and the history of other Christians" was the history beyond her own family that interested her most; "the death of Jesus" was the historical event that "changed my life"; and Jesus was the historical figure who most affected her by "teaching me how to live my life."

A 52-year-old south Florida salesman also exhibited a vivid sense of a living Christian past. He said that he regularly studied the past in his church group and learned biblical history so that "I can understand the future better. The things of the past are related to the biblical prophecies that are related to things that are happening today. . . . What is happening today was prophesied 2,000 years ago." Asked about a book that made him feel connected to the past, he immediately answered, "the Bible." Asked about a historic site that made him feel connected to the past, he described how "in Greece you went up to Corinth and that's where Paul preached to the Apostles, and I sat on the rock that Paul sat on when he preached to the apostles, and that was an emotional experience, just to be where he was when he was preaching." What person and event from the past had an important effect upon him? Jesus and the crucifixion. Did family gatherings connect him to the past? Yes, "because our family is all together, except for the ones who have gone to be with the Lord . . . and we're [still] close to them. I go by every day to the graveyard [and] say 'Hi Grandpa.' "

For evangelical Christians, a religious understanding of the present suffuses their view of the past, highlighting the importance of particular events like the birth, death, and crucifixion of Christ, particular historical figures (primarily Christ but also some biblical figures like Joseph or leaders of some churches), particular historical sources (the Bible and some preachers), and particular historical periods ("the period of time when Jesus Christ was on the earth," as a man from South Carolina put it).[13]

Part of the appeal of the Christian past may lie in its unchanging answers to the questions about morality, immortality, identity, and agency that trouble almost everyone. Not only does religion deeply influence the way many Americans understand the past, but a distinctive interpretation of the past underpins their religious, social, and moral commitments in the present. Asked what he learned from his knowledge of Christ's era, a 31-year-old UPS driver replied: "I learned that I am a sinner, and that Christ died on the cross for me, and as a result of that, I am going to Heaven when

I die." Speaking of "the death of our Christ on the cross," a 39-year-old Arizona housewife said, "Because of that event, I have salvation."

Though the similarities in these answers are striking, religious Americans brought a range of perspectives to the relationship between present and past.[14] Nonevangelical Christians too described views of the past and present that were shaped by religion. A number of Mexican Americans, for example, gave a more social interpretation of the Christian past. Asked what she learned from the birth of Jesus, a 30-year-old woman from Laredo, Texas answered: "He had the choice to be rich and power-ful and he chose to be born in a poor family."

Some of those who rated religious history as particularly important did so more out of a sense of personal spiritual commitment than a sense of col-lective identity. A 30-year-old accounting assistant from Irvine, California said the history of religion was important to her, even though she had no specific religious affiliation or upbringing, because she wanted to be able to "teach her [child] things about Christianity." For this woman—and for many of the people we interviewed—an excursion into histories beyond their family often led back to the same intimate relationships that they said defined their lives.

Kennedy "died on my birthday": Personalizing the National Past

Generations of commentators have assumed that the history of our nation-state is the history people have been most likely to know and use—or at least is the history they *ought* to know and use. The recent debate over *The National Standards for United States History*, as well as the general alarm over the teaching of U.S. history, has proceeded from the assumption that a knowledge of national history is essential to civic life. The authors of this book belong to a profession premised on exactly those assumptions—a profession that encourages required survey courses on American history, publishes scholarly journals arranged around the national story, and orga-nizes itself along national historical lines. One of the most important con-tributions of professional historians has been to foster the idea of national-ism, and the rise of nationalism has in turn fostered the practice of profes-sional history. "Historians," as Eric Hobsbawm wryly observed, "are to nationalism what poppy-growers in Pakistan are to heroin-addicts: we supply the essential raw material for the market."[15]

Our respondents did not share historians' assumptions about the nation-state. When forced to say whether the past of their family or the past of the United States was most important to them, Americans chose family history more than three times as often as their country's history. Not that they were uninterested in or unaware of U.S. history: they repeatedly demonstrated their familiarity with our national past. Many of them brought up the importance of celebrated national figures (especially Abraham Lincoln, John F. Kennedy, and Martin Luther King Jr.); talked about feeling connected to the past on national holidays like July fourth; said it was necessary for children to learn about our national heritage; acknowledged the effect that key national events (World War II and the Vietnam War, for example) have had on their lives; described meaningful visits to national shrines like the Smithsonian, the White House, the Alamo, Plymouth Rock, and the Liberty Bell; and said they participated in patriotic societies like the Veterans of Foreign Wars and the Daughters of the American Revolution.[16]

Respondents identified their approaches to the national past most intriguingly when we asked them to name events that had greatly affected them. That two fifths named events from their personal lives (like the divorce of parents) and one fifth named national events (like World War II) might lead us to conclude that most saw the personal and the national as separate realms. But an additional two fifths of the respondents named public events and then volunteered one of two ways they had participated in those events. Thirteen percent of all respondents remembered that they had taken part in it (serving as soldiers in a war, for example); 29 percent said that they had had a memorable social experience in hearing about and making sense of the event (crying with other fifth graders when they heard of Kennedy's assassination, for example).[17]

Among those who selected public national events as the most memorable of their lives, two thirds talked about them as things they had experienced and engaged for themselves, on their terms. A 30-year-old Florida fund-raiser said she was uninterested in history when she took formal classes in school, but "as soon as I got out I wanted to know more history." Soon after graduation she began exploring one of the most national of all historic sites, the Civil War battlefield at Gettysburg, which she enjoyed because "it was done on my terms rather than being force-fed it in school." She added, "I've lived some history"—by which she meant "I can remember how I felt" as a resident of Washington when she heard about the Watergate investigation and discussed it with friends as it unfolded.

A 34-year-old salesman from the New York suburbs said he'd researched for himself "what it was like to be a common soldier in the American Revolution" and then reenacted what he'd learned for public audiences. He described the experience as much more engaging than studying the Revolutionary War in school: "It's a form of living history rather than just reading a book, which is rather static. It brings out other senses, like feeling, touching, smell, taste." A Johnstown, Pennsylvania homemaker in her sixties complained that books about the depression had given factual overviews, but that "it is difficult to place yourself in that time period because there are no personal stories, just facts and dates." She came to understand what the depression had meant from her parents' accounts of how "my father lost his job and they had to live with his parents, and it was very difficult." A Pennsylvania laboratory technician in her twenties could understand the depression when "my grandparents start telling stories. They grew up in the depression. They tell how [my grandfather] got food because they were so poor. He tells the story and I get to paint a picture in my mind."

In explaining how they reached out to wider pasts, many respondents focused on the experience of individuals—themselves and others. A Kokomo, Indiana truck driver defined history as the story of "the people [and] the changes they've gone through." A 75-year-old retired man from Westfield, New Jersey recalled:

> There are two things that have had a profound effect on my life. One was the Great Depression. My father lost his job and I . . . had to go to work rather than go to college when I was 16 years old and help support the family. The second was the Second World War. I was enlisted in the Marine Corps and served four years and really started my career well behind the people who had not served in the armed forces. I think that it makes you a stronger person from having lived through adversity and having overcome it.

While textbooks might present the depression and war as different phenomena in different chapters, this participant recalled that the two events had a strikingly similar impact on him. With his eye on what people experienced, a 65-year-old retired man from Massachusetts said that he "was never thrilled by history courses in high school. . . . I think perhaps my interest in history is in what one might call vulgar history, ordinary history, history of people, what people do, not so much what nations do." When we interviewed him, this indifferent former student of history was finishing his third year as president of his local historical society.

As respondents tried to find "our place in history," in the words of a Sebring, Florida firefighter—to see how individuals related to each other in contexts beyond the intimate—some also acknowledged the limitations of national or international histories told only by participants. After interviewing her German grandmother about World War II, a 33-year-old New Jersey psychologist noted, "My grandmother was able to tell me about the war in Germany but she was not part of the Holocaust—so she can give me a part but not all of it." In addition, what her grandmother saw and reported lacked critical distance and was limited by her personal biases. Asked to rate her grandmother's trustworthiness, the psychologist answered: "We'll give grandma a 7 for her slightly romantic view."

Although we at first tried to classify events into "personal" and "national" pasts, our respondents often made national stories personal, personal stories national, and formal settings for studying the past intimate. A 19-year-old student from New York City liked making a family tree as a project for her U.S. history class. And a 44-year-old woman from Toms Rivers, New Jersey said she had become interested in studying the Holocaust as she worked with her daughter on a school project. In assembling a "baby book for my daughter," a 32-year-old technician from Houston included an account of the burial of Richard Nixon "because that will be a part of her history."

A 64-year-old Fort Lauderdale homemaker concluded that she could not separate family from nation: "When you talk about the family, you talk about lifestyle, the family's lifestyle, the country's lifestyle, and it is a wide area. It covers so much, your background, everything is grouped into one. To me it is all one." A Washington, D.C. woman liked a TV documentary on the history of the atomic bomb because her home town is near Oak Ridge, Tennessee; a Georgia woman liked books about World War II because "we were young during World War II" and lived in Germany "during the occupation." In these narratives, national and international events form a backdrop for dramas played out within more intimate realms.

This tendency to make sense of history with a capital "H" through personal and familial frameworks can be seen in respondents' descriptions of what they had learned from important events in the past. Although some Americans drew lessons about patriotism from the experience of World War II, a much larger number drew personal lessons. The war was background for dramas about enduring family separation, moving to new places, meeting spouses, and gaining maturity. A 71-year-old Omaha man observed, "I was a 19-year-old kid when I went in and came out four years later, and was pretty mature by that time." A slightly younger Michigan man noted that "there weren't many men. Most had gone to war. So I had the opportunity when 16 or 17 to be a man." In such narratives, the important lessons about maturity and self-reliance were drawn from the battle to achieve personal autonomy, not the battle to defeat fascism.

When asked what lessons they had learned from past events, most respondents—especially white Americans—spoke of personal rather than political messages. They generally used the past to think about how individuals should live, not how society should be organized. Respondents showed a similar tendency when they answered our question about a person from the past who had particularly affected them. Only about one fourth of white Americans selected figures from the national past, and some of the names—Brigham Young, Howard Hughes, Wallace Stevens —fell well outside the conventional pantheon of "great" national figures. Kennedy and Lincoln were the only national leaders cited by a significant number of white Americans (6 percent chose Kennedy and 4 percent chose Lincoln). If Americans have a consensus about the important figures from the past, it is that they come from their own families. More than twice as many white Americans selected their fathers as chose John F. Kennedy; three times as many chose their mothers as Abraham Lincoln.[18]

Those respondents who selected national figures often treated them like family. They saw national figures as inspirational role models for proper and moral behavior. A Colorado woman said Lincoln's life taught her about "integrity, courage, maybe simplicity, and definitely love for fellow man." An Oklahoma woman said Kennedy's life taught "the meaning of pride" and the need for "enough guts to stand up against everyone and anyone for what was right." From Columbus, Napoleon, and Lewis and Clark, a Georgia carpenter in his twenties learned to "make your own way, trust your judgment." Other respondents constructed narratives in which a national leader offered messages about whether you could make a difference in the world. John F. Kennedy showed an Illinois woman "if you work hard enough you can always get it" and made a Bronx woman "feel hopeful," but led a Colorado man to worry about "what's wrong" when "someone so magnificent in his appeals for peace" gets shot.

Respondents often talked about how people from the past (whether relatives or public figures) taught them lessons about good living and proper behavior. They learned to stand up for themselves from a brother or from Martin Luther King Jr. They learned persistence from an aunt or from Harriet Tubman. A few respondents used the stories of famous historical figures to draw explicit conclusions about the nature of American politics. A 67-year-old West Virginia widower talked about Franklin Roosevelt by way of explaining the wisdom of the Social Security system: "I highly respected FDR, at that time I was an honor guard at his funeral. . . . He was the one behind Social Security, and it's proven in fact. I am drawing it now. It's proved to be a great benefit. He was a wise man. Any man would be wise that had the ability to stimulate the social Security benefits. He was the one that done it." Even in the interviews, the national past moved into personal realms.

Many respondents who brought up public figures cast them as bit players in personal dramas. A Catskill, New York man said he had met Kennedy when "he came to our neighborhood in Brooklyn" in 1960; he also said Kennedy "died on my birthday." A Yonkers woman told a story that started with Kennedy but turned out to be about her own participation in the aftermath of the Bay of Pigs operation. Three people in their late thirties or early forties framed Kennedy's importance as part of a narrative of their coming to political awareness. In general, respondents presented narratives of personal or familial progress or decline; they wrote their own versions of American history.

The most significant exception to this reluctance to invoke an abstract, holistic national historical narrative is, in effect, the one that proves the rule. It came in answer to the question: "What about the past do you think is important for children to know?" When confronted with the prospect of official transmission of the past, many Americans fell back on prepackaged civic ideology: almost twice as many respondents chose U.S. history as chose family history.[19] Even here the lessons that respondents most wanted children to learn were about morality and identity; still, just under half emphasized collective lessons about, for example, group identity, national principles, or mutual understanding.

"I think that children should always know that people have fought for their freedom for this country," a 42-year-old Maryland floral designer told us. A 43-year-old Philadelphia man also made his point in the language of high school civics: children should know "the basic principles upon which our country was founded, particularly I feel everybody should know what the Constitution is about, the basis of our laws, how over time . . . the times influenced those concepts and beliefs." A 42-year-old Montana caterer reported that for her the "most fascinating periods in history" occurred "when people were fighting for their belief in freedom."

These patriotic sentiments are doubly ironic. First, they offer a different hierarchy of importance than the one most people erect when they describe what they themselves think about the past. Both the Maryland woman and the Philadelphia man, for example, listed family history as more important than U.S. history. Second, the patriotic sentiments conflict with what respondents told us about feeling disconnected from the past when they studied the same civic principles in school. Having found their own history classes boring or irrelevant, some Americans are still prepared to insist that their children have the same education. Why? Perhaps the conventional narrative of national history is so much a part of American consciousness that most people don't comment on it unless it is threatened or questioned—as it was when we asked about what children should learn. Perhaps respondents were speaking more out of obligation than conviction. Or perhaps what they disliked in school was process as much as content—the forced memorization and regurgitation, the lack of participation in learning about their own pasts.

In the less ideologically guarded precincts of leisure time, respondents offered less obviously nationalist answers. Of those who mentioned specific holidays that connected them to the past, only one quarter talked about national and patriotic celebrations like July fourth, Memorial Day, or Veterans Day. And even among that small group only half said the patriotic significance was what made them feel connected to the past. The significance and utility of national stories emerged in the context of narratives about the lives of family and friends. A retired Michigan man associated July fourth with family vacations at a lake rather than Thomas Jefferson writing the Declaration of Independence. A 40-year-old Georgia woman said, "I feel that I have nothing to do with gaining our independence—that was done for me. I appreciate it, I celebrate it, but I did not have any relatives that fought for it or signed the Declaration of Independence."

In her evaluation of what was most significant about the past, this woman constructed a hierarchy of importance very different from the ones used by professional historians, textbook authors, or conservative critics of the history standards. The issue is not Americans' lack of knowledge about the past or their sense of disconnection from it. Rather, it is that most Americans simply do not recognize themselves and their families in a distant narrative that stretches from election to election, war to war, and equates our national past with the history of nation-state.

"The government was a bunch of liars": Is National History Weakening?

If individual Americans are divided within themselves about the importance of our national history, the differences among groups of Americans
are even more striking. When we asked which area of the past was important to respondents, their answers revealed the most prominent demographic variations we encountered in the survey (see table 5.1).

TABLE 5.1

Percentage of selected groups listing U.S. history as most important

Men 65 or over	42%
Household income over $75,000 per year	31
White Americans without high school diploma	31
All men	29
People 65 or over	28
White Americans	23
Post-college education	22
All Americans	22
Mexican Americans	22 (minority sample)
Women	16
18–29 year olds	13
Household income under $15,000 per year	12
African Americans	13 (national sample)
African Americans	11 (minority sample)
African Americans without high school diploma	7 (minority sample)
African Americans under 30 years old	6 (minority sample)
Pine Ridge Sioux Indians	5
Pine Ridge Sioux Indian men	1

Though the contrasts in every demographic category are suggestive, the
differences between generations seem particularly revealing.[20] People over
age 65 were more than twice as likely as those under age 30 to describe the
history of the United States as most important to them. Is widespread loss
of faith in the state a relatively recent development? Though our evidence
on this contentious question is far from definitive, the survey responses
lead us to speculate that American nationalism (and a concomitant interest in the narrative of American national greatness) has significantly
eroded since the mid-1960s for a variety of reasons—among them the
globalization of the economy, the absence of unifying events like World
War II or the Great Depression, and the socially divisive fallout of the
1960s.[21]

Three quarters of people over 65 cited public or national events (rather than personal ones) as having most affected them; only one third of people under 30 made that same choice. Four events or periods were mentioned by more than fifteen respondents as especially influential in their lives: World War II (40); Vietnam (27); the assassination of John F. Kennedy (22); and "the 1960s" (18). Those who selected World War II were on average 61 years old; those who selected the other three events were on average 46. So few respondents in their twenties mentioned a public event that it is impossible to discern a defining historical moment. People over 30 mentioned the Gulf War just about as often as those in their twenties did.[22]

Members of different generations tended to take different meanings from the historical events they mentioned. Although most people told personal stories about World War II, about one sixth (all of them over age 65) depicted the war as a moment of public unity and patriotism. A 70-year-old Tulsa man who fought with the navy in the South Pacific described his wartime experiences in great detail and concluded that he had "learned the American people, when they are confronted with a catastrophe . . . will do everything within their power to come together for the common cause to defeat the enemy." A 75-year-old New Jersey man who served four years in the marines said, "I learned a lesson in extreme patriotism which I have never regretted having." Such answers help explain why men over 65—many of them World War II veterans—were more than three times as likely as 18–29-year-olds to put U.S. history above the history of family, community, or ethnic/racial group.

The lessons baby boomers learned from the 1960s left them considerably more skeptical about the nation-state. Most of their comments emphasized defeat, disunity, and betrayal. A 49-year-old New York woman summarized the conclusions of many in her postwar generation. Asked what period or event from the past most affected her, she replied, "The 1960s, because that's when my eyes opened up about the hypocrisy within our government. . . . Up until the 1960s, I basically believed everything about history that I was taught in school. I thought our country was always right, but with the Vietnam War I saw that we aren't always right."

The assassination of John F. Kennedy—mentioned by respondents who were on average 17 years old when he died—evoked bitterness. "I was a very young child," said a 39-year-old Massachusetts woman, "and very disillusioned, that's probably where I acquired a great deal of my cynicism." She learned "not to believe everything you see and hear—not to trust the newspapers or the government." Another New York woman, age 44, put matters more starkly: "Well, Kennedy was sort of this savior, this prince, and they called his administration Camelot. And when he died it seemed that he took the dreams—I was 13—the dreams of the future generations were shattered when he was killed. . . . I've never looked at government and politics in quite the same way after that. I no longer think that our elected officials are competent."

Baby boomers constructed narratives from the Kennedy assassination that had two different, but connected, messages. On one hand, they used the event—like so many drawn from their personal and familial pasts—to assess the degree to which they could make a difference in the world. In that sense, theirs were troubling stories about the problems of agency. Kennedy, they noted over and over, tried to make a difference and was shot down. On the other hand, respondents also drew messages from the assassination about whether government could be a positive force for change. Most people thought the answer was "no." They almost universally interpreted the Kennedy assassination as a moment of betrayal—an event from which they learned not to trust politicians.

The stories respondents told about Vietnam have an even stronger flavor of political betrayal. Almost all of those who mentioned Vietnam as the historical event that had the greatest impact on them (people who were on average 20 years old at the time of the Tet Offensive, 1968) talked about it in purely personal terms or viewed it as a lesson in the futility of war or the mendacity of government. A 48-year-old Ohio railroad conductor, who had served in Vietnam and complained that vets "were treated like dirt," told us what he learned from the war: "Never trust the damn politicians. I just don't trust any of them, period. If he's talking, he's lying." A 46-year-old Rhode Island musician who had protested the war as a college student put his lesson in one word: "distrust." Asked, "Of whom?" he answered, "Of government." A 45-year-old Illinois contractor who had neither fought nor protested came to a similar conclusion: "The government was a bunch of liars about the whole thing. . . . I just don't have as much faith in my government anymore."[23]

Except for a handful of people who recalled protest movements of the 1960s, Americans told us depressingly consistent stories about a decade that had robbed them of hope. When they remembered the 1960s, they thought not of freedom but of threats and barriers to positive social change. And events in the years since had given them little reason to put their faith in the nation-state.

TABLE 5.2

"Other areas or groups" that were "very important" to people
(selected by five or more people)

Church/religion/Bible	45 people
History of other ethnic, racial, religious, or cultural groups	38
World history	33
American Indians	21
Mankind/earth/evolution/natural history	21
History of other specific countries, regions, or continents	18
Ancient history/Egypt/Greece	11
History of spouses, fiancés, and their families	9
Job/occupation	9
Friends	8
History of the country my family came from	8
Music	8
My state/region	8
Women	7

"When I was younger there wasn't all this gangs and violence":
Other Narratives of Historical Change

Though professional historians have traditionally built their narratives around national history, there are obviously many ways to tell stories about the larger past. To get at some of them, we devised a catch-all question. Having asked about the past of family, nation, community, and ethnic/racial group, we added: "Is knowing about the past of any other area or group very important to you?" Almost three fifths of the people we surveyed said yes. We followed up with half of them and asked what specifically they had in mind (see table 5.2).

When respondents offered reasons for their interest in other histories, about three fifths explained it in terms of personal connections. A retired Texas man, for example, talked about his interest in Middle East history, which dated back to the seven years he spent on a State Department mission that monitored peace agreements between Israel and Egypt. A 35-year-old Tennessee woman attributed her interest in American Indian history to living in "part of the Trail of Tears," where "lots of people . . . have Cherokee ancestry." A 79-year-old Chicago woman described an interest in "the past of Russia because we still haven't found . . . the last uncle in my mother's family," who disappeared in Siberia in 1945.

Explaining their interests in historical books and films or hobbies and collections, most respondents also began with personal connections and questions and then moved outward. "I read a lot of stories by Flannery O'Connor and about the South in the 1920s and 1930s," said a 29-year-old Washington consultant, because "I'm from the South and my grand-mother's young adulthood was similar to those stories." Hobbyists and collectors tended to associate their passions with relatives who got them started or with memories of their youth. A 43-year-old Philadelphia human services worker said he collected Beatles outtakes because "it was happy music, being at the time I was 11 and 12 years old falling in love for the first time and hearing songs and lyrics that helped to identify those feelings and helped to express those feelings as well." But more than that, the old songs were for him "a link to my past, an explanation and part of who I am or how I became who I am."

Many respondents explained that their historical interests helped them grapple with the same set of questions about identity, relationships, morality, immortality, and agency that are at the core of their engagement with intimate and familial history. Some of them said they believed history could help them make sense of the present and understand cultures unlike their own. "I don't think you can have a clear understanding of what is happening with Native Americans or any other group of Americans unless you know of past events . . . that have repercussions for what happens today," concluded a Minneapolis mortgage underwriter who had visited the site of the Little Big Horn battle in search of clues to present-day relations between Indians and whites. By exploring larger contexts—different view-points toward and experiences with the same event—some respondents gained empathy. A 25-year-old receptionist from Carmichael, California was glad that the Pearl Harbor memorial display told "both sides." Seeing Japanese perspectives "helps me understand them and their actions."

Some were convinced that history could deepen understanding of the present—despite their experiences with history in school. "I always hated history class," began a 26-year-old Denver chemist who said she had sub-sequently become "interested in the past of other countries." She started to look into the history of Spain because her husband was a Spaniard and into Russian history because she'd read a book by Alexander Solzenitsyn. And "I was always fascinated with the sixties," she reported, because she was born in 1968, because "people were trying to speak out against the govern-ment and . . . were finding themselves," and because "I seem to really like a lot of the music from that time." Explaining that he liked to explore the history of a range of topics, a retired Texan identified the common denominator in his interests: "If I was there that is what makes it." Visiting his mother's sister in Iowa, he was eager to learn about his mother's ancestors. Visiting London, he tried to understand how the English had survived World War II. Visiting sites in the present whetted interest in the history of both the intimate and the remote.

Over and over respondents told stories that reflected the intersection of their families and the wider world. Professional historians often use families and individuals to illustrate some larger historical theme: rural versus urban deprivation in the Great Depression, the impact of World War II on women on the home front, the religious basis of the civil rights movement. But our respondents tended to start with the immediate, personal, and familial and then reach out for larger narratives and explanations. And they were less likely than historians to assume that families and larger trends were moving in the same direction. Respondents' narratives appeared to differ from traditional textbook stories in another respect as well: they did not chart the course of progress. Like respondents' narratives about Vietnam or the 1960s, their stories of rising crime or decreasing discipline tended to be framed as narratives of decline.

A 50-year-old black woman from Decatur, Georgia offered one example of how respondents interwove personal stories with these larger narratives. "I was remembering when we growed up. When we came up we had good parents and things," she said, adding: "It makes me feel good" to think of how she and her siblings "grew up together." From their upbringing they learned that "the past, the present, and the future, all of it comes down to one thing—you are going to heaven or you are going to hell." But good parents left them unprepared for a tragic intrusion from the outside world: the woman's brother was robbed and killed. Even now, years later, she couldn't understand. "I was wondering about why would someone just rob someone and kill them?" The shock of a good person from a good home suddenly being murdered by a stranger took its toll: "We changed over the years. I was slender and I gained a lot of weight. My face hasn't changed, but I used to weigh 95 pounds. Now I weigh 200."

Many respondents said that the largest threat to families came from the rise of crime and gangs. An Iowa mail-room employee saw the "start of gangs" in her community as the development that most affected her: "Gangs from different towns [are] coming in and trying to recruit high school kids, any kids. I'm not afraid for myself. I'm afraid for my [8-year-old] daughter," she began. The possibilities were so disturbing that she could not finish her sentence: "If something gang-related happens to her, if a gang got to her, with what's going on here, if she walks somewhere, if they get her . . ." "When I was younger there wasn't all this gangs and violence," reported a 37-year-old Sioux woman from Pine Ridge. "It really makes me watch out for my children because things are getting more ridiculous with the drive-bys they are having." "Things were different in the past than now," said a retired woman from Fresno, California. "There's too much crime. . . . When I went to school the teachers were stricter; now it is too lenient."

For many respondents the erosion of social authority represented by the rise of crime was a symptom of the larger spread of selfishness and hedonism. "There's no more respect or morals," observed a 43-year-old maintenance worker. "We're seeing more abortions and more sexual diseases. I feel that a lot of that has to do with the way the generation is going about it. You see a lot of divorce, and marriages aren't lasting. There's no respect between parents and children." A Mexican American from San Antonio said she grew up in "a very strict family because I was raised by my grandmother. They were very strict. They wouldn't allow us to play out of the yard." But these days "parents let their kids run wild, not all but some. They get into gangs. We have a lot of drive-by shootings around here. They kill a lot of little kids around here." "A lot of our problems today" are caused by the decline of "discipline and punishment," observed a Kentucky airline supervisor. "The juveniles have all the rights. The adults have no rights. We are raising these little juveniles. You can't even discipline them any more. Spare the rod, spoil the child. I am not saying beat them till their eyes fall out, but a spanking never hurt anyone," declared a 46-year-old Tampa woman who had joined Parents Against Gangs.

Many blamed television and popular culture. "I don't see close-knit families like we used to. They sit around watching TV now, but home life long ago meant playing games together and sitting around together, singing together, reading the Bible together or eating popcorn at night. We get together once in a while," but mostly "the family is scattered," said a widow from Monticello, Iowa. A woman from Idaho reported: "When I was growing up families were closer. Now both parents have to work and a lot of children are raising themselves. . . . My father was a carpenter, and he taught us to make our own toys. We taught our children the same. The grandchildren laugh because they don't know how to build. They just know how to go to the store and buy."

Along with these variations on the theme that declining discipline and rising crime prevented them from taking care of their families, respondents offered another narrative about conflicts inside the home. In this narrative the younger generation became agents of change and the older generation defenders of tradition. At stake were the transmission of values and the family's capacity to sustain itself in the face of adversity. "We were very poor" during the depression, said a Mexican American woman from Montebello, California, "but we appreciated what we had, not like kids today. You give them a dollar and they say, 'What's this?' and expect more." According to some respondents, the spirit of pitching in seemed to be slipping away; here, as almost everywhere else in the survey, participation was seen as the key.

As they linked their family stories to larger historical themes and modes of analysis, some respondents explored how technology had changed their lives. Thinking about "how hard things were" for his grandparents and parents, an African American auto worker from Southfield, Michigan felt "lucky that I was born in the time now. . . . It makes me appreciate that I don't have to go through so many things that they had to go through." But in talking about technological advances, many respondents added a critical spin. A man from Ravenswood, West Virginia invidiously compared his life with his grandfather's: "They used to have to split firewood just to cook, and . . . no inside plumbing. It makes me realize how easy we have it today." A teacher from Irvine, California took her grandmother as the reference point. She "cooked and cleaned and ironed. And this was when you had to scrub clothes on a wood board! No washing machines. No electricity. I don't know how they heated a thing to iron. And there was no running water. I'm too spoiled by modern conveniences."

Stories of progress rather than decline are hard to find in our survey, particularly from white European Americans. (By a rough count, four out of every five white respondents who talked about progress or decline emphasized change for the worse.) Again and again we heard that things are getting worse—more crime, less morality, less trustworthy government. Both in their choice of larger narratives (the story of crime and television rather than the rise of the welfare state or the globalization of the economy) and their mode of narration (moving out from the particulars of their family into wider realms, concentrating on decline rather than progress), white Americans departed from the narratives of professional historians. Like all Americans, our respondents continually constructed historical narratives of change and continuity; the form and content of those narratives illustrate the divergences between popular and professional historymaking.

"We have struck a balance": Mexican Americans in the Borderlands

Our interviews with Mexican Americans add up to a revealing case study of the intermingling of family stories and larger narratives of progress and decline. The special sample of 196 Mexican Americans, which included 55 interviews in Spanish, was confined to the states with the largest Mexican American populations (primarily Texas and California) and to Mexican American areas within those states. This vast "borderland" separating the 90 million residents of Mexico from the 220 million residents to the north and east is home to more than four fifths of the nation's 13.5 million Mexican Americans. Like most borderlands, it is a permeable region that allows Mexican Americans to move back and forth between the nation of their parents or grandparents and the nation in which they now live.[24] It is also a figurative borderland where the extended family mediates the claims of multiple cultures and multiple pasts.

Like its geographic equivalent, this mental borderland is a place of movement and interchange among competing traditions. And as Mexican American respondents described their pasts and their uses of the past, they repeatedly moved onto the borderland between family stories and larger narratives. Their modes of narration—in particular, their lack of emphasis on standard themes, figures, and events of Mexican and Mexican American history—were not precisely what professional historians might expect.

Our respondents clearly felt a sense of historical connection to the past of their ethnic group and their native land, though they drew upon those historical resources ambivalently in everyday life.[25] Like most European Americans, Mexican Americans were more likely to use their familial pasts than their ethnic past as they sorted out fundamental questions and built primary relationships. Yet like most African Americans and American Indians, they also drew upon ethnically and nationally rooted historical materials. And Mexican Americans often constructed a traditional narrative of linear progress that was very different from the narratives of decline offered by most white respondents. For Mexican Americans, the extended family seemed to provide an arena in which they could sift through the claims of many pasts and many heritages—Mexican, Mexican American, American, and those of their own families.

The Mexican American pattern in using the past could be said to fall somewhere between that of white European Americans on one hand and those of American Indians and African Africans on the other. A statistic that suggests this positioning can be found in the responses to our question about the relative importance of different areas of the past. Among Mexican Americans, 10 percent selected the past of their "ethnic or racial group" as most important, compared to 4 percent among European Americans, 26 percent among African Americans, and 38 percent among American Indians.[26]

Other quantitative measures reflected Mexican Americans' struggle to mediate among the claims of different pasts so they could accept their Mexican heritage while embracing their new home. One quarter said they shared "a lot" of "common history" with other Americans; one third said they shared only "a little" or "no" common history; the most frequent answer was "some."[27] When Mexican Americans talked about what they did share with other Americans, they often pointed to a heritage of freedom and opportunity. African Americans, by contrast, tended to explain that what they shared with other Americans was the experience of oppression and struggle. Only one tenth of Mexican Americans told us that the past of Mexico was more important to them than the past of the United States. African Americans indicated a stronger sense of identification with Africa than Mexican Americans did with Mexico, despite the vastly greater geographic and temporal distance in the connection.

Most Mexican Americans were unlikely to think of Cinco de Mayo (celebrating the Mexican victory over France in the Battle of Puebla) as a day that made them feel particularly connected to the past. No one mentioned it spontaneously when we asked about holidays, whereas one tenth—almost the same as among white European Americans—mentioned July fourth. When pressed to say whether they felt more connected to the past on Cinco de Mayo or July fourth, fewer than one sixth selected Cinco de Mayo.[28] Unlike either African Americans or American Indians, Mexican Americans gave little evidence of a sense of alienation from July fourth as a holiday celebrating the birth of the American nation.

Mexican American respondents were not only more likely to celebrate American holidays than Mexican ones; they were also more likely to name Americans rather than Mexicans as the historical figures who had affected their lives. Like white Americans, they mentioned John F. Kennedy most often; only a scattering of people cited Pancho Villa, El Cid, or Hernando Cortez. Benito Juárez, the Mexican president from 1858 to 1872, was cited by three people. Jesus Christ, Abraham Lincoln, Adolph Hitler, George Washington, and Bill Clinton were named by as many or more Mexican Americans. In response to our question about an event or period that had affected them, Mexican Americans were more likely than any other group (including white European Americans) to cite an event from their personal past. And Mexican Americans who chose public events made choices similar to those offered by European Americans: the Gulf War, World War II, and the assassination of John F. Kennedy.

Mexican Americans answered our open-ended questions in more patriotic tones than Americans in general. Some of these answers reflect the defensiveness of people who were confronting growing anti-immigrant sentiments (Proposition 187 was on the ballot in California at the time of the survey) and who may have thought we were questioning their patriotism—or even their citizenship—when we asked "In what ways do you feel you share a common history with other Americans?" (Some Spanish-speaking respondents, one of our Spanish-language interviewers later observed, needed "substantial reassurance that information would not be relayed to immigration officials.")

Somewhat testily perhaps, a 74-year-old San Antonio man answered: "I served in World War II. I think I earned the right to be among the people that call themselves American." Asked if he had anything further to say on this question, he added: "Well, I'm a taxpayer for one, aren't we all?" A 34-year-old El Paso woman whose parents were born in Mexico put it this way: "I was born here, raised here, went to school here, married here." A number of respondents went further and talked passionately about "freedom" and "our country." A 37-year-old nurse who lives thirteen miles from the Texas-Mexico border said, "We should be proud" of the United States "because of everything we have." "During Desert Storm," she recalled, "I had my little yellow ribbon in my door."

When Mexican Americans were asked to tell us what children should learn about the past, a number of them emphasized conventional lessons of civics and patriotism—as did Anglos. A 42-year-old machine operator from a small south Texas city whose father was born in Mexico thought that children needed to learn "how hard our ancestors fought for the country [the United States] for them to have their freedom, and how hard they worked so we can lead the kind of lives we do now." A 36-year-old foreman from Laredo, Texas who had immigrated to the United States as a child also argued that today's children needed to learn "the way people fought for freedom." And a 28-year-old Texas housewife who had come to the United States from Mexico at age 8 and was not yet a U.S. citizen answered: "It is important . . . they should know how independence was won and I think they should know the history of the United States. . . . I feel happy to be in the U.S. and I think it is a very blessed country; it is not like in Mexico."

Of course, Mexican American respondents acknowledged that they and their compatriots had faced injustice at the hands of white Americans. A few respondents noted that large areas of the current United States were once part of Mexico. And a few mentioned stories of personal discrimination. Asked about stories told at family gatherings, a 30-year-old Houston office manager said: "When my brother was about to be born . . . the hospital here in the U.S. wouldn't let my mother deliver here. They had to cross the border into Mexico and deliver him there, but they actually lived in the United States."

Still, relatively few Mexican Americans talked about discrimination or complained about the presentation of their history within mainstream American society—a particularly sore subject for African Americans and American Indians. Some of that unhappiness over the portrayal of blacks and Indians in films, books, museums, and schools is reflected in a lack of trust in these sources of information about the past. Mexican Americans, by contrast, rated museums, books, films, and high school and college teachers as more trustworthy historical sources than African Americans, American Indians, and white European Americans did.[29] Most Mexican Americans offered neither distinct public historical narratives of their own nor sharp critiques of the history offered by mainstream historical sources.

At times, Mexican Americans did embrace ethnic history. Asked on what occasions they felt particularly connected to the past when studying history in school, some described learning about the Mexican Revolution or the glories of the Maya and the Aztecs. A 40-year-old watchman from south Texas recalled that he felt particularly connected to the past when he learned about Pancho Villa, because he had once "met a man . . . who was the father-in-law of my aunt and he used to ride with Pancho Villa and he would tell us stories and in the book they would say something and the old man would tell us something similar to it. And I'd think, man, look at that: he knows about this . . . he was there." A 19-year-old California man who had recently graduated from high school noted that "when they talked about Mexican history, I tended to listen up."

Some Mexican Americans described their efforts to preserve Mexican cultural traditions like tamale making. Others put a Mexican American spin on American holidays like Thanksgiving. A 60-year-old retired woman from El Paso explained that on Thanksgiving she felt connected

to the Pilgrims who came to America but also to the people who "are coming to the United States . . . now."

As these examples suggest, efforts to preserve Mexican cultural traditions took place within family settings—often within large and extended
family networks. Mexican Americans attended more reunions than any
other group in the survey. More than two thirds of the Mexican Americans
we interviewed said that they had taken part in a reunion during the previous year. About three quarters of those were family reunions, many of
them large, multinational gatherings of kin.[30] A 33-year-old Brownsville,
Texas sales clerk who had immigrated to the United States as a young girl
reported that her extended family from both sides of the Mexican border
gathered at least every other month. And a 24-year-old San Antonio
woman who was born in the United States of American-born parents
described a reunion of 120 family members who traveled to San Antonio
from as far away as Florida and California.

This tendency of Mexican Americans to draw on Mexican, American,
and Mexican American historical traditions and experiences as they sort
out questions of identity is in line with what Gloria Anzaldúa calls a "mes-
tiza" worldview marked by "a tolerance of contradictions, a tolerance for
ambiguity." Or, as George Sánchez concludes in *Becoming Mexican
American*, "to be Chicano, in effect, is to be betwixt and between."[31]
Certainly, that is an analysis shared by a 42-year-old Laredo law enforce-
ment officer who was asked what about the past of his ethnic group was
important to him: "I'd say the migration, the acculturation, and finally the
assimilation into society—our society, the American society." Asked to
elaborate, he offered an eloquent personal summary of Mexican American
history: "Well, that brings into play our family history, because my grandparents migrated from Mexico during the Mexican revolutionary war, a
lot of people did. They migrated here to south Texas, and they settled here,
and brought with them a lot of culture. And our culture has permeated
this area, as well as the American culture has also permeated our ethnic
group. We have struck a balance. And now, we have sort of like a best of
two worlds, we have kept values, family values from our own culture, and
yet now we have a justice system, and the values that create a strong
nation, community service, and all that."

Although the Laredo lawman emphasized the "balance" and harmony
between a Mexican background and life in the United States, many of our
respondents described the tensions and ambivalences of living at the border between these two nations, cultures, and histories. A 43-year-old

school counselor from Brownsville, Texas talked about dual allegiances: "I'm Hispanic and will never be a Caucasian or Anglo" but added, "when you ask me, 'which one do you like the most?' it's like asking a child do you love your mother or father more. I've been living here now for six years and am having my history here—maybe in the future, this will be my past." He noted that he celebrated both July fourth and Mexican Independence Day. When our interviewer pressed him to say which made him feel "most connected" to the past, he refused to choose: "As a Mexican, I feel more connected to the 16th, when I hear the music and so on. Now that I'm living in the U.S., I try acculturization. Because I'm living here, I am celebrating things that I never did before—like Thanksgiving, it's a part of my life."

Many Mexican Americans spoke of working through multiple allegiances by telling stories about their own and especially their families' histories. Like other Americans, they tended to start with family stories and then reach out to larger narratives and frameworks. Because they often placed their family histories within the framework of movement and migration, the family became a medium for navigating between personal and group identity, between its own history and the history of Mexican Americans. In some ways, these stories are similar to stories told by all our respondents: Mexican Americans construct narratives as a way of answering such basic questions as "Who am I?" "How will I be remembered?" "How should I behave?" and "How can I make a difference in the world?" What seems distinctive is their comfortable fit within the framework of traditional, linear historical narrative.

Two story lines stand out. One, about declining traditional values, emphasizes questions of morality; the other, about economic progress, foregrounds questions of agency. For Mexican Americans, telling these two historical narratives is a way of dealing with claims of a traditional culture in Mexico and a less rooted but more economically rewarding life in the United States. Perhaps equally significant, the second of these stories demonstrates the persistence of the traditional historical narrative of progress—a narrative that's hard to find among white Americans of European descent.

The Mexican American declension narrative is almost always about the ways that the modern (and American) world threatens traditional family discipline, which demands that individuals respect and obey authority. Mexican Americans gave particular emphasis to this story, but it appears among all the groups we surveyed. Although a number of Mexican

Americans thought it essential for children to learn about American struggles for independence and freedom, more respondents emphasized lessons about morality, values, and, above all, respect. "To respect people" and to learn traditions "from your religion, from your ancestors" were the historical lessons children needed to learn, according to a 31-year-old teacher's aide who lived on the Arizona side of the Mexican border. She thought that kids today "get away with so much stuff," whereas when she was growing up "my Mom used to blink at me, and you'd know you were in trouble. And it made me a good citizen."

This sense of a decline in values seems to be shared across generations. A 72-year-old Brownsville, Texas carpenter wanted children to learn the importance of the family as "a good backbone" and to "get back to the old traditional family." A 33-year-old sales clerk in the same city agreed that in the United States, unlike Mexico, "the younger ones" are "not that respectable for the older ones." Many respondents seemed to believe that this moral decline had occurred both over time and across space—in the migration from Mexico to the United States. A 56-year-old refinery worker who came to the United States as a young adult explained that he has tried to teach his daughters and grandchildren "to be good American citizens," but also "not to forget their heritage" as Mexicans. Asked what traditions he had in mind, he talked briefly about the Spanish language and then turned to "the way the traditional family in Mexico behaves— respect to the elders, a real tight family unit."

Mexican Americans' fear that they or their children have lost a traditional Mexican culture that upholds the family ran through dozens of interviews. Yet it was only half the story that they told about their pasts. Many of them were also devoted to a narrative of economic progress that contrasts the poverty and restrictions of Mexico with the economic opportunities and freedom of the United States. Both are stories of change and continuity—the dominant frame for all the narratives we heard in the survey—but the first emphasizes how change threatens what was good in the past and the second emphasizes how change opens up new possibilities.

Often enough, these two stories were told by the same people. They were two sides in an internal dialogue or even an imagined conversation with friends and relatives who stayed behind in Mexico. In effect, those who told the story were asking whether they (or their parents or grandparents) had done the right thing when they uprooted themselves and their families and moved to the United States. And while many bemoaned the loss of traditional values, they seemed content with the choice they made. The most important event from her past, explained a Brownsville woman who immigrated in 1987, was "the decision to come to the U.S. . . . Balancing the pros and cons, I think that I made the right decision to come to this country."

Thus, Mexican Americans' most common story is the very traditional one about chasing (and sometimes catching) a piece of the American dream. A 25-year-old Houston construction worker who came to the United States as a boy described a typical conversation at a family gathering: "Well, all we talk about is the hard times, and everything that was going on. But mostly my grandparents are from Mexico, and they talk about all the poverty, and the government stealing from them, and all the hard times, and then they talk about coming to America, and being grateful that they had a chance to redo their life." A 56-year-old California housewife said that her Mexican-born parents "respect Mexico but they love America very much. Here, they were able to work and buy themselves a new house and you know a car, a TV set, and things that people who are poor in Mexico don't have. . . . My parents said that no matter what people in this country say, it's still the best country in the world."

This potent narrative of upward social mobility, of individuals taking control of their lives, can be found even among relatively recent and poor immigrants. A 54-year-old California field worker, who left Mexico in 1968 and had a family income of less than $15,000 a year, explained (in Spanish) that he had come to the United States "to look for a better life," because "I was poor and suffered a lot of hunger" and "had no future in Mexico at all." "Now," he concluded, "I see there are more opportunities in life, better horizons."

Sometimes the narrative of economic progress is framed in terms of personal advancement. "I'm self-educated," a California refinery worker commented. "I couldn't make it in my own country, so I had to come to America to realize my dreams." But more often the story is told in familial terms: "We didn't have what we have now." The "we" does not usually reach beyond the extended family; this is not the story of group progress. Though they use the past to ground their concern about what has been lost and their satisfaction about what has been gained, to affirm bonds with loved ones, and to grapple with multiple identities and heritages, Mexican Americans do not generally use the past to connect with others of a similar background. The collective past—understood implicitly as the shared experience of leaving Mexico for America—turns up in a migration story that they render in ambivalent but still positive terms. In this, Mexican

Americans depart from the dominant white European American pattern, which uses the past in more purely personal and familial ways and eschews linear narratives of progress. But as the next chapter suggests, they depart as well from the pattern of African Americans and American Indians, for whom the collective past is an even more looming and powerful presence.

At family gatherings, African Americans transmit "wisdom," as one respondent put it, from one generation to the next. "When the old people get with the young people," a 37-year-old St. Louis warehouse worker told us, "the old people tell the young people how it was when they were growing up." "It's usually the older folks that have the stories to tell," agreed a self-employed man from Pinetop, Arizona. The same could be said of white families and indeed all the families we heard about in our phone calls. People of varying backgrounds talked about their energetic pursuit of the past through looking at photos and writing in diaries, their powerful sense of connection to the past at family gatherings and holiday celebrations, and their strong trust in historical information from older relatives.

Yet black "older folks" also told some different stories and told them differently; so did the 186 Pine Ridge Sioux we called. Individuals from both groups often started with their families and their intimate pasts but then drew upon a broader set of cultural and historical materials. A 33-year-old Memphis photographer illustrated how stories about the past of a particular family become stories about the history of African Americans and how both sets of narratives offer guidance for living in the present. Asked by our interviewer to name a person and an event from the past that had a major impact on her, this woman talked about her grandmother. She described her grandmother's death as a turning point—a "Pandora's box"—that taught her "that love was more strong than I had ever imagined it to be." This moment reinforced some basic lessons she had absorbed from her grandmother: "I learned from her that regardless of whatever you do as a person you have to learn to genuinely like people. And she taught me that people around me (some I would not like), taught me to tolerate them, tolerate things you don't like. And that goes now in my life. You have to tolerate things you don't like or you'll go crazy. She was a loving person and to this day her memory is with me as if she were still alive."

Earlier in the interview, when we asked why this woman felt intensely connected to the past at family gatherings, she quickly extended the story of her grandmother into the story of slavery and of racism. "My family is a part of me," she explained, "and my grandmother and great-grand-mother are part of the past. I might not have lived then but I am a part of it. My great-grandma, her parents were slaves, she used to tell us about liv-ing on the plantation. And as a kid you learned to stay out of people's way . . . the white man's way. You grew up very quickly."

For this woman, family stories about "slavery times" were not some abstract history lesson; a century and a half later, they helped her make sense of her own life. "We sit and talk about slavery, we bring it up and wonder. My old relatives, I really respect them for what they went through and it makes my life seem not so bad. I think back to what they had to go through, the struggles. I went through struggles, but it's nothing like that. You can't even put them in the same breath—there is no comparison." For this young woman, then, the living past included not only her grand-mother but also much more distant relatives who struggled to survive. And she recognized that slavery was an experience her family had in com-mon with millions of other African Americans.

This collective and wide-ranging sense of the past gives particular force to the same woman's complaint that her high school teacher did not pro-vide "black history" that was as "in depth" or as "interesting as the other history she was teaching." "There wasn't enough information to tingle in the mind," she said, explaining why history classes made her feel almost entirely disconnected from the past. She didn't see her family history as unrelated to the history that was taught in school, but she said her teach-ers failed to make that connection. "Knowing about my family," she observed, "that's part of blackness." And knowing about the past of the United States is part of the same package: "I feel it goes together in some way, because I'm black and an American in the community, and I feel it's all blended into one."

As they thought about questions of change and continuity, life and death, many African Americans turned to the experiences of their grandparents and to the experiences their grandparents shared with other African Americans. When we asked a 34-year-old black woman from suburban Maryland to select the past she found most important (the past of her family, her ethnic or racial group, her current community, or the United States), she selected "family" but quickly pointed out the artificiality of the question. "The past of your family is also the past of your racial group," she said. With innumerable variations, our 300 black respondents (76 from the national sample and 224 from the special African American sample) used materials from both their families and their culture for resolving questions like "Who am I?" "How will I be remembered?" and "Can I make a difference in the world?"

Similarly, the Oglala Sioux we interviewed blended the stories of their families, their tribe, and American Indians. "In our culture," remarked a police officer on the Pine Ridge reservation, "family is the most important thing." But then he added, "The racial group would be the same thing. While you find out about your family, you find out about your culture." He harked "back to when we lived in tepees. A strong warrior would kill four buffaloes—he would take for his family and would give the rest to the tribe." Connecting family and tribal identity came easily to Pine Ridge Sioux since the two histories were so closely intertwined. One young man proudly noted that "my mother's father wrote the tribal constitution," that "Crazy Horse married my great-great-grandmother," and that "we have five uncles and three aunts . . . on the tribal council."

All Americans use the past to build and affirm primary relationships; African Americans and American Indians also use the past to affirm and build ties to their communities. They not only see themselves as sharing a collective past, they sometimes use these collective pasts to construct the sort of progressive narratives—history with a capital "H"—that seem harder to find among white Americans. And in some ways American Indians and black Americans also connect their narratives much more explicitly to the American national story than most white Americans do, even while they dissent sharply from its traditional formulations.

"Our race, our people": African Americans and Their Collective Pasts

We could hear black Americans blurring the boundaries of the personal and the public, the individual and the collective, when they spoke of "roots." Whites who mentioned "roots" were usually referring to their family tree. African Americans were also interested in their "family roots"—almost one third of them reported investigating the history of their family in the past year.[1] But "roots" meant something broader.[2] Explaining why she shared "common history with other African Americans," a Brooklyn woman said, "we all come from the same place. Our roots are all the same." Discussing the importance of family history, a black woman from Maryland commented: "It's your beginning . . . your racial and roots heritage." To talk about your family history was also to talk about the history of your race; to listen to a grandparent describing the struggle of your family was to listen to a description of black history. White respondents rarely spoke about their family history as a microcosm of the history of the nation, their region, their local community, or their ethnic group, but black respondents often described their family history as an exemplar of the black experience in America.

The black Americans we interviewed tended to blur the "I" and the "we." White respondents often talked about "I" or "me" in explaining why family history is important; when they spoke of "we" or "us" they were generally referring to their family. Black respondents peppered their answers with collective pronouns that intended broad meanings. When a 34-year-old Detroit postal worker noted that "other Americans" had experiences "similar to the things we went through," he added a clarification: "We—meaning my race of people." Most respondents didn't need to explain. Those who spoke about "how we came to be in this part of the world" or how Martin Luther King Jr. "made a mark in history for us," led struggles "to get us equal rights," and fought for "our race, our people" showed again and again how their sense of a collective past enabled them to claim a collective voice in the present.

Asked which area of the past (family, nation, community, or ethnic/ racial group) was most important to them, more than one quarter of African American respondents chose ethnic or racial history—a proportion almost seven times greater than among white Americans.[3] Even that figure—because the question forced people to choose between family and race—understates the powerful differences. The collective cast to the answers given by black respondents pervaded the survey. In an interview almost two hours long, a 50-year-old high school counselor from Alabama told us about how she explained the civil rights movement to her children and grandchildren, how she felt visiting the Birmingham civil rights museum, what she thought of films like *Mississippi Burning*, what she learned about slavery in school, what winning the right to vote meant to her, and how Martin Luther King Jr. personally affected her. Not surprisingly, then, when we asked her, "What specifically about the past of your racial or ethnic group is important to you?" she grew slightly exasperated. "They'll know. I already said that. I seem like I'm answering the same thing."

Our questions may have tried the patience of some respondents, but their answers painted a clear picture of how African Americans use a shared set of historical events, figures, commemorations, sites, and even sources. Although we did not hear a unified "black" narrative, African American respondents described patterns and drew on historical references that distinctly set them apart. Racial identity was like a watermark that invariably showed through the pages of the transcripts. We realized this as we read the responses in the national sample and could tell without checking the demographic data, which was in a separate database, when we were reading an interview with an African American. Later we heard the same distinctive voice in the 224 interviews in the special black sample. (Appendix 1 discusses the sampling procedures we used.)

"He is no father to me": Black Counternarratives of U.S. History

Black and white respondents drew distinct timelines for American history. Asked, "What event or period in the past has most affected you?" the two groups gave significantly different answers. Vietnam, World War II, and

TABLE 6.1

An "event or period in the past that has most affected you." African American and white European American differences in relation to selected events:

Event	Black	White
Civil rights	30 (22.4%)	9 (5.4%)
Slavery	15 (11.2)	2 (1.2)
WWII	9 (6.7)	21 (12.5)
MLK assassination	6 (4.5)	0
Assassinations of the 1960s	6 (4.5)	1 (.6)
Vietnam	6 (4.5)	19 (11.3)
JFK assassination	2 (1.5)	14 (8.3)
Gulf War	2 (1.5)	9 (5.4)

(Percentage is of blacks and whites who chose any public, rather than personal, event.)

civil rights made the top six choices for both, but whites were twice as likely to choose Vietnam and World War II, and blacks were four times as likely to choose civil rights. Black respondents talked largely about key moments or periods in African American history: the civil rights movement, slavery, and Martin Luther King Jr.'s assassination (see table 6.1).

African Americans talked about these historical moments when answering other questions as well. Asked what children need to learn about the past, almost half mentioned themes and topics in black history, from slavery to segregation to civil rights. Although many insisted that the schools needed to teach these stories, they also wanted "kids to learn this from their parents or grandparents or their relatives." A 55-year-old civil servant from California complained that in school "nothing was taught about the slaves or the black man other than we were slaves." But from his grandparents, he learned more positive lessons about blacks under Reconstruction through stories about "a great-great-grand uncle named George W. Murray, who was the last black congressman from South Carolina."[4]

When white Americans incorporated well-known historical events or people into their family narratives, they often appeared as the backdrops for more intimate tales—how we learned self-reliance during World War II, for example. In the black narratives, famous people and events figured much more centrally. Asked why family gatherings made him feel connected to the past, a 63-year-old Washington, D.C. man began rather blandly: "We talk about relatives that are dead, events that happened years and years ago." Pressed for a specific example, he recalled:

> When my ma was a small girl—10, 11, 12. She wasn't very big and lived in southern Illinois. Grandfather built a home for them. The assumption was that he, as a black, was building it for someone white because of the quality of the home—special leaded glass from New Orleans. When the whites realized the family was black, the Klan came to burn them out and my mother and grandpa went out on the road and stood on either side of the road. And when the Klansmen came down the road with torches to burn the house down, my ma and her father were hiding in ditches on the side of the road and fired into them. So it appeared that many people were there. So many Klansmen were wounded that they turned and ran.

The Washington man told us a family story about his mother and grandfather's triumph, but he linked it to a much wider racial context, as did dozens of others who described their family's experiences with slavery, sharecropping, Jim Crow, and civil rights.

Asked to name "a person, either a historic figure or one from your personal past, who has particularly affected you," just under half of the black respondents chose a historic figure. Of those, half chose Martin Luther King Jr., who appears to stand far above all others in the black historical imagination. Indeed, King was selected by more than five times as many black respondents as the second choice—Jesus Christ. Aside from Christ, only a handful of whites were mentioned.[5] Most of the rest of the votes went to a scattering of black leaders, from Frederick Douglass to Malcolm X.

A government worker from suburban Maryland denoted this distinctive historical pantheon (as well as the racial exclusiveness of the dominant narratives) when he told us, "This has always been a stickler with me . . . the reference to George Washington being the father of the country. . . . Being black, he is no father to me. . . . When it is put that way—'the father of our country'—that has no meaning to me. The first president, I can understand that, but the father of our country, no. Then, another thing: Abraham Lincoln—my perception of the Emancipation Proclamation— freeing the slaves—was only done to win the war. They needed bodies and who was on the front line? The black troops."

Not only did African Americans venerate particular historical figures, many of them also seemed to have a stronger sense of a public (and especially American) past than white Americans did. So even as black Americans asserted a counternarrative of famous black figures and events, they also implicitly recognized a traditional American narrative that white Americans eschewed. In answer to our question about a person from the past who had affected them, about one quarter of white Americans but two fifths of black Americans selected a recognizable public figure from American history. White Americans more often cited a parent than all the national historical figures combined. By contrast, more black Americans chose Martin Luther King Jr. than any particular relative.[6]

White Americans simply do not have a shared, revered public figure comparable to Martin Luther King Jr. Nor when they talk about public figures like Kennedy or Lincoln do they make them powerful living presences within their lives, as blacks do with King. A student born five years after the civil rights leader's death embraced him as a "role model" and "a hero." King's life offered lessons for how individuals should live and how society should operate. He taught a 70-year-old Cleveland woman that all people need to "get along together in this world." A 69-year-old Detroit man heard a more personal message: "I had been kind of hothead, fighting here and there. As the times developed and I found out things about Martin Luther King, I learned that sometimes you have to take things and that gave me a good example to my life. I kind of got myself together to the point now where I'm almost a preacher." King's life offered lessons for both self and society. "I loved his nonviolence movement of trying to change the way things were by not fighting or being violent," said a retired Maryland woman. "He influenced me a great deal, that just made me want to better myself and my family."

Not surprisingly, African Americans regard King's birthday as an important national holiday. Asked to make a choice between July fourth and Martin Luther King Jr. Day, they chose King's birthday by a margin of almost four to one as the day that made them feel more connected to the past. Some black respondents said the fourth of July fell well outside their historical vision. A secretary from Grambling, Louisiana talked about Juneteenth, which celebrates the freeing of Texas slaves.[7] But of July fourth, she said: "To be honest, when I look at that particular holiday, it is more of a white holiday . . . a white thing. I do celebrate it, but I think back to when it actually took place, I look back to the people who were actually in it back then. Where were we back then?"

Ironically, most whites view July fourth as a distant or largely irrelevant historical event, an excuse for familial celebration; black Americans, by contrast, warmly testified to their direct connections to Martin Luther King Jr. Day. They told stories that made the emergence of King and the civil rights movement into crucial turning points when they personally, along with other African Americans, took more control over their lives. "The fourth is the celebration of America's independence from Britain many year ago," noted a 42-year-old car salesman from St. Louis. "But that doesn't mean I was free. [That's] what Martin Luther King did for me personally and what he did for black people in general. I was 16 years old when he died, and I lived my whole life with him up until that point." A 63-year-old West Indian man explained that he felt more connected to the past on King day than on July fourth, "because I struggled through that era. . . . I worked in south Florida. I could not go in restaurants and mix with the white people." King, a 51-year-old Georgia man agreed, "helped us not have to go to the back of the bus."

Many African Americans fashioned their distinctive historical consciousness by celebrating holidays like King's birthday and constructing a black historical landscape. Unlike white Americans who tended to visit history museums and sites serendipitously on trips to someplace else, African Americans often deliberately sought out and commemorated the black past. Virtually every black respondent who mentioned a museum or historic site talked about black history. The civil rights museums in Birmingham and Atlanta, the Frederick Douglass House in the Anacostia neighborhood of Washington, D.C., and the Schomburg Library in Harlem imparted powerful messages to black visitors. Even when black respondents talked about visits to "white" institutions, they described a quest for African American history—an exhibit on black women at the St. Louis Museum or on black music at the Missouri Historical Society. Asked which historic sites made him feel connected to the past, a 50-year-old Milwaukee businessman replied: "I visited the old slave markets in Carolina, where I felt very connected, whereas I visited the old landings of Christopher Columbus in Jamaica or the Bahamas and I felt no connection."

African Americans often described pilgrimages to black shrines. "I always go" to "the Martin Luther King museum here in Memphis" on April 4 (the day King was assassinated), a Tennessee woman told us. White Americans often found visits to historic sites and museums meaningful because they allowed the family to talk about the past. Black respondents tended to directly connect their personal and family narratives to the specific public historical narratives that these sites presented.

African Americans were also more likely to connect deeply with particular historical films and books; they often integrated materials from these sources into their personal sense of the past. Though the historical books and films mentioned by whites were too scattered to suggest any conclusions about reading patterns, black respondents repeatedly brought up the same books—especially Roots and The Autobiography of Malcolm X (both, in effect, written by Alex Haley)—and films and television programs (again, Roots but also Mississippi Burning and Spike Lee's Malcolm X). Black Americans drew upon Roots in a way that few white Americans did for any book or film; some offered detailed memories of the TV series even though they hadn't seen it for many years. Others talked about the show's lasting effects: "When I first saw Roots," said a 33-year-old Tennessee woman, "it had an impact on me—left my imagination open and wondering. Being an African American, I wondered. You had to wonder. Even with the information out there about slavery, I had to wonder. When I went to Mississippi and saw where the plantations used to be, I envisioned myself being there. . . . I had a mental vision. I could see the women on the porch washing the clothes, the kids, the men in the fields."

For these black Americans, a rich oral historical culture modifies and reinforces the historical narratives provided through books, films, and museums. A 30-year-old custodian told us that he felt especially connected to the past when reading history books. Asked for a specific book, he first mentioned a biography of Martin Luther King Jr. but then explained how his mother's memories had amplified its meaning: "I remembered what my mother was telling me, because she lived back in his days. . . . And she would explain to me what happened and how everything took place. . . . She told me what kind of man he was, how he was trying to stand up for what was right so that people no matter what color, they'd all be equal." A government worker and retired military officer from Sacramento who was twenty-five years older described a similar process, even while talking about more distant events. Asked why reading a collection of slave narratives, *Bullwhip Days*, made him connect with the past, he explained, "Being a black man . . . I could identify and also having been reared by my grandparents, who were of the first generation born free, I could identify with and understand the book better. . . . My great-grandfather was six years old when slavery was ended."

For many African Americans this orally transmitted history—as well as particular, trusted books, films, and museums—competes with an "official" version of the past that is often distrusted. African Americans judged high school and college teachers, museums, and books as significantly less trustworthy than did white Americans; but they more favorably evaluated accounts from eyewitnesses and relatives. Black Americans described themselves as more connected to the past than white Americans when gathering with their families but less connected when visiting museums, reading books, or studying history in school.[8]

Many African Americans criticized the history taught in school, which they said "ignored," "distorted," or even "lied" about the black experience. An Atlanta firefighter who gave studying history in school a 2 on the 10-point connectedness scale and high school history teachers a 3 on the 10-point trustworthiness scale explained his answers: "I'm not saying that I didn't trust a history teacher. It was the material they were giving that I did not particularly trust. Basically, just being an African American, our contributions to history are not presented. They are left out. If you are presenting history you want to include everyone, but African Americans are often left out."

Despite this forceful critique of mainstream history, African Americans still placed their experiences within American history. When we asked black respondents, "How much of a common history do you think you share with other Americans?" only 7 percent said "none." Almost three quarters said they shared "a lot" or "some," and another one fifth said "a little."[9] When we then asked what common history they shared with other Americans, they generally avoided conventional sentiments about freedom and democracy. Instead, they found common ground in the history of migration or struggle against oppression—identifying with other immigrant and poor Americans rather than with dominant social groups or mainstream political ideals.

"Your ancestors, my ancestors," a 44-year-old Memphis mail carrier said to an interviewer whom he correctly perceived to be white, "all came from the east side of the world—Africa, Great Britain. My forefathers, your forefathers all came to America. They had one common goal, to live here. Some came as slaves. There were slaves that were white, called indentured servants. The ones who weren't were truly slaves. We all share a certain situation of coming to a new country. That's how I can identify with . . . other Americans. The only ones who I can't are the Indians." "We're basically all . . . born of immigrants," said a Petersburg, Virginia woman in a phrase used by several others, "whether the original immigrants were free or not." "Well," observed a Brooklyn tap-dance instructor in her twenties, "everyone has gone through a struggle in one way or another."

This sense of a shared history in the United States helps explain why relatively few black respondents identify primarily with Africa rather than America. When we asked whether the past of any other place in the world seemed more important than the past of the United States, only about one fifth said yes—although of those, almost three quarters named Africa as that place. Many black Americans sympathize with and support Africa, but fewer than one sixth placed their strongest historical associations there. A retired Memphis woman who is quite involved in the history of her family and the black community told us, "I'm an American, born in the U.S. . . . I don't feel African American, I feel black American."

Their powerful sense of racial identity did not prevent African American respondents from talking about the mulatto nature of American culture. Though our minority sample included only those who identified themselves as "black or African American,"[10] more than 10 percent of this self-selected group mentioned racial mixing in their family's past. Half of those who mentioned interracial family pasts (and most of those with stories about the more distant past) referred to Indian ancestors. A Texas man in his twenties noted that he had been trying to learn more about "where I come from because I have a lot of Indian in me."[11] Such stories seemed to reflect an effort to root African American history more firmly in American soil, to question clear-cut racial categories. A Georgia man whose great-great-grandmother was a Cherokee made the point sharply: why do white people think they are superior to blacks, he asked, when "we all have the same blood?"

"How we struggled to where we are today": Black Narratives of Group Oppression and Progress

Like other respondents, African Americans found the past a particularly useful resource for thinking about whether they could make a difference in the world. Like other respondents, they constructed narratives in an effort to understand how and why things change and how they could themselves effect change. They differed from white respondents in that they often used a broad set of cultural materials in thinking about those questions, and they pushed the question of personal effectiveness into issues of group agency—asking whether or not they could join with others to make a difference in the world.

This merging of the personal and the political was evident when a black state worker and community activist from Connecticut talked at length about writing in his journal, an intimate form of historymaking for most other respondents. "My journal," he explained, "is basically information about what I've done in the community in the past and poetry, tidbits of poetry, because I like writing poetry. It's based on, I'd just say cultural plights, like slavery, or what a lot of people feel is a systematic oppression in America of certain ethnic groups." Out of this private record, he crafted a public narrative of black history by writing a newsletter and running a community organization aimed at "enhancing awareness to the people who had been through my same plight" and "uplifting the African American community in which I live." Of his community work, he said: "I thought it was my duty, because every individual who exists on this earth today is definitely a part of history. It does not matter whether he's a butcher or a baker, the president or the low man on any totem pole, he is a part of history."

Black Americans like this man tended to share three types of stories in response to the question "What specifically about the past of your racial group is important to you?" (In fact, the same sets of narratives reappeared throughout the survey.) One was the story of oppression, discrimination, and racism: slavery obviously plays a central role in such narratives, but so do later episodes of racial violence and discrimination. Indeed, a vaguely worded question about the past of the respondent's racial group evoked very concrete and personal stories of oppression. A 72-year-old Chicago man answered rather matter-of-factly: "My father's cousin was tarred and feathered in the South—no reason given, because he was black." A Gary, Indiana man of the same generation began his answer with a general statement about the importance of learning "the way the black man is treated in the United States—so far as opportunities, denial, the hate, the bigotry." But then he described how, when he "was living in Mississippi, I was drafted into the service for one reason—I was told for fighting for my country. But I didn't know how could I consider this my country, when I couldn't even vote, I had to go into the back door to get something to eat or drink, and I had to bring it out. I couldn't even stay in there. And I had to fight for my country. That was very hard for me to understand when I was 18. Still is."

Although African Americans often recounted this depressing and ongoing tale of racial discrimination, they also talked about how particular individuals overcame oppression and made important contributions to crafts, agriculture, or science. In discussing this second type of story, three different people brought up Dr. Charles Drew—not a well-known name among white Americans. Drew, according to a 34-year-old postal worker, "invented blood transfusions but he died from a car accident, and the reason he died was because he wasn't admitted into a hospital to receive a blood transfusion that would have saved his life."[12]

The third, and most frequent, black historical narrative combines the first two by describing group struggle to overcome the racism and oppression of white society. Often, it is a hopeful story about group progress that suggests how individuals can take control of their lives. As a Dallas housewife put it, "From slavery times—things that I had read—it made me think about how far my children have come from the past of the children back then. It helps to overcome any of the hostilities that you might feel . . . and to look toward to the future."

To a startling degree, black Americans constructed a story of progress when they looked at the past—a rather traditional story that was hard to find among white Americans. When they named public events that had affected them, about one third of the African American respondents talked about change for the better or worse, and of that third, almost three quarters described change for the better. (By contrast, more than four fifths of white respondents described change for the worse.) Asking themselves whether it was possible to make a difference in the world, African Americans answered that "we" can, that groups and movements can alter a seemingly unchanging regime of racism and discrimination and push history into a new trajectory.

They often used metaphors of distance or travel when they drew lessons from past events, talking about how we "have come a long way," "how far Martin Luther King brought us," or "where we came from to how we struggled to where we are today." To some extent, emancipation from slavery offered the paradigm for this progressive narrative. Asked to name the period or event that had most affected him, a young Arkansas steelworker chose "the era of slavery with an emphasis on the abolition of slavery resulting in black Americans or black men, in particular, being able to have full rights and privileges as Americans, especially the right to vote." Asked to draw a lesson from that era, he replied: "If there is a strong enough desire in the community at large, inevitably that change is going to take place because of our system of democracy and each individual's power to make that change happen."

Black respondents most often found a story of progress in the civil rights struggle. A Detroit woman spoke about "freedom" and then defined it by saying, "Thank God we're able to drink from the same fountains as other races, we're able to vote, and we're able to go places." For a 65-year-old Detroit woman, the changes could be summarized in two incidents separated by six decades. The first was from her Arkansas childhood: she and father were run off the road and threatened by a white man who was angry because he'd been turned away at a country store that had given her father credit. "We didn't deal with white people too much," she said of those days. The second was a recent shopping trip: "When we got groceries, a young [white] man took our groceries to the car.... I think it's so nice. It's just so different now."

Black respondents employed similar narrative strategies when they talked about advances won under Martin Luther King Jr.'s leadership. King "fought against blacks sitting in the back of the bus," a pipe fitter from Newport News, Virginia explained. King "opened the doors for better opportunity for the black man," agreed a Georgia math teacher. King, many concurred, taught about not only equality and nonviolence but also resolution in the face of adversity. King "kept on marching on," said the math teacher. King "taught persistence," added a Chicago man in his mid-thirties. "It's like he never gave up his quest for civil rights no matter what obstacle stood in front of him."

Not all black respondents drew such affirmative messages from history. With the death of the Kennedys and Martin Luther King Jr., a 61-year-old Chicago man argued, "the dream was lost, and blacks are back twenty or thirty years, back before he started his dream." King's birthday, agreed a 57-year-old unemployed Massachusetts woman, "makes me sad because I feel the man died for nothing, because what he was killed for, people are not doing what he set out to do or to try to get better jobs, schooling, rights, and education for everybody."

Just as some read the story of civil rights and King as that of a dream betrayed, others told the story of slavery with an emphasis on brutality and oppression. Slavery, in the words of a 33-year-old Baltimore retail manager, "has torn me away from a lot of heritage, a lot of heritage I will never know . . . a crime that has never been answered for." A 26-year-old Detroit waitress provided the sharpest version of this alternative interpretation of the black past when she described what she learned from her boyfriend, who is "really into history": "He feels like black people wouldn't be the way they are if it weren't for slavery—the things that the white people did. He blames everything on the white man. I don't agree with him, but he does."

These interviews were exceptions: most black respondents found hope rather than despair in the past. From the civil rights movement, a 21-year-old Brooklyn student told us, "I learned that people can overcome no matter what the obstacles are." The progressive view of most African Americans is remarkable not simply because they *have* faced enormous oppression in America but also because we cannot locate a comparable optimistic public historical narrative among white Americans.[13]

Even when white Americans drew more directly upon the substance of national historical events like Vietnam and the Kennedy assassination, they often constructed privatized, fragmented, or pessimistic narratives. Asked what lessons they drew from public historical events, few offered narratives about ordinary people acting together to change the world. White Americans had not experienced anything as empowering as the civil rights movement; they made the Vietnam War and the Kennedy assassination into stories about betrayal—stories about the world spinning out of control. By contrast, some black respondents found hope even in tragedy. Asked to describe the lessons he learned from King's assassination, a 35-year-old black army officer said: "Even in death, great things can occur from that. I think that the country as a whole became more sensitive, or more in tune with what Martin Luther King was trying to espouse."

"We're all basically related": The Oglala Sioux and Their Pasts

The 186 Oglala Sioux from Pine Ridge reservation in South Dakota shared with all respondents an emphasis on family as the primary source of personal identity and locus of historical memory.[14] Like whites (and African Americans and Mexican Americans), they told us that the past of their family was "most important" to them and that they felt "most connected" to the past when gathering with their families. More than half of them had looked into the histories of their families during the previous year—a dramatically higher figure than for any other group in our survey. Yet the Oglala Sioux also spoke in the kind of collective voice that came easily to African Americans. The Sioux referred to more than their own families when they talked about "we," "us," or "our." They repeatedly talked about "our history," "our heritage," "our culture," "our tribe," "our language," and "our traditions." The Sioux were almost ten times as likely as white Americans to describe ethnic/racial history as most important to them; indeed, a higher percentage of Sioux than African Americans made that choice.

Even more than black Americans, Oglala Sioux stretched their connections from their families to more collective identities as members of a tribe, as residents of Pine Ridge reservation, and as American Indians. Asked to explain why she had rated the history of her family as the most important, a 48-year-old Pine Ridge woman answered, "My family leads down to my Indian culture and that leads to the history of the United States. I guess it all connects." A 53-year-old homemaker offered a similar response: "You learn the past of your family and that branches out to many things, and that would include your community and your ethnic group, and not to mention the history of the U.S. too." Oglala Sioux believed that they shared a blood tie to other members of their tribe. "In the Lakota beliefs," explained a 28-year-old cook, "we're all basically related." "Around here," noted a 30-year-old fireman, "everybody treats you like brothers, sisters, moms and dads . . . even as far as the fifth and sixth cousins." To a 48-year-old professional, the most important thing for children to know about the past was "who their people are, how they came to be here, how we're all related."

Since "we're all related," gathering with family or investigating family history meant affirming a larger collective identity. "We all feel the . . . spirit of our ancestors on a daily basis," said a 42-year-old unemployed woman. "When we are all together, it is a really strong feeling. We have ceremonies where we feed our ancestors. Invariably, everything we do has connection to our ancestors. The Native American culture thrives and lives by ritual because we're part of this oral history, and everything we do, we tie it into the past." These connections with a wide circle of ancestors as well as the reality of life in a relatively small community meant that many Pine Ridge residents reported familial ties to key figures in the local past, especially prominent chiefs. Asked to identify a figure from the public or personal past who had a major impact on them, Oglala Sioux respondents offered names that fell in both categories: "my grandpa, Chief Red Cloud"; "my sixth generation grandfather, Chief Big Foot"; Chief Spotted Tail, a relative "from my mom's side."

Yet even those Oglala Sioux who did not claim lineal descent from a prominent leader constructed family histories linking themselves to the tribe. This tie between family history and tribal history had a bureaucratic component—the Bureau of Indian Affairs required people who want to enroll as members of the tribe to prove their ancestry. "In order to be a member of a tribe," a 47-year-old man explained, "you have to do a history of your family in order to see if you have the right ancestors." Thus, most Pine Ridge residents had researched their family history. But even when the Sioux complied with a government requirement they reinforced their group identity as members of a particular tribe—what respondents variously described as Sioux, Lakota, Oglala Lakota, Oglala Dakota Sioux, or, most often, Oglala Sioux.[15]

Many Sioux used family history as a vehicle to move beyond their tribe to an identification with other American Indians. By looking at his family tree, reported a 42-year-old Pine Ridge resident, he "found out that I am related to people out in other reservations," because "the cavalry separated us into separate reservations so that there wouldn't be a big group of them." Asked to define his race, the same man told us that "the Lakotas are Native Americans, that is what we call ourselves." A 32-year-old woman noted that she had looked into her family history "to get my oldest son enrolled into our tribe," but that in the process she had "found out that I was related to some people from the Northern Cheyenne."

Some Sioux created historical narratives that undercut notions of "pure" or fixed racial identity. Like African Americans, they used the past to juggle multiple identities—which, in the context of reservation life, sometimes proved difficult. A teacher, for example, had learned from talking to "elders on my father's side" that one of her distant relatives was a Lindbergh. Although she thought this discovery was "kind of neat," she acknowledged that there are still "a lot of full-blood Indians that look down on it if you have some white blood in you. People who have white blood are called 'Iyeska' and sometimes it's a bad word." Another school employee in her twenties who had both "white relatives and Indian ancestors" was "looking up her genealogy" so that her children could know where they came from and "avoid some of the prejudice I've grown up with."[16]

Though some Sioux respondents reported their kinship with white Americans, most viewed whites as "the other," as "them" or "they." Asked to explain who she meant when she talked about "how they used to treat us," a 20-year-old women answered simply "the white people." Sometimes this presentation of white Americans as the "other" partook as much of curiosity as hostility. A 31-year-old game warden noted that he would "like to know about the white society. I know they came from overseas, but I'd like to know exactly where they came from—France or wherever."

"Pretty much opposite": The Sioux Rewriting of U.S. History

For the Oglala Sioux, a strong sense of group identity both drew upon and reinforced a distinctive sense of the past—a shared set of historical references to particular events, places, and people that they repeatedly invoked and used, albeit not always in the same ways. Asked about an event or period in the past that "has most affected you," the Sioux drew their answers from a specifically Indian historical chronology. Almost two thirds cited events from American Indian history, with most of them talking about the 1973 occupation of Wounded Knee, the 1890 massacre at Wounded Knee, the confinement of Native Americans to reservations, the signing and violation of various Native-White treaties, and Columbus's arrival in the New World. Not a single white respondent cited any of these events.

The Sioux described a historical landscape just as distinct as their time-line. More American Indians (about two thirds of our sample) than any other ethnic or racial group reported that they had visited a museum or historic site during the previous year. They almost always chose such places as the Wounded Knee massacre site, Crazy Horse Mountain, Little Bighorn Battlefield National Monument, and the Sioux Indian Museum in Rapid City, South Dakota. At least twenty-six Oglala Sioux noted that they visited the giant sculpture of Chief Crazy Horse that is being carved in the Black Hills. Only fifteen mentioned visiting nearby Mount Rushmore, and most of them did so only in the context of a visit to the Crazy Horse monument. Or they put a distinctive spin on the trip. For a schoolteacher from Pine Ridge, a trip to Mount Rushmore was memorable because her granddaughter got to sit in the lap of Ben Black Elk, "a great Indian leader . . . who took a job of going to Mt. Rushmore each summer dressed in his native costume and having his picture taken" and who had given this woman and her husband their Indian names when they were themselves children.[17]

When we asked about a person from the past who affected them, the Sioux's most popular choice by far was Crazy Horse. Not a single white or African American cited the Sioux warrior, who was stabbed to death at age 35 by an American soldier.[18] (Whites and blacks did share the Sioux interest in men who could be considered martyrs: white Americans put Kennedy, Lincoln, and Christ first and black Americans overwhelmingly selected King.) The Sioux set themselves apart not only in the people, places, and events they cited but even more in the way they talked about them. Sioux stories reversed the conventional narrative, establishing different key turning points or viewing conventional turning points in an entirely different light. A 37-year-old Pine Ridge man described his sense of the past as "pretty much opposite" that of "most of the Americans." "Well," he pointed out, "when they were fighting the Civil War, we were fighting the cavalry and when they were homesteading the West, we were stuck on the reservations. . . . Whereas they gained their freedom, we lost ours."

In presenting their story as "pretty much opposite" the traditional narrative, the Sioux differed from African American respondents. Members of both groups offered sophisticated counternarratives of U.S. history. African Americans, however, most often saw themselves as part of the traditional story, which they told in conventional Americanist terms of emancipation and progress; they demanded inclusion in the basic narrative and complained of white failures to live up to the nation's principles. The Sioux seemed to reject the traditional narrative structure altogether, defining themselves as a separate nation with a history that followed a dramatically different trajectory.

This conviction that you needed to "reverse history" to tell the story of American Indians, as one person put it, ran through many of the interviews. "Because American history began in 1492 and Native American history began long before that, we have different histories," observed a teacher. A man who worked for the federal government said Columbus's arrival in the New World was "more or less the beginning of the downfall of the Indians"; a 38-year-old woman called it the start of "genocide." A 26-year-old student, conscious that he was talking to someone of his own generation but of a different race, declined to offer much detail about the lessons he drew from the "discovery of America." "I don't really want to be offending, so I'll have to skip that one," he explained.

The bitterness of the Sioux narrators increased as they came closer to the present. Eleven of them talked about July fourth, for example, as having either no meaning or a reverse meaning for Native Americans. "The fourth of July," noted a schoolteacher, "is supposed to be Independence Day, but we never got independence. We have nothing to celebrate about." A 33-year-old man described the founding of the United States as "the beginning of genocide of the natives of this land."

White injustice toward Native Americans, our respondents told us, intensified in the nineteenth century. White respondents said little about nineteenth-century events, except for occasional references to the Civil War, but the Sioux spent considerable time talking passionately about things that happened more than a century ago. Many of them could detail a history of broken treaties. Pine Ridge residents attached particular importance to the Fort Laramie Treaty of 1868, which had given the Sioux control of the Black Hills. The U.S. government's blatant violations of the treaty, they told us, signified that "Native Americans, in the eyes of whites, are expendable" and that "European colonists cannot be trusted."[19]

Not surprisingly, Pine Ridge residents celebrated the Battle of Little Bighorn, where in 1876 Sioux and Cheyenne warriors under Sitting Bull and Crazy Horse wiped out General George Armstrong Custer and his Seventh Cavalry. One respondent called it "the greatest victory of the Lakota people" and another "our victory, our only victory." Among the Sioux, Little Big Horn Day (June 25) is a holiday celebrating "the day that Custer got killed." Yet some Pine Ridge Sioux cast even this victory within the tragic mode that characterized their overall public history. A 35-year-old unemployed man, describing how high school history classes degraded "our people," observed that teachers described the battle as Custer's "last stand, but it was ours. We lost a way of living; after that, we were sent to the reservations."[20]

Sioux spoke most mournfully about Wounded Knee, where the U.S. Seventh Cavalry massacred 146 Sioux men, women, and children on December 29, 1890—the last military engagement between whites and American Indians. More respondents had visited the local memorial to the massacre than any other historic site. More respondents mentioned Wounded Knee as the historical event that affected them than any other but one. And that exception was the 1973 American Indian Movement occupation of Wounded Knee—a confrontation that itself drew upon and reinforced the powerful historical associations that residents had with the event and the site. More than half of our respondents mentioned Wounded Knee in the course of their interviews. And these references weren't casual; respondents graphically described how "soldiers came in and killed women, children, and babies" and said they had learned from this not to "trust the United States government" and "how cruel people can really be to another race."

When we later asked our interviewers what they particularly remembered about their interviews with the Pine Ridge Sioux, one pointed to the way that such stories about the past are deeply embedded in the present: "Their everyday life becomes the past, the past becomes their everyday life." He recalled a woman who explained to him, "We're still talking about Wounded Knee like it happened today."

Despite—or because of—their bitter criticism of the American government, Pine Ridge residents were more directly engaged with the traditional national narrative than most white respondents, even while placing themselves distinctly apart from that narrative. To a greater degree than any other group we surveyed, the Oglala Sioux cited public rather than personal events as the ones that most affected them. And more than white Americans, they talked about events—treaties signed and broken, presidential orders, actions by federal troops and agents—from our national political history. Pine Ridge Sioux more often invoked events and people from U.S. history, conventionally defined, than white Americans, though the perspective on those people and events was not exactly the one that advocates of teaching the canonical names and dates would want.[21] In contrast to the indifference with which white respondents viewed textbook narratives of American history, the Sioux spoke with the passionate interest of the outside critic.

In fact, the Oglala Sioux sometimes seemed to enjoy giving our interviewers their take on cherished symbols of Americana. A 62-year-old Pine Ridge man who described himself as "a history nut" noted that "I'm not too high into . . . how Washington chopped the cherry tree. I'm not too much into that. . . . I don't think my kids are into it either. They have to study it but they're not much into it." Recalling his own grade school education, he commented on how they used to "beat into you" things like Longfellow's "Hiawatha," but that even as "a little fourth grader I thought it was a lot of bullshit."

"I was taught that Abe Lincoln and other forefathers were great men," remembered a man who grew up in the 1950s, "but . . . in real truth they were part of policies that were to wipe out Native Americans." Like this man, other Sioux respondents described their disillusionment when they discovered that Lincoln did not live up to the historical reputation that they had been taught in school. "When I learned that Lincoln had hung twenty-four Sioux in Mandan, North Dakota," a 39-year-old woman told us, "I was pretty mad. . . . He had freed the blacks and still allowed genocide to happen to Indians." A teacher said that in grade school "I was taught to praise and look up to" men like Lincoln. But while Lincoln is "most widely known for freeing the slaves . . . in fact on the day he signed the Emancipation Proclamation, he also ordered the death by hanging in Minnesota of the group of men, women, and children Native Americans for defending their camp."[22]

Although every group we interviewed rated high school history teachers, nonfiction books, and movies and television as the least trustworthy historical sources, Native Americans ranked them significantly lower than anyone else. Interviews with the Oglala Sioux resonated with deep anger over the way that their story has been misrepresented in these sources— "just lies," as more than one put it. When African Americans talked about official versions of the past, they protested about exclusion; Native Americans talked about distortions. "The way they show us in schools makes us look like cavalry killers," observed one man. Instead, he argued, the schools "should teach the kids how the greed came from the immigrants coming into our country and taking our land." Movies and television, added a 23-year-old woman in a comment echoed by many others, invariably portrayed Indians as "stupid or savage." History books, an administrative assistant noted in another typical comment, "don't really tell the accurate history of our people. . . . When Columbus came over, they really made us out to be savages and murderers, when really our people helped Columbus and his people survive those first winters."

Some respondents condemned those who propagated dishonest views of the past. "Whenever a schoolteacher starts the class with the saluting of the American flag and not telling the children what happened under that flag to the Native nations," said one Pine Ridge man, they are "in the same category as the gas chamber attendants at Auschwitz." Although not all Oglala Sioux would go as far as this man, most expressed anger and pain at the way mainstream historical sources depicted American Indians. Some Pine Ridge Sioux felt so angry that they initially refused to talk to white interviewers. One woman, who at first declined to be interviewed, offered the explanation, "I hate all of you; I want to kill all of you."

When we asked white Americans what they thought children should be taught about the past, many offered relatively bland answers highlighting patriotic pieties. American Indians often had a simple yet passionate answer. As one retired man put it, children need to learn "the truth. The way it really happened and if it's right or wrong, you know, the truth." When he went to school all he learned was the "white man's version of the past." But today, he argued, history books could tell how whites "got this country. They didn't get it because God gave it to them. They stole it. Tell the truth. Tell the way it happened." No white respondents used the word "truth" in answer to the question about children and the past, but at least ten Native Americans did.

Oglala Sioux turned to alternative historical sources to challenge what they saw as the mainstream historical narrative. They sharply criticized most history books and historical films. Though some of them praised books like *Black Elk Speaks*, *Bury My Heart at Wounded Knee*, *In the Spirit of Crazy Horse*, and *Lakota Woman* and films like *Dances with Wolves*, *Thunderheart*, and *Lakota Woman*, they tempered this praise with insider criticism. Many endorsed *Dances with Wolves*, which was filmed nearby, for its favorable and nonstereotypical portrayal of Native Americans as well as its use of Lakota language, but a few complained that it was overly "romantic," reflected a "one-sided" "Anglo-American" perspective, and inaccurately portrayed Indian dress and ceremonies.

Pine Ridge residents found material artifacts and oral evidence more trustworthy than books or film. Like others we interviewed, the Sioux put particular faith in museums that presented "a lot of artifacts" and especially "our things." A 33-year-old office worker praised the Sioux Indian Museum in Rapid City as "factual" because "they have this Indian lady's stuff, they had her buckskin dress, her beads and information about her." Many talked about what they had learned from historic sites like the

Wounded Knee massacre memorial and the Little Bighorn Battlefield National Monument.

The Oglala Sioux, like black, white, and Mexican American respondents, valued historical evidence that came out of "personal accounts from grandparents or other relatives" and "conversations with someone who was there." But the Sioux sharply differentiated between oral and nonoral sources. White Americans, on average, rated oral sources 16 percent more trustworthy than films, books, museums, college professors, and high school teachers; the Sioux gave them a 42 percent higher ranking. Put another way, Pine Ridge residents thought the gap between the value of the two sets of sources was more than twice as large as white Americans did.[23] "Our grandparents say our history," explained a Sioux police officer, "and we listen to all they have to say. . . . It is part of our culture to listen to what our grandparents have to say." "In my tradition," added an administrative assistant, "our past has been passed on orally." In "my culture," noted a range technician, "we were not given books to read—history was given through stories, from accounts that were given by word of mouth I can remember. When I was very young, it was passed on to me."

So powerful was this veneration of oral accounts passed on from trusted relatives and elders that Pine Ridge residents used this evidence and this way of knowing the past as the standard against which to judge other historical sources. A nurse endorsed the Sioux Indian Museum as "pretty much accurate . . . because it was part of the way things were told by our ancestors, by our elders." A maintenance man praised a particular high school history teacher because "he was an older fellow when he started teaching history, and he just seemed like he had more experience, from his grandparents, or something." And a young woman rated "college professors I've spoken to" as trustworthy sources because "they've talked to a lot of older people who really know what happened."

"You can see it from here": The Integrated Sense of the Past at Pine Ridge

Because the Pine Ridge Sioux draw their sense of the past from people, places, and artifacts they regularly encounter, their everyday lives reinforce a shared historical identity. They don't limit this engagement with their collective past to particular holidays or particular settings—as white Americans do when they study history in school or visit museums. The

Oglala Sioux experience and use a group past with the same depth and intimacy that white Americans reserve for the history of their families.

Wounded Knee, a topic mentioned in more than half of the Sioux interviews, illustrates the way a common historical consciousness is reinforced at Pine Ridge.[24] (White Americans spoke of no public historical event with remotely comparable frequency and passion; African American respondents didn't assign the same prominence even to the civil rights movement.) In part, these dense connections to Wounded Knee stemmed from its powerful physical presence for Pine Ridge residents. One 28-year-old woman could not avoid contemplating the Wounded Knee massacre site while she talked to our interviewer: "As I look out my living room window," she reported, "you can see it from here."

Sometimes a familiar historical site simply blends into the background; many Washingtonians walk or drive to work past the Jefferson or Lincoln memorials without thinking about their significance. But the familiarity of the Wounded Knee memorial reinforced its importance to Pine Ridge residents. "You see it and you look at it and it is a hurt because of what happened to the people who were there who were killed. . . . Those of us here seem to grieve over and over again." A 35-year-old man said he went to the site regularly "to pray for the people who got killed." "I just go there to think about how it was back then. I like to stand there and think about how it was. . . . It was my people who got killed there, the Cheyenne River Lakota. They were killed there. They were my people."

At least 18 respondents (in a sample of 186) brought up relatives who were present at the Wounded Knee massacre. Those personal connections made Wounded Knee a force in the lives of Pine Ridge residents more powerful than recent events like World War II and Vietnam in the lives of white Americans. A 48-year-old woman, who described the Wounded Knee massacre as "the epitome of racial hatred" and who had recently helped commemorate the event, noted that she "began hearing about [Wounded Knee] from the time I was a really small girl from my parents and grandparents." The same young woman whose house looked out at the massacre site reported discussing family history with her mother while they sorted some old photos. "My mother is a descendant of Wounded Knee," she explained. "And we talked about how the massacre to this day has influenced her, even though it was her grandmother who was shot. She was not killed. She was a child at the time. She was hit, but most of the bullet hit her shawl." A 43-year-old woman whose relatives died in the massacre said that she learned about it through "talking to different people, mostly elderly." As a result, the events of more than a century earlier were a haunting daily presence for her: "You can almost hear the voices, you can almost see the events taking place."

An event that few white Americans could identify (the massacre site doesn't even rate a mention in the AAA guide to South Dakota) is a shaping force in the lives of almost all the Sioux residents of Pine Ridge reservation.[25] Through events like Wounded Knee, the Oglala Sioux bring together personal and collective pasts into a single shared past that is reinforced as they move through the reservation and talk with friends and relatives.

This integrated sense of the past gives the Oglala Sioux a self-confidence and self-knowledge that many white Americans seem to lack. The white Americans we interviewed turn to the past as part of a struggle to define who they are; the Oglala Sioux's clear sense of the past gives them a firmer expression of self and group identity. Unlike black Americans who struggle with W.E.B. DuBois's dilemma of "double consciousness," of being black in a white society, the Pine Ridge Sioux appear—at least to outsiders—much less conflicted over matters of identity. One of our interviewers thought that his conversations with Native Americans were memorable precisely because of this secure sense of the past. "The interviews that stand out most in my mind," he told to us after the study was over, "are the minority interviews and especially the American Indian interviews because not only were they the longest because they had the most experience with the past (the past of their family, the past of their ethnic group) but they almost all had hobbies or had taken some initiative to learn more about their society or family background." He found that many Indians seemed to know "the answers before I got done with the questions; they knew what they were going to say. It was like they had been thinking about it so much that it was 'old hat' when we asked these questions."

"We survived": The Sioux Triumph over the Past

The Oglala Sioux respondents presented a shared past, but not one free of internal conflicts. Residents of Pine Ridge have deep political disagreements—so deep that they erupted in a virtual civil war in the 1970s.[26] Many respondents used the past to debate issues of assimilation and accommodation versus resistance and tradition. Some celebrated Crazy

Horse to argue that you can't "trust the white man" or that you should never "give into the white man." Others marshalled stories about Spotted Tail, who was chief when the Sioux were put on the reservation, to contend that assimilation and education are the only routes to "a better life." Many debated resistance and accommodation as they commented on the 1973 confrontation at Wounded Knee and the 1975 Pine Ridge shoot-out that resulted in the death of two FBI agents and the imprisonment of Leonard Peltier.

Like everyone else in the survey, the Sioux used the past to deal with more personal issues as well. Their intimate uses of the past, however, differed from white respondents' because of the broader range of cultural resources they deployed. White respondents typically addressed a problem like alcoholism by thinking about personal and family histories. But Oglala Sioux respondents, who talked a great deal about alcoholism (a major problem on Pine Ridge reservation) almost invariably reached back into the past of their group when they looked for explanations and solutions.[27] They often blamed the "Europeans," the "boarding schools," "the white people," or the reservation system. And they offered solutions drawn from the Indian past. A 44-year-old Pine Ridge man maintained that a combination of family and native history would help to defeat "poverty . . . alcohol and drug abuse." Only by giving children of the "native nations" a "complete understanding of where they came from, their great-grandfathers and grandmothers," he argued, "can we circumvent a lot of the problems" like alcoholism.

Sioux respondents repeatedly told two different kinds of stories as they used the past to live in the present. They described the oppression whites have imposed on Indians starting in 1492. And they talked about how Indians have survived and taken control of their lives and culture despite the barriers imposed by white society.

The first narrative, which has innumerable variations, draws conclusions from the past about both the immorality of white settlers and the ways they have restricted the possibility of change for Native Americans. Thus, the lesson that Pine Ridge residents draw from the stories of the 1868 treaty, the death of Crazy Horse, Wounded Knee, and numerous other Indian-White encounters: "Do not trust the United States government"; don't "trust the white people"; and "never trust the European." In this emphasis on trust and the betrayal of trust, the story of broken treaties becomes the governing metaphor for understanding the history of Native Americans since 1492. In effect, Pine Ridge residents seem to be saying to white Americans: You have abused us for centuries and then lied about the abuse.

But more often than this cautionary tale about betrayal we heard a positive and affirming tale about survival, persistence, and progress. Over and over, the Pine Ridge Sioux spoke with pride—and sometimes wonder—that they had survived despite the long history of white oppression and perfidy. The important message of the Oglala Sioux past, a Pine Ridge man explained, was "just the survival, that we survived. . . . They took our land away and put us over here where we are now. We're making do with what we have now."

The Oglala Sioux defined survival largely as the preservation of their culture—language, customs, traditions, and beliefs. Asked why he, like so many others, worked on "our cultural native crafts, things like beaded belts," an accountant explained, "It's part of our culture. We just enjoy doing it because it's within us, it's something built within us and we enjoy doing it to save our culture. [It's] part of preserving our culture." A 39-year-old who worked with children urgently insisted that "without our beadwork, without our culture and our language, we are no longer a people, we are no longer distinct."

This work of cultural preservation includes making and preserving traditional objects like beadwork, studying and teaching the Lakota language, maintaining rituals like sun dances and sweat lodges, and simply preserving the past itself. Like most efforts at cultural preservation, this one also involves recovery and reinvention; the interest in "traditional" culture has greatly increased at Pine Ridge since the early 1970s.[28] A 32-year-old student described his hobby as collecting "songs and stories that were told by our grandfathers." A 28-year-old woman explained why her mother and her sister worked with the Wounded Knee Pine Ridge Survivors Association: "That is our identity, part of our culture. A way of life that we have to teach our children." "Well," she concluded, "this is who we are. If we lose our culture then we cease to be Indians." (The Pine Ridge Sioux were more likely to participate in organizations interested in the past than any other group in the survey.)

This woman, and many other Pine Ridge residents, described the past as not simply "usable" but essential to group and individual survival. The Pine Ridge Sioux looked to the past to explain individuals' alcoholism as well as the poverty of the whole reservation. The future of their tribe, they said, depends on the lessons about adversity, struggle, and progress that they draw from the past.[29]

"You can't allow the past to be lost": American Indians Beyond Pine Ridge

Because we talked to almost 200 Oglala Sioux on a reservation with fewer than 25,000 people, we are fairly confident that we have been able to capture their distinctive sense of the past. But can these be described as "Indian" responses? Are these typical of what we would have heard if we had called Native Americans across the United States?

In certain respects, they are not. Many Oglala Sioux respondents talked about the specific history of the Pine Ridge Sioux—the repeated references to Wounded Knee or Crazy Horse, for example. Their conversations reflected the experience of people living in a community with other people of the same group. Urban Indians might not have the same intense sense of connection to a particular place.

We can't provide a full comparison, but we did interview 28 American Indians from Minneapolis, whom we located by calling phone numbers in the census tract with the highest concentration of Native Americans and from the membership lists of several Indian organizations. We also interviewed 31 American Indians in the national sample and as a result of calls made in the other minority samples. Given the nonsystematic methodology in the first case and the small numbers in the second, the results must be regarded as suggestive rather than definitive.

Urban Indians in Minneapolis and American Indians in the national and minority samples shared with the Pine Ridge Sioux a conviction about the importance of the past of their ethnic/racial group. Thirty-eight percent of the Pine Ridge residents and 27 percent of those reached in other samples said that the Indian past was more important than the past of family, nation, or community—which means that Indians expressed a greater interest in ethnic history than any other group in the survey. Both groups of American Indians, however, put family at the top of their list; thus, they shared the tendency of all groups in the survey to say that family history was most important to them. Indeed, the single exception was the sample of 28 Minneapolis residents, who were equally likely to choose family history and ethnic/racial history—perhaps because a majority of them were members of Indian organizations.

The Minneapolis Indians—most of them members of the Ojibway (Chippewa) tribe—shared the Oglala Sioux's skepticism of mainstream history. Asked to rate their sense of connection to the past in school or while watching movies and television on a 1–10 scale, they came up with a lower score than any other group in the entire sample. "It was very painful to listen when [instructors] talked about when my forefathers were savages," said a 47-year-old man. "When I was in school there was a lot of racism. So I have these white instructors/educators telling us that. It was very difficult as a child to continue hearing that." The Minneapolis American Indians were also more skeptical about films and television programs than any other group in the survey. For a 31-year-old woman, the film *1492: Conquest of Paradise* "glorified those who were seen as discoverers when in fact they are stepping over the bones of many people to serve their own interests." Although American Indians in other samples were less critical of mainstream presentations than the Minneapolis group, they distrusted movies and high school teachers much more than white Americans did.

Not surprisingly, Indians outside the reservations did not have the strong collective sense of "we" and "us" that is so apparent among Pine Ridge residents, who live in a tight geographic community. When non-reservation Indians investigated family history, they seemed to be trying to establish a sense of personal, rather than group, identity. Yet despite these differences, they echoed the Pine Ridge narrative of cultural survival. A lawyer from a large East Coast city described her work with the Osage Language Association, which is developing a computer program to document, preserve, and teach the language. "You can't allow the past to be lost. We all have a responsibility to protect our history," she explained. Minneapolis Indians frequently talked about their interest in Indian crafts and beadwork and in organizations devoted to studying and preserving the past of their tribe. Asked "what specifically about the past of your racial or ethnic group is important to you," a Native American living in Minneapolis offered a five-word answer that summarized what many Pine Ridge residents said at greater length: "That we are still here."

Roy Rosenzweig: Everyone a Historian

History professionals—like most professionals—tend to emphasize the differences between themselves and others. Those who "do" history for a living (whether schoolteachers, university-based historians, museum curators, historic preservationists, documentary filmmakers, staff members at local historical societies, or other public historians) sometimes see nonprofessionals as ignorant of and uninterested in the past. In his 1989 presidential address to the members of the American Historical Association, the leading bastion of professional historians in the United States, Louis R. Harlan deplored the "present public ignorance of our cultural heritage." "This ignorance and indifference," he argued in a statement that has been echoed by many other history professionals, "has alarming implications for the future of our nation and our historical profession."[1]

The 1,500 people we have quoted in these pages refute the idea that Americans don't care about the past. Two fifths of our respondents, for example, reported that they pursue a hobby or collection related to the past, and they spoke of those pursuits with words like "love" and "passion." An Oklahoma man summarized his reasons for collecting old motorcycles in one sentence: "It is my life." Two thirds of our respondents described themselves as deeply connected to the past at family gatherings; and the stories they told indicate how the past figures in some of the most intimate corners of their lives. A northern Virginia woman said, "I always loved to hear my mother tell stories about the past," and her comment was typical. Like professional historians, these popular historymakers crafted their own narratives, albeit as dinner-table conversations or family trees rather than scholarly monographs. They preferred constructing their own versions of the past to digesting those prepared by others, and they viewed other sources and narratives with sharply critical eyes. Everyone, as Carl Becker famously observed, is his or her own historian.[2]

Moreover, there is nothing abstract or antiquarian about popular historymaking. In these interviews, the most powerful meanings of the past come out of the dialogue between the past and the present, out of the ways the past can be used to answer pressing current-day questions about relationships, identity, immortality, and agency. Indeed, this was a point that Becker recognized back in 1931 when he wrote his essay about "Everyman His Own Historian" and used the example of popular historical practice to argue that historians need to "adapt our knowledge" to "the necessities" of the present rather than "cultivate a species of dry professional arrogance growing out of the thin soil of antiquarian research." Thus, our interviewees implicitly join Becker in insisting on something that professional historians can too easily forget—"our proper function is not to repeat the past but to make use of it."[3] For our respondents, the past is not only present—it is part of the present.

Such observations about how popular historymakers use the past and what they share with professional historians may contradict the conventional wisdom. Yet they are also commonsensical; anyone who reflects on his or her own experience of family and holiday gatherings—or indeed everyday life—will realize how the presence of the past saturates all of us. Whether surprising or commonplace, these findings have important implications for the practice of history and even for the future of American society. To sort out these findings and their implications would take much closer scrutiny of patterns of popular historymaking than a national telephone survey permits. What follows is one brief effort to describe the significance of what we heard, particularly for history practitioners. Inevitably, this personal statement reflects my own experiences as a scholar and teacher who has worked in a university for the past two decades and has also been involved in trying to present the past in nonacademic forums, including museums, films, oral history programs, CD-ROMs, and the World Wide Web.

For historians who want to engage with diverse audiences, this study offers encouraging news and useful advice (as well as some sobering cautions). The interests and passions that our respondents have described suggest bases for forging new connections, alliances, and conversations with those diverse audiences. Of course, many good teachers and history professionals are already aware of these conclusions about popular engagement with the past, about the power of the intimate past, and about the ways audiences actively and critically relate to the past. Our survey strongly supports their most creative approaches to presenting the past and connecting with audiences. This is hardly surprising: the most thoughtful teachers, museum curators, and historical writers listen carefully—if perhaps not always systematically—to what their audiences have to say. The endorsement that this survey provides for their insights and efforts is nevertheless important, since many innovations have recently come under attack from those who seek to reinforce traditional approaches.

Schools have been among the most hotly contested arenas in what have sometimes been called the "history wars."[4] Our respondents had a great deal to say about history in school; they told us that they felt less connected to the past there than in any other setting we asked about. "Boring" was the most common description of history classes. An Alabama man's vivid recollection of high school—"my teacher was 70 years old and she carried a blackjack"—summed up the views of many.

While the history wars have often focused on content—what should be taught in classes or presented in exhibits—our respondents were more interested in talking about the experience and process of engaging the past. They preferred to make their own histories. When they confronted historical accounts constructed by others, they sought to examine them critically and connect them to their own experiences or those of people close to them. At the same time, they pointed out, historical presentations that did not give them credit for their critical abilities—commercialized histories on television or textbook-driven high school classes—failed to engage or influence them.

Given this preference for history as an active and collaborative venture, many respondents found fault with a school-based history organized around the memorization of facts and locked into a prescribed textbook curriculum. Their comments implicitly rejected the recommendations of conservative commentators on history in the schools. For these conservatives, the reason students don't know enough "history" (as defined by standardized tests and textbooks) is the rise of multiculturalism and the decline of a traditional curriculum based on the patriotic story of the American nation—the very curriculum our respondents described as insulting to their ability as critical thinkers. Even if one shared conservatives' desire to cram more facts into students, this survey suggests that the revival of traditional stories and traditional teaching methods conservatives advocate isn't the way to do it.

What respondents told us runs counter to the narrative of declension that says Americans are disengaged from history because cultural radicals have captured the schools (and museums) and are teaching gloomy stories about our nation—stories about McCarthyism rather than America's triumph in the cold war, about Harriet Tubman rather than the Founding Fathers, about destroying Indians rather than taming the West.[5] If only we would get back to the good old facts of American triumph (and the old-fashioned methods of teaching those facts), they maintain, then Americans would be reengaged. The people we interviewed said that they are already quite involved with the past—through formal activities like going to museums as well as informal pursuits like talking with their families. They liked history in museums and didn't like history in schools—not because Harriet Tubman has been added, but because the schools require dry recitation of facts instead of inspiring direct engagement with the "real" stuff of the past and its self-evident relationship to the present.

The fading of the traditional nationalist story has much deeper roots than shifts in school curriculum—one might look at how American misadventures in Vietnam or the racial divisions of the 1960s undercut nationalism, or how the globalization of the economy has made it harder for nation-states to deliver on promises of prosperity for all.[6] Some regard the waning of nationalism as a threat; others see it as an opportunity.[7] Whatever one's position, there is no need to equate history with the nation-state, even though that equation has long been at the heart of professional historical practice.[8] The past, our survey respondents suggest, has many mansions, and in America at least, the past is very much alive, even if traditional textbook narratives of the national past seem to be dying out.

Some teachers are already demonstrating that the narrative of national greatness is not the best way to engage students with the past. Veteran North Carolina high school teacher Alice Garrett tries to help her students develop "personal meanings" of the past through research projects, reenactments, and exposure to firsthand sources. Breaking with "the rigidity of the state's curriculum," she explains, "almost always brings about different power relationships. The teacher becomes a learner; the student becomes a teacher. The parent becomes an expert consultant, and the most energetic individual student in the class emerges as a group organizer."[9]

Garrett is not alone in trying to teach outside the canon. Many other teachers around the country have tried to reshape the formal study of the past by encouraging students to interview members of their families, to explore sites of historical events, or to assume the roles of particular individuals in the past. David Kobrin and his collaborators in the Providence schools transformed the U.S. history curriculum so that students could "grab the power of the historian for themselves rather than rely on the anonymous authors of a textbook." Working from primary documents, teams of students wrote their own histories. Particularly when they could see the connections between the historical issues and their own lives, Kobrin recalls, they worked "past the bell."[10] Creative teachers are tapping into the most resonant patterns in popular historymaking by allowing and encouraging students to revisit, reenact, and get close to the past through encounters with primary documents and living historical sources. "When I teach American history," observes a perceptive high school teacher, "I ask them 'What will your grandchildren ask about you?' History is a living story. It's your story."[11] Such approaches are far from new, of course. In the early twentieth century, "new historians" (like Becker) and supporters of "social studies" advocated historical instruction that closely connected the past and the present and that paid attention "to the present life interests of the pupil."[12]

Teachers who want to connect past and present and to turn students into historians are offering the kinds of classrooms that many respondents told us they wanted. Some public historians (filmmakers, preservationists, museum workers) who speak to largely adult audiences are also aiming to make history less of a top-down enterprise. Implicitly, and sometimes explicitly, our respondents endorsed such attempts to see historymaking as a more democratic activity that allows amateurs and professionals to learn from each other.

One fruitful metaphor for reimagining the relationship between history professionals and popular historymakers is what Michael Frisch has called "shared authority." Frisch urges us to break down hierarchies by redistributing and redefining the meaning of intellectual authority for crafting historical narratives. Scholars and public historians, he argues, "need better to respect, understand, invoke, and involve the very real authority their audiences bring to a museum exhibit, a popular history book, or a public program." The audience's "authority," he notes, may be "grounded in culture and experience rather than academic expertise," but "this authority can become central to an exhibit's capacity to provide a meaningful engagement with history" and to forge a dialogue "about the shape, meaning, and implications of history."[13]

In the 1980s some museums took the notion of shared authority directly into their exhibit halls and created what the Chinatown History Museum in New York called "dialogue-driven" exhibits and museums. Reclaiming the "neglected past" of New York's Chinatown, writes one of the museum's founders, John Kuo Wei Tchen, "must be done in tandem with the people the history is about" so that "personal memory and testimony inform and are informed by historical context and scholarship." The Chinatown History Museum, for example, has found "reunions to be an excellent way to link the felt need for history directly with historical scholarship"—an insight confirmed by our survey. The museum has focused on reunions of Public School 23, since the museum occupies its former quarters. "A dialogue between museum staff, scholars, and P.S. 23ers," Tchen reports, "developed and drove much of the organization's planning during the late 1980s and early 1990s."[14]

Likewise, when the Minnesota History Center in St. Paul opened in 1992, it involved visitors in "active participation with history as a process of inquiry and exploration," according to former assistant director Barbara Franco. Its planning for "A Common Ground: Minnesota Communities" proceeded along "three parallel paths—scholarly discourse about the nature and definition of community, audience research about public perceptions of community, and active involvement of community members in the themes and content of the exhibit." In order to portray an "insider's perspective" on the Winnebago Indians, the curators met frequently with a community advisory board, which helped find artifacts and photos, suggested oral history questions, and shaped the focus of the exhibit. The curators were able to provide "important background information and research skills"; in the process they gained the "trust of the community so that the Winnebago individuals and families were willing to share photographs, precious keepsakes, and personal stories."[15]

Such approaches have influenced curators outside the United States as well. In the late 1980s, organizers of the People's Story Museum in Edinburgh set out to involve local "people in the presentation of their own history." "The term 'People's Story,' " they explained, "was taken literally, as the story was to be told as far as possible in their own words and in this way the museum may be seen to be returning history to those who created it . . . in effect a handing over of some of the power of the Curator to the public." They launched an impressive set of partnerships, particularly with older residents of the community. One project, for instance, brought together "a wide range of community groups, from an Asian girls' sewing club to Adult Training Centres to primary schoolchildren" who created a banner that featured "contemporary people sharing their history with each other, surrounded by the objects, photographs and words which hold most meaning for those individuals who have created this work of art."[16]

Many earlier neighborhood and community history projects also embodied this ethic of shared authority. Such ventures—oral history programs, photo exhibits, walking tours, documentary films, union history classes—often grew out of the social movements of the 1960s and 1970s. Professional historians who were caught up in those movements tried to infuse a more democratic ethos into their historical practice. Frequently with support from the National Endowment for the Humanities (NEH) and its offspring, the state humanities councils, scholars collaborated with amateurs to collect and present stories of people who had been invisible in traditional national histories. Some of these efforts either originated as or became means of creating usable collective pasts for feminists, gays, or union workers.[17]

In the 1980s, funding for these collaborative and noninstitutional projects became harder to find; some were derided as "populist" rather than "serious" and "scholarly"; NEH shifted its funding away from them, although a number of state humanities councils continued to provide support. In the 1990s a growing chorus of voices has even argued that the government has no business funding the arts and humanities, that the private sector can do it better. Some conservatives have also made their own "populist" argument, which concludes that public agencies like NEH, the National Endowment for the Arts, and the Corporation for Public Broadcasting concentrate narrowly on topics of interest only to elites. Our respondents didn't agree. They put more trust in historical presentations funded and sponsored by public agencies and nonprofit organizations— especially museums, which they regarded as the most trustworthy sources of historical information. (Our survey shows that an interest in history museums cuts across lines of income, education, and race.) Such views offer strong support for continued government funding of museums, documentary films, historic preservation, and other public humanities programs that bring together popular historymakers and history professionals in dialogues about the past.

Why not increase collaboration between professional historians and popular historymakers? Why not set up public humanities programs that bring together Civil War reenactors and Civil War historians? Why not make use of the World Wide Web, which has emerged as a popular venue for amateur historians, to create virtual meeting grounds for professionals and nonprofessionals?[18] Why not connect professional archivists with popular historymakers who document the past through photos and diaries? Why not tap into the intimate ways that people use the past? By assembling wills and treasured objects passed between generations, museum exhibits might illuminate the ways people use the past to address matters of immortality. The personal connections people draw to public historical events—like the Kennedy assassination or World War II—would make excellent subjects for exhibits, class projects, public humanities programs, or documentary films.

All this is easier said than done. Our survey emphasizes not only the commonalities between professionals and popular historymakers but also the differences. The curator for the Winnebago exhibit noted the difficulty of becoming both a trusted insider and a dispassionate outside expert: "There were two sets of ethics operating in this exhibit development process—people ethics and historian ethics."[19] Some history professionals will feel ill-equipped to deal with the intimate issues that popular history-making can easily unearth. After workshops at the People's Story Museum repeatedly evoked painful memories from older participants, staff members decided they needed a family therapist to teach them more about confronting wrenching memories.

There are other differences as well. Professional historians, by training, have often been more suspicious of oral sources than of written documents.[20] And we professionals have also been deeply invested in stories about the nation-state, institutions, and social groups—unlike the people we surveyed, who especially valued the past as a way of answering questions about identity, immortality, and responsibility. Our respondents talked at great length about the past as a source for moral guidance, but morality is not a category that has lately figured in our professional discourse, where relativist notions prevail. Consider the profound engagement with the past that we heard about from evangelical Christians. What does a largely secular group like historians have to say to them? Is there a basis of conversation across such fundamentally different notions about the past?

These differences should not be exaggerated; professional historians have talked about love, tragedy, and morality, just as the historymakers in our survey at times talked about the rise of the nation-state or the experience of social groups. Not surprisingly, history practitioners have found that biography, oral history, and microhistory—which intermingle the everyday and the intimate with larger social and political events—can bridge the gap between professional concerns and popular interests. Still, our professional training often teaches us to shun rather than embrace the moral and personal questions that seemed so important to respondents.[21]

Sometimes historians are also unprepared to deal with the political issues raised by efforts to share authority. Listening to the "community" does not necessarily solve the problem of deciding who speaks for it. The creation of a community advisory board can be a highly political process. And giving a platform to people not usually heard can provoke counterreactions from those who have traditionally had more power in shaping historical accounts.[22] In 1997, for instance, the Smithsonian Institution's National Museum of American History planned an exhibit based on notions of shared authority, which was called "Between a Rock and a Hard Place: A Dialogue on American Sweatshops, 1820–Present." In a gesture of respect for those whose story was being told, the exhibit organizers planned a section on the notorious El Monte, California sweatshop to be told in the "participants' voice." Apparel manufacturers were also invited to contribute their perspective to the exhibit, but they refused: the exhibit, they said, gave too much attention to sweatshops and included the views of trade unionists. "Sharing a platform with the union and giving them undue recognition and credibility is something I do not want to get involved with," announced Joe Rodriquez, executive director of the Garment Contractors Association.[23] Can authority be shared with people who are interested in victory rather than conversation?

Popular historymakers are also likely to raise unfamiliar and uncomfortable questions of their own. "I have found it more difficult to write about Chinese New Yorker history with and for fellow community members than for fellow academics," writes Tchen.[24] Linda Shopes captures some of the tensions that can result from a dialogue between professionals and nonprofessionals in a perceptive commentary on the Baltimore Neighborhood Heritage Project of the late 1970s. She analyzes the many strains and misunderstandings between professional historians and community residents over what was important in the community's history, how to collect and interpret residents' stories, and finally how to report the results. On the one hand, in their collection of stories local residents lacked "the historical background and analytical framework to pursue certain subjects in sufficient depth." On the other hand, the professional historians "failed to appreciate the tapes' value. They used the oral testimony simply as a source of specific information, illustrative quotations, or interesting anecdotes that fit their own analytical framework. They were unable to penetrate beneath the surface of the informants' words."

Shopes concludes that "the deepest impediment to sustained collaboration between the project and the community" was the professionals' "primary affiliation . . . with a nationally organized profession" and their lack of "social commitment to a specific locale."[25] My own experiences in the 1970s with filmmaker Richard Broadman confirms Shopes's point. When we began working on an oral history film about the impact of urban renewal on his Mission Hill neighborhood in Boston, Richard's neighbors were not eager to participate; he was a "newcomer" who had only lived there for five years. Only after another seven years of work on the film and of joint participation in community projects did local residents come to see it as "their" film as well as ours and told their stories for the camera.[26]

The differences are not simply ones of community affiliation. As Shopes recognizes, nonprofessionals have their own blinders, their own resistance to new approaches. Baltimore residents, for example, wanted histories to avoid anything "even mildly critical of the neighborhood" and to favor a "booster spirit" that made the scholars uncomfortable. Our survey respondents often used the past in complex and subtle ways, but their approach was sometimes in tension with my historical training and preferences. For example, I found their emphasis on the firsthand, the experiential, the intimate, and the familial to be confining as well as illuminating. At times respondents seemed primarily concerned with their own and their family's pasts; the stories of others were often ignored. This privatized version of the past, I worried, can reinforce rather than break down barriers between people, resist rather than promote change. Many respondents were struggling to reach beyond the firsthand, to think themselves into wider histories, and to scrutinize sources of the past that originated outside their immediate circles. Still, I sometimes found their views of the past (as well as they can be judged from these interviews) as narrow and parochial as those of the most traditional professional historians.

Even when popular historymakers avoided overt parochialism, they still tended to draw the circles of their historical interests narrowly. In interviews with white Americans, "we" most often centered on the family rather than other social groups—whether class, region, or ethnicity. The understanding of the past that white Americans get from their families is an enormously potent resource for living in the present, a way of coming to terms with personal identity and of gaining personal autonomy. But white Americans, it seems to me, less often use the past to reach beyond their families and recognize their connections to wider groups of neighbors and fellow citizens. Just as Americans seem to be bowling alone, as political scientist Robert Putnam argues in his commentary on the decline of civic society, they also seem to be writing their histories alone—or at least in small familial groups.[27] Many white Americans understand and use the past in ways that make them suspicious of outsiders.

Black Americans and Sioux Indians drew the circle of "we" more broadly and saw themselves as sharing a past with other African Americans or American Indians.[28] A distinctive view of the past enables both of these groups to maintain a collective identity in the present. Their understandings of the past help them live in an oppressive society. Black Americans, for example, are sustained by a progressive, enabling historical vision rooted in the story of emancipation and civil rights. And for Native Americans, an understanding of their cultural survival in a hostile world is a source of strength for both individuals and the community. Yet even here, the connections drawn—at least in these interviews—often stopped at the boundaries of their own group. Multiculturalist visions of easy border crossings and rich mixings need to confront the suspicion with which these borders are sometimes guarded.

Nevertheless, when people do let down their guard, the common patterns of historymaking that we observed can allow individuals to identify and empathize with others. Moreover, the past can provide a safe, because distant, arena in which people can imagine alternative identities and explore different points of view. We need to marry experience with imagination and enable people to connect with "imagined communities" beyond the ones that they have learned in family circles.[29]

Reading the survey interviews, I also worried that popular historymakers who emphasize the experiential and the firsthand may sometimes underestimate larger structures of power and authority. Families can nurture their members, but many individuals need to earn their livings in exploitative workplaces. And family breakups are often the result of economic crises rather than the failures of individuals. Historical narratives that start (and sometimes end) with the personal cannot readily take account of categories like capitalism and the state—categories, I would argue, that are useful to more than just history professionals.

A history grounded in the immediate and the experiential also runs the risk of neglecting important stories that are temporally or geographically distant. And valuing the experiential can obscure the degree to which reports of "experience" are mediated by existing structures of language and power.[30] As Shopes observes, "Popular ideologies of independence, individual achievement, and respect for the 'self-made man' " shaped the memories reported by participants in the Baltimore project, just as popular ideology, language, and culture (for example, respondents' frequent invocations of "the family") surely stamped the interviews that we conducted.[31]

At stake here, at least potentially, is not simply whether one's sense of the past is rich in context, comparison, and complexity—whether, for example, one sees similarities between one's own experience and the experiences of others or recognizes how employers and politicians might have affected the course of family history. Such understandings of the past have a potential bearing on action in the present. Is it possible to build movements for social change without imagining a set of past and present connections to groups of people who aren't kin and ancestors? Is it possible to work for change without a vision of other alternatives that the past can provide? Is it possible to work for change without an understanding of the structures of power that support the status quo?

By providing context and comparison and offering structural explanations, history professionals can turn the differences between themselves and popular historymakers into assets rather than barriers. History professionals can help to enrich popular uses of the past by introducing people to different voices and experiences. They can help to counter false nostalgia about earlier eras. They can make people aware of possibilities for transforming the status quo. Recognizing how the civil rights movement broke the fetters of a stable and racist social order or how the CIO challenged entrenched notions of management "rights" can inspire people to work for social change in the present. We need a historical practice that is somehow simultaneously more local and intimate and more global and cosmopolitan, more shaped by popular concerns and more enriched by insights based on systematic and detailed study of the past. And, as our interviewees would insist, that historical practice needs to link the past and the present in an active and continuing conversation.[32]

My concerns about the presence of a privatized and parochial past in some of these interviews grow out of a belief that the past should be a vehicle for social justice. Obviously my perspective is not shared by all history professionals or, indeed, by most of the popular historymakers with whom we spoke. The past for many of them (particularly white Americans) is more a source of personal identity and empowerment than group identity and empowerment. Indeed, the prevalence of narratives of declension and defeat among white Americans suggests their understandings of the past may sometimes be disempowering. Their emphasis on stories of declining discipline and rising crime and their celebration of the family as a bulwark in a changing world could much more easily support traditionalist and conservative programs than movements for social change.

Yet this is not a nation of acquisitive and atomized individualists, as some libertarians would want us to believe. Our respondents cared deeply about morality, forging close relationships to others, and leaving legacies for the future. These values and priorities are an important foundation for mobilizing people for a better society—or really for people mobilizing themselves.

Of course, definitions of the "good society" vary widely, and historians play only a small role in bringing about larger social changes. Our respondents told us of beginning with the personal and the intimate, and historians too must begin with their immediate worlds—the places where they teach and talk about the past. The most significant news of this study is that we have interested, active, and thoughtful audiences for what we want to talk about. The deeper challenge is finding out how we can talk to—and especially with—those audiences. History professionals need to work harder at listening to and respecting the many ways popular historymakers traverse the terrain of the past that is so present for all of us.

David Thelen: A Participatory Historical Culture

This book furnishes evidence that academic history differs from everyday history. Readers of an earlier draft called this finding both "exciting" because our respondents described rich alternatives to current professional practice and "troubling" because those alternatives sometimes violated academic norms. We are not the first professionals to discover this gulf. In his "Everyone a Historian," Roy points to pioneering initiatives by other professionals that seek to adapt professional practice to popular uses of the past.

Over the past year, as I have discussed our survey with others, I have been increasingly struck by a second finding: Using the past is as natural a part of life as eating or breathing. It is a common human activity. What we have in common as human beings is that we employ the past to make sense of the present and to influence the future. From this perspective it matters little whether "the past" consists of a 200-year-old narrative, an account from a textbook, a display at a museum, or a tale recounted by a family member over Thanksgiving dinner.

In this essay, I will use our survey responses to illustrate some of the features of this common process, and point out some places where professional historymaking diverges from it. And I will try to sketch a participatory historical culture that surrounds us—a culture in which using the past could be treated as a shared human experience and opportunity for understanding, rather than a ground for division and suspicion.

The "history wars" of recent years have subverted the development of a healthy, participatory, fundamentally historical culture because they have politicized history as a struggle among claims to authority. In the debate over the National Air and Space Museum's proposed exhibit on the Enola Gay, for example, people were asked to choose between the authenticity of a pilot's memories of wartime service and the accuracy of written sources recovered by a historian. In a fundamentally historical culture, both would be respected and treated for what they are: different uses of the past introducing different perspectives and different individual voices.[1]

Commenting on an earlier draft of this manuscript, Michael Frisch wrote: "This book virtually opens up a whole new front in the culture wars by deepening our appreciation of history's capacity to bring us together in dialogue and respect, grounded in dimensions of family, community, national, and human experience that are . . . understood and engaged in fundamentally historical ways by most people most of the time." This,

Frisch continued, provides "ground for a deeper engagement with what history can mean as a resource for our common life and how it can be developed and engaged as such."

What are these "fundamentally historical ways" in which we are alike? How can we learn to see them instead of just our highly visible differences? How can we use our similarities and differences in pursuit of a better common life?

In historymaking practice, terms and even whole languages often get in the way of recognizing our more fundamental similarities. The very word "history" was associated by many respondents with their most unpleasant experiences with the past. Indeed, "forced regurgitation" or "spitting back" of "meaningless" and "boring" facts and dates on exams in school were their most common associations with the word. To call something "history" is to describe it as dead and irrelevant, completely useless. For professionals, however, "history" is both alive and useful. The term is practically synonymous with our occupational identity, and we associate it with rigorous discipline and the authoritative use of the past. The word that seemed to have more meaning to our survey respondents—"experience" —is dismissed by many professionals as random, private, shallow, and even self-deceptive.

From our interviews, I have concluded that the greatest danger from professionalization—a danger that is great because it is often invisible—is that its self-enclosing thrust has made it harder for us professionals to recognize which of our practices resemble "common," "local," or "everyday" knowledge and perspective and which have evolved into jargon that makes sense only to other professionals. If we wish to construct serious dialogues about the past with nonprofessionals—who are, after all, our fellow citizens and human beings—we may need to go back and revalue our first languages, the ones we were taught to leave behind when we entered the professional world. By recognizing patterns in our historymaking practices that we share with others, we can more effectively contribute to the larger historical culture we all inhabit.

I believe our findings support the conclusion that the foundations for a more participatory historical culture already exist. In section I, I report public rationales that people gave us for connecting experience with history when we asked them what about the past adults had the responsibility to pass on to children, probably the most central issue for any culture. In section II, I sketch outlines of existing patterns in which our culture already seems to connect history and experience. And finally, in section III,

I try to imagine a participatory historical culture in which, by using the past on their own terms, people can reshape the civic forum to better hear their voices and meet their needs.

I

I want to begin to recognize existing foundations for a more participatory historical culture by reporting themes our respondents themselves identified when we asked them what about the past should be passed on to their children. The 60 respondents who received this question in the national sample emphasized several recurring themes as they answered this open-ended question.

By far the most common rationale for passing things on to their children—mentioned by 33 of the 60 respondents—was to help them understand "why things are the way they are today," in the words of one of the people who talked with us. "Without history we wouldn't know who we are. . . . Knowing the past gives continuity and meaning to life," observed a 67-year-old salesman from Fort Worth who turned to history to understand his family, ethnic group, occupation, state, and nation. "The past gives a good indication of how people are going to act tomorrow," reported an art installer from Long Island. "To understand the past is to understand the present, and to know why you are what you are, and hopefully project that into the future and possibly know how things could be in the future." By assigning a historical culture the responsibility of illuminating the present, respondents argued that everything that mattered—personal identity, religious values, civic practices—could be better engaged in everyday life when individuals understood where they came from and why they had developed as they had. In order to approach the past on their own terms—not as a classroom progression from election to election, war to war—respondents grounded historical inquiry in present circumstances, perceptions, and needs.

Since an awareness of how people had passed through experiences in the past helped respondents to understand them in the present, one sixth of those answering this question volunteered that it was as important to understand strangers' pasts as it was to understand their own. A Jamaican-born Illinois woman told us that on her arrival in New York it was "fascinating to me" to learn about how people from "all types of groups and backgrounds came here . . . how they survived in their country and how we survived over here." As she talked about experiences with her new neighbors, she learned "actually it was not much different" for her and other Jamaicans than it had been for immigrants from other backgrounds. Interested in understanding "people [who] come from different areas and have different beliefs," a Charlottesville, Virginia student in his twenties maintained that it was "important to know why they came here, what they left behind, and how their culture affects how they act and live here today." Understanding the past was a first step toward respecting, engaging, and even embracing unfamiliar people, practices, and faiths. A Scottsdale, Arizona stockbroker in his forties said, "I was raised Catholic and my child should be raised Catholic"; but he wanted his daughter to "know of other religions so when she gets older she could compare them and choose which one she wants to follow."

The most common narratives or themes about the past that respondents hoped to pass on to their children—mentioned by one quarter of respondents—centered on the struggles of individuals to make a better world for themselves and those who came after them. By presenting history as a story of struggle, by insisting that blessings from political freedom to personal wealth were the fruits of dedication and hard work by real individuals, respondents described not only a content of history but also a responsibility they wanted users to feel when they engaged history. They wanted younger people to feel responsible for determining the course of events instead of merely accepting their fates as automatic rights or unearned gifts. A New Jersey collection analyst in her fifties wanted children to know "how hard the struggle was for grandparents when they came to this country, how difficult it was in the neighborhoods they lived in, the ethnic separations of the people in the communities, the language barriers and the lack of education" because she believed that "the children of today think that everything was just given to them, that our parents were just given everything they had, that they didn't have to work for it." If they could see that the past was a story of dedication and struggle, she hoped children would learn that "education, sharing and sacrifice within the family are necessary" for future survival.

A 42-year-old Maryland floral designer wanted children to draw the same conclusion about why they had political freedom: "They should know how people have struggled for freedom for this country. . . . We don't want them to think that life is always easy . . . they have to work for what they want . . . everything isn't handed to them." The material ease and cultural tolerance they enjoyed would last only if they assumed responsibility for sustaining them. Respondents wanted children to grow up like those before them to become active citizens, take responsibility for maintaining freedom and democracy and, if called on, to make "the supreme sacrifice" (in the words of a retired man from Louisiana) so that heritage could live.

The real issue for respondents in teaching about sacrifices and struggles at the core of civic heritage was the same as for family heritage: Did people feel these were personal inheritances they were compelled to defend and assert? Or were they merely distant conventions to be memorized for an exam or harmless stories with which to indulge Grandma at a holiday dinner? Participation was the center of historical culture.

A quarter of respondents who answered this question worried that people needed to be able to transmit experience, values, and heritages across generations at a time when popular culture and classroom curricula segmented tastes and values by generations. "My children should know what we have gone through to where they appreciate all they all have," said a retired woman from Chesterfield, Missouri. Focusing on separation of generations, many respondents said the problem of transmission of perspectives and experiences was central for a culture that would make history a resource for shaping the future. The cultural stakes were clear, observed a Montclair, New Jersey teacher in his thirties, because "kids today will be leaders later and will hopefully be able to then save civilization."

A quarter of those answering the question talked about their responsibilities to identify mistakes and prevent similar events from recurring. From learning how individuals fell into self-destructive behavior to learning how regimes permitted disagreements to end in wars, many respondents believed that history should teach how tragedies might have been avoided and might be prevented in the future. "Our generation should realize the mistakes that have been made in the past and try not to do those again," said a retired woman from Pleasant Hill, Missouri in her sixties. A 43-year-old medical supervisor from Las Vegas wanted her son to study the Holocaust "so as to make sure nothing like that ever happens again."

Respondents envisioned a participatory culture in which their children could sort out how and why individuals in the past had tried to make a difference in their worlds, how and why they had made things better and worse. From these explorations people would learn not only how they could make things better and worse in the future but also how to be active users and interpreters of the past. Both popular culture and formal history classes mediated between them and actual experiences from the past, frequently conveying distortions, lies, and inaccuracies. Respondents said they wanted a culture in which individuals took responsibility and acquired skills to interpret history for themselves.

II

What common perspectives on the past frame a profoundly historical culture that already exists beneath what may appear to be differences between professional and amateur historymakers, themes that make the past our common resource? To begin with, it may be helpful to distinguish uses of the past from contents. The "intimate past" (content) is not the same as intimate uses of the past. At Christmas gatherings families talk about national things as well as family things. The national narratives that made up the content of exams that respondents had hated as students were less the source of their alienation than the exam format—the fact that they had been forced to spit back meaningless material. What mattered was not that the subject was intimate or national but that outside of class the students were active participants and in school they (and often their teachers, they complained) were required to absorb abstractions and facts that made no sense. What mattered was whether they could actively participate in using the past.

I'm much more certain that respondents participate actively and use the past intimately than I am that the pasts they use are intimate or private. The central issue in a fundamentally historical culture is participation or passivity, active and firsthand engagement or mediation by others who had mysterious or untrustworthy agendas.

To find the common ground among respondents, then, we should look for occasions when they participated voluntarily and enthusiastically, situations where they felt invited to use the past on their own terms. History museums present an obvious example. Respondents trusted them as much as they did their grandmothers. They felt as connected to the past in museums and historic sites as they did at family gatherings. And the keys were that they could go when and with whom they wanted, and interpret artifacts how they wanted. More than half the respondents in the national sample had visited a museum or historic site during the previous year. Museum artifacts and historic sites invited them to revisit experiences at other times and places, to imagine how they might have felt and acted, to reflect on how the earlier experiences or circumstances might have changed or been changed by those who had originally participated in them.

Hobbyists and collectors—two fifths of our respondents—are another obvious group of historymakers who practice history for the love of it. Some hobbyists tried to imagine their way into the Civil War by sleeping on rope hammocks or firing Civil War muskets or reenacting battles. Others tried to understand why postage stamps at a particular time commemorated presidents or pop singers, were printed in different inks or perforated in different ways; they asked and answered questions that require remarkable attention to details of documentation. Hobbyists, like museum visitors, chose the arenas and terms of their participation with the past.

I came away from reading respondents' stories with the strong sense that popular historymaking was intensely social and intensely intimate, that people relied heavily on those they felt closest to as they engaged the past in ways that mattered most to them. With individuals they trusted or at least knew, they probed experiences and constructed the traditions they wanted to sustain. In these relationships they discovered what they shared and did not share with others, shaped and reshaped memories into trajectories, made and changed commitments to sustain and change heritages, and generally created the perceptual world they wanted to inhabit. In finding the will to overcome the destructive habits and inertia in their lives, several respondents told us, favorable experiences with Alcoholics Anonymous had helped—demonstrating that many people needed the intense encouragement and shared experience of others who had been through what they were about to undertake. Far from mechanically storing and retrieving fully formed representations of the past, respondents constructed and used pasts as products and by-products of living their lives. In order to steer through dangers and opportunities as they imagined how to move from past toward future, they needed to focus their critical and empathetic skills on making sense of the present. The point of engaging the past was to understand choices in the present to shape the future.

When we approach the more familiar content of academic history, we need to investigate how in their intimate relationships individuals used and did not use, went along with and defied larger "historical" trends. At this level the dichotomy between "intimate" and "national," public and private, dissolves into dynamic and reciprocal interaction. Respondents more often mentioned public experiences than private ones as the most formative of their lives, but they mentioned those public events most often as intimate experiences. What they remembered was the personal contexts in which they engaged the public events (teachers and students in a fifth grade class weeping when they heard of Kennedy's assassination) or their own participation in those events (fighting in a battle in World War II). They often drew personal meanings when they recalled public figures as the most important individuals in their lives. In distinguishing between those experiences that still live in active memory, passed on orally from individual to individual because people believe that they continue to provide meaningful anchors for the present, on one hand, and those experiences now remembered only in writing—in books, written by professional historians—Pierre Nora draws a more important distinction than that between personal and national pasts. What matters is whether something lives for participants in the present.[2]

In other words, walling off public from private pasts doesn't make sense. When not forced to choose between family and national pasts, half the respondents who wanted their children to learn their family heritage also wanted their children to learn their national heritage. They connected these heritages, intimate with public, each time they toured a museum or visited a site with family or friends, each time they reenacted a battle or showed objects they had collected to others. They named both national figures and family members as influences; about the same number of people in the national sample (24) named John F. Kennedy as a formative influence as named their grandfathers. Many worried about how larger historical developments—economic insecurity, waning of discipline—might have eroded the family, turning it into a source of disintegration instead of support. Respondents gave meaning to large phenomena like immigration or economic depression by describing how they had changed and been changed by passage through those experiences.

A fundamentally historical culture centered on individual participation would invite members to explore just how individuals conform to and resist larger historical trends, how the rhythms and narratives of family life fit or do not fit those of changing power and institutional arrangements in the larger society. It would envision individuals as more than examples of large and impersonal cultures and institutions. It would take seriously how they live lives and meet needs in relationships driven by forces different from those that power institutions and cultures. The best microhistory does this already. In *Mr. Bligh's Bad Language*, Greg Dening tries to reconstruct events leading up to mutiny on *H. M. S. Bounty* by speculating from observation around him about how forty men might relate to each other when confined in cramped space over a long period of time. But Dening places these timeless observations about personal relationships in the context of the late eighteenth century, when authority was being challenged in new ways by the French and American revolutions and British civilization was encountering Polynesian cultures for the first time.[3]

Not until this century did scholars begin to understand the defining importance of primary relationships to larger phenomena. Social scientists began to peel back large formal institutions like factories and armies, large cultures like Irish-American immigrant communities, mass media audiences, and student movements of the 1960s to discover that in each case the real source of creativity and productivity lay in the myriad primary groups whose members took responsibility for the larger whole.[4] And for scholars, as for respondents in our survey, the question was often how much and what kind of control they had or could imagine as individuals and in groups. Workers formed unions, audiences shaped television content, blacks acquired rights in circumstances they had not chosen. They probed their pasts to imagine how they had made a difference then and might in the future.

Respondents said that their families and friends both exemplified and resisted larger historical trajectories. Sometimes they saw their families as swept along by a larger thrust of history, toward greater tolerance and encouragement for women and members of minority groups, for example. But sometimes they saw their families as trying to resist a thrust of history—toward greater crime, permissiveness, or materialism, for instance—that seemed to threaten their cohesion and even survival. When they talked about religion—especially evangelical religion, which had an appeal so powerful that it seems the most likely common ground on which some respondents from different cultures can recognize each other—they told agonizing stories of struggles to bring their own trajectories into line with a single, eternal master narrative that extended from the creation of the earth to the end of time.

Respondents identified a fundamentally historical way of viewing movement through time by emphasizing change and continuity when they talked about themselves and their worlds. In contrast to the few who viewed human nature as fixed and unchanging, greed or racial hatred as timeless themes, most emphasized change as a basic fact of life. They believed it was important to identify the causes, direction, pace, and consequences of change, to locate turning points when new directions were introduced.

And they had a deep sense that values and contexts changed over time.

They reported that grandparents lived by different values than they did. They measured how older values had ebbed and new ones had replaced them, how the world seemed to move faster than before. Fearing that changes in the larger society might erode their capacity to sustain values their parents had taught them, they wondered how individuals could preserve those traditions in the face of erosion in the larger society of values like freedom, morality, or neighborliness. But they also spoke of themselves and their parents as products of their times. Some described individuals as products of prejudices formed in earlier times against women, racial minorities, and homosexuals, or as products of the financially insecure thirties or socially conformist fifties or politically rebellious sixties.

By placing individuals at the center as both actors in and observers of history, we can build a historical culture around participation. Individuals, after all, experience, interpret, revisit, reinterpret—in short, they remember and forget. Nations, cultures, and institutions can't, even though politicians and pundits pretend that they can. Individuals can discover, recognize, ignore, cross-examine, fear, dream, hope. Moving the focus of history from texts to interpreters turns historical culture from a spectator sport into something created by participants. A Florida fund-raiser reported "being force-fed" history in school and disliking it, but finding history "more interesting when it was done on my own terms" after leaving school. Better yet, by comparing their experiences and interpretations with those of others, individuals create empathy that permits them to enter into the experiences of people from other times and places, people from other backgrounds. Indeed, as observers from Charles Horton Cooley to Zygmunt Bauman and Arne Vetlesen have pointed out, people develop their empathy toward strangers not as political choices or philosophical abstractions but from intimate contacts with people around them.[5]

This focus on individuals reminds me of Norbert Elias's brilliant, counterintuitive point that individuals are larger than groups because individuals contain within themselves so many different identities. An individual could be a woman, lawyer, Republican, Chicagoan, lesbian, Irish-American. Each piece of her identity carries with it materials and traditions that the individual, alone or with others, could turn into a collective past with constantly evolving individual variations. And yet to describe any one of these groups is also to fall far short of describing any individual who contains so many potential identities and locations between identities with which to describe where he or she has been. While some individuals and group leaders draw circles around poles of identity and try to keep members from straying and strangers from entering, many people describe themselves as "betwixt and between" identities, to use George Sánchez's description of Mexican American life—as border crossers who construct their lives between Mexican and American, Republican and Democrat, gay and straight.[6] Choosing among potential identities, locating themselves at poles or somewhere along continua between poles as circumstances inspired them, individuals revealed stunning creativity as they made and remade their narratives of where they had come from and were heading. This intimate work was so hard and creative that from time to time they sought out resting places built by others who seemed to have followed paths like their own, places where they could rest from individual labors and find social support.

I too am attracted by the collective pasts that black and Indian respondents presented in this study. But I fear that emphasizing different racial contents may obscure basic similarities in how respondents from all groups constructed their pasts. Among African American and Indian respondents as well as whites, a majority said that their family pasts were their most important pasts. For all races, family provided both the content and the context where respondents talked about identity, morality, and agency. The major difference was that black and Indian parents and grandparents tended to incorporate experiences of the race into family materials they presented youngsters, while whites tended to limit their accounts to extended families. In both cases the challenges of making trajectories and taking responsibility were those older family members wanted to instill in younger ones as they tried to teach them how to use the past to live their lives.

Respondents brooded about this question of whether and under what circumstances individuals could develop a sense of a common past and a common future. Looking back, a retired Tulsan thought that the most remarkable lesson to be learned from his experience in World War II was that "the American people when they are confronted with a catastrophe . . . will do everything in their power to come together for the common cause to defeat the enemy." As he reflected on what he had just told an interviewer, he paused, compared the 1940s to the present, and posed a troubling question about whether individual Americans would be likely in the 1990s to come together to make a nation. "I'm not too sure that would hold in today's environment," he said. "I think people put too much emphasis on themselves as individuals."

Instead of inheriting or retrieving fully formed collective pasts, individuals felt bursts of recognition when they suddenly felt common points of identity with others in the present that they made into shared experiences and trajectories. Across affiliations, from family to race or religion, from sex or sexual orientation to nation or humanity, individuals experienced moments when they felt more and less connected, more and less alone, when they recognized shared experiences. From a personal trauma, a television program, or a new acquaintance they suddenly felt connected to others, with a bond of family, race, or nation. Indeed, the changing possibilities for discovering what they shared with others often inspired the most empowering—and discouraging—uses respondents made of the past.[7]

A fundamentally historical culture would recognize that there are seasons when people use the past differently. As children and young adults, respondents were eager to figure out where they came from and where they were heading: their identities. As adults, they stood between generations and worried about how they could shape their lives and take responsibility for those older and younger who depended on them. And as they aged, they worried about leaving a legacy so that the next generations could learn and use what they had learned.

In such a culture people would face basic historical questions. Some people were attracted to the past on its own terms, because of its pastness, its otherness. For them the past could be an object of curiosity, a source of old traces like fossils or arrowheads, or a reservoir of alternatives to the present. But for others the past offered links to the present, not breaks from it.

In a participatory historical culture members would explore whether things from the past were like and unlike the present, the sources of change or continuity. By revisiting or reliving the past they could reinterpret it as they unearthed new sources but also as they experienced new needs in the present. In their interpretations and narratives, respondents felt torn between a desire for authenticity (that the story meet present needs) and for accuracy (that it conform to what happened at the original moment). They sought sources to verify contested accounts, so they could decide whom to believe. In debates recognizable to professional historians, respondents argued about change and continuity, authenticity and accuracy, as they constructed and reconstructed narratives of their lives and times.

A fundamentally historical culture, in short, would be one with many levels, uses, points of access, recognitions. It would recognize similarities and respect differences in grandmothers' stories, museum exhibitions, and manuscript collections as trusted sources for approaching the past.

III

I can't leave a discussion of participatory historical culture without exploring implications of our findings for history's traditional civic mission. Since the days of the Israelite, Greek, and Roman cultures, we have assigned history the task of defining nation or creed, of proclaiming core values, and of teaching citizens to connect their personal aspirations with their civic heritages.[8] With these traditions of giving visibility and voice to people as they have tried to assemble their experiences and advance their needs, history appealed to me in graduate school in the 1960s as a natural field in which I could contribute to making a better society.

The hard civic challenges for a participatory culture grounded in history revolve around how people might move outward from their intimate worlds, connect with others, recognize common experiences, and settle on common narratives. Those challenges have become much more difficult over the thirty years since I attended graduate school. In the 1960s it was easy for citizens to find and engage each other. Unprecedented numbers of people mobilized into highly visible social movements through which they spoke collectively and acted to engage everyone in public contests. Over the next generation, as those social movements have receded, new industries have emerged to reshape the very meanings of "political participation" and "civic forum." They have tried to change who participates in the civic forum and on what terms. They invented means for finding and listening to people—market research, opinion polls, focus groups—and the means for talking—advertising, public relations, spin doctoring—that transferred the initiative for shaping the civic arena from citizens to opinion managers. They manufactured an arena in which public "conversation" took the form of raising issues that mattered to opinion managers, measuring denominators that turned individuals into a mass, and then crafting appeals to move the mass. As opinion industries have come to define where and how citizens and politicians engage each other, they have driven both voters and legislators away from the civic arena in record numbers. Indeed, the new opinion managers possess the arena by dispossessing citizens and politicians. They leave citizens unsure even where to enter the civic arena.[9]

Before I could imagine how professional historians could assist in building a participatory historical culture, I had to sort through some heavy baggage that history has been carrying around since the inventors of professional historymaking in the nineteenth century defined the mission that set themselves apart from amateurs. The story of history, they taught us, should be above all the story of the nation and of national institutions, events, policies, and cultures. In the 1960s, when I was in graduate school in Madison, the nation was self-evidently the central unit of historical analysis and the policies and institutions of the nation-state obviously provided crucial vehicles for shaping society.

Over the next thirty years, changes in the economy and culture increasingly knocked out these important props. Most of the people we talked with from all backgrounds saw history differently. The nation or national institutions and events were not the prime movers or actors or themes; they and their lives were. In questioning the centrality and authority of institutions, our respondents provided independent confirmation of the growing need for history, even if it is to be the story of the rise and fall of power centers, to interrogate its traditional starting places.

The nation-state still has policies and institutions, but it is by no means clear that these provide the most necessary, desirable, creative, or responsible arenas in which people can control their lives or fulfill a civic heritage.[10] As we explore challenges to the core of historical practice and its traditional civic mission—the increasingly global transit of people, capital, goods, and cultures; the decentering of authority and truth in scholarship and life, raids on the regulations and safety net of the state—historians can contribute simply by doing what we do well: we can explore where and how the nation-state has actually touched people's experiences, what it has done well and poorly, to what or whom it has lost resources and authority, and what people have expected and trusted, as well as what they no longer expect and trust, from its traditions and institutions. We can investigate what people want and fear to replace the nation-state to focus authority and common will in ways that the nation has done in the past.

Precisely because the props of professional history have been knocked out, it is crucial at this time that we not create an essentialized dichotomy between "historians" and "people" and that we interrogate and explore common ground from which to use the past to reshape the civic arena according to popular concerns. Our respondents profoundly distrusted many large institutions, including the nation-state, reflecting a deepening pattern of popular alienation that began in the 1960s and 1970s and increased dramatically in the 1980s and 1990s. The percentage of

Americans who told Gallup's pollsters that they can "trust Washington to do what is right all or most of the time" fell incredibly from 78 percent in 1964 to 19 percent by 1994. By a 75–19 percent margin Americans told pollsters in 1994 that "government is pretty much run by a few big interests looking out for themselves."[11]

Since both institutions and national narratives seemed so far removed from everyday experiences and needs, respondents retreated into their intimate relationships as places where they could trust and use the past. They kept the civic heritage alive not by choosing sides in political conflicts over institutions they didn't trust and over issues and images that mattered mostly to opinion managers, but by using the past actively in their intimate relationships to shape their lives. They developed superb foundations for a participatory civics: they learned that people could change or be changed by experience and circumstances, that things have been and might be different than at present, that encounters with others could become bonds through which they took responsibility to change political direction. They recognized that history indeed possessed the valuable "powers of the past" that Harvey Kaye has listed as perspective, critique, consciousness, remembrance, and imagination—all powers many people told us they also valued and practiced.[12]

The basic civic challenges for a participatory historical culture take place as people move beyond individual experiences to widen narratives and imagine how they might make a difference in the larger world. As I imagined how to address these challenges, I soon realized that I was faltering when I focused on political institutions. Instead of envisioning how existing political arenas might assemble individuals, I kept being drawn— as I had from the first time that I listened to these interviews—toward the classroom as a more natural place to experience and explore the making of public narratives and progressive civics.

In imagining how a participatory historical culture could help people reach from the personal to the collective, I suggest three tentative observations about how we might use the past and then illustrate them with possible applications to classrooms. First, we can find where people are and how they want to be heard by listening hard to the voices and styles they select as they use the past. Second, we can imagine how to improve our present circumstances by turning to the past for alternatives. And finally, we can use the past to develop institutions and programs that better reflect our needs.

The ways people use the past can help us find and converse with real people at a time when opinion industries, scholars, and pundits have tried to subordinate people to their agendas. Two discoveries emerged from our study of how people use the past. The first is that everyone uses the past for similar and fundamentally human purposes—such as to establish identity, morality, immortality, and agency. People use the past to imagine how they might change and be changed by other people and by circumstances. And they use the past critically, creatively, and actively, in making and testing narratives of change and continuity. They re-examine trajectories of their lives and imagine how they might fit differently into their worlds. The second discovery is that individuals create a stunning variety of content and conclusions: as unique individuals, as products of collective circumstances and traditions, as human beings. Historical narratives thus follow Clifford Geertz's observation that "thought is spectacularly multiple as product and wondrously singular as process."[13] In the classroom, students could write and compare accounts of experiences, and study autobiographies. With such exercises they would face the challenges of history to civics: to seek the core, the commonality, the singularity of processes that recur and then to contrast that core with individual and group variations shaped by particular moments and contexts. In the tension between the unique individual and the group, the past and the present, people presented how they wanted to be seen and heard. By exploring how all biographical stories are both alike and different, we can recognize and respect both common and different needs as individuals experienced them.

The past is a reservoir of alternatives to the present, many survey respondents told us in pointing toward a possible use of the past for people to shape a civic arena. In perhaps the most far-reaching claim for history's ability to make available all human experience to any individual, Ralph Waldo Emerson wrote that "Who hath access to this universal mind is a party to all that is or can be done. What Plato has thought, he may think; what a saint has felt, he may feel; what at any time has befallen any man, he can understand."[14] By recovering things from the past or by looking at experience differently we can see how to think and act differently in the future. The past can challenge us with eloquent, brilliant, troubling material that widens our present experience and wisdom. It provides perspectives to engage, accounts to cross-examine, and opportunities to hone skills of empathy, compassion, and reflection.[15] Good history teachers have long presented students with documents, artifacts, pictures, and films in which people address issues of identity, narrative, and agency, thereby introducing students to a variety of perspectives on moral issues, political alternatives, and ways of making individual and collective narratives.

How can we develop sympathy for others when "we have no immediate experience of what other men feel?" asked Adam Smith, as he sought to explain how empathy might be compatible with his larger conviction that the common good came when individuals pursued their self-interests. The answer, he reasoned, was "by conceiving what we ourselves should feel in the like situation": "by the imagination we place ourselves in his situation, we conceive ourselves enduring all the same torments, we enter as it were into his body, and become in some measure the same person with him, and thence form some idea of his sensations, and even feel something which, through weaker in degree, is not altogether unlike them."[16] By trying to imagine how other people experienced something, we can develop a moral sympathy for others.

Since respondents seemed naturally to begin narratives with reflections on how they had changed and been changed by experiences, I see another major use of the past in the dynamic interactions between individuals and larger institutions. From time to time institutions have provided participatory and interpretive centers of autonomy, but our study suggests that at this moment most people don't trust them and that the work of building autonomy and making interpretations now takes place intimately, in primary relationships. Students could use these institutions in different ways, to explore how national events or institutions changed the lives of different individuals and in turn how individuals shaped the events and institutions. In what ways did the rhythms of their intimate lives converge and diverge from those of larger phenomena like immigration, moral decline, war, depression? By supplementing the conventional classroom focus on the rise and fall of institutions with timeless human experiences—tragedy, hope, fear, love, loss—students can inquire about connections between living fulfilling lives as people and trying to change and sustain institutions.

By starting historical inquiries with experience, students can measure how institutions and programs and cultures have succeeded and failed to meet people's needs and expectations. Students can imagine more responsive institutions and politics by exploring how people have discovered, recognized, shared, and mobilized experiences and presented them as common narratives in the civic arena. Readings and discussions could focus on moments in the past when people recognized common experiences and mobilized to create more responsive politics.

We historians might gain a sense of our own choices by studying how political debate has evolved to force individuals to do the work of interpreting and mobilizing what in the past century was done by cultures, parties, and groups. We might explore how and with what consequences opinion managers have come to shape the public arena, and get a comparative perspective by looking at which individuals, groups, cultures, and institutions at other times and places did the work of interpreting and mobilizing experiences. With cases from the past, we might imagine how political policies could begin not in ideologies or institutions but when people insist that policies or public spaces reflect their own experiences and narratives. A politics that values active individual engagement over group, ideology, institution may be built by listening for and to the deepest needs that individuals present, in places that presently elude pundits and pollsters, as they use the past to sustain and change the course of their lives and the world.

How We Did the Survey

This study takes up a subject that is at the heart of the historian's inquiry (the past) but investigates it at a moment in time (the present) that historians generally leave to sociologists and anthropologists. In our foray across conventional temporal and disciplinary borders, we were guided by our talented colleagues at the Center for Survey Research (CSR) at Indiana University, who helped us design the survey, carried it out, and ensured that it followed the highest professional standards of academic survey research. Indeed, throughout the book, we use the generic "we" to denote not only our own collaboration but also our collaboration with the CSR's director, John M. Kennedy; its field director, Nancy Bannister; its assistant field director, Kevin Tharp; the project managers for this survey, Barbara Hopkins and Christopher Botsko; and the more than sixty energetic interviewers who made the hundreds of phone calls so essential to our study. That "we" also includes research assistant Andy Draheim, our day-to-day intermediary with the CSR, who worked intensely with them on every phase of the study and then worked closely with us on the analysis of the data, especially the quantitative analysis embodied in the tables.

Because we wanted this book to be inviting to readers not trained in social science, we have tried not to burden it with excessive methodological or statistical discussions. After reading the overview in this appendix, some readers might want more detailed information on the survey methodology and results. For them, we offer two additional sources of information. First, we invite them to consult a Web site that we have set up (http://chnm.gmu.edu/survey), which contains additional statistical tables as well as the full text of the survey questionnaires. Second, we are happy to respond to further questions, which can be directed to rrosenzw@gmu.edu or thelen@indiana.edu.

Discovering What to Ask and How to Ask It

To move from the idea of a survey to implementing it required figuring out the questions to ask—and the way they should be asked—about a subject that no one had seriously studied. We assembled the first list of possible questions in October 1990 in a meeting at the Smithsonian Institution's National Museum of American History, and early the next year a venturesome group of 15 public history graduate students at Arizona State University tried out and refined the questions in one- to two-hour face-to-face interviews with 135 people in the Phoenix area; subsequently, a smaller group of graduate students at the University of Toledo did the same. We put together a written questionnaire based on this initial project and sent it to 75 people who, in turn, administered it to 75 history professionals and 75 nonprofessionals. Lois Silverman, then the director of the Center for History-Making in America, played an important part in organizing and summarizing the written questionnaire. After the Spencer Foundation and the National Endowment for the Humanities agreed to fund the survey in 1993, we further revised the questions and systematically tested them in seven nights of telephone interviews carried out by the CSR. To widen the circle of discussion, we solicited comments on our draft questionnaire from survey experts as well as more than 40 public and academic historians.

This extensive piloting and pretesting taught us two crucial lessons. First, we needed to ask broadly framed questions if we were to learn what people were thinking and doing. That meant, in turn, that we had to ask people about "the past" and not just about "history." Our pilot survey showed that three quarters of those we interviewed thought of "the past" and "history" as different concepts, with most people defining the past in more inclusive terms and history as something more formal, analytical, official, or distant. As Melissa Keane, one of the Arizona graduate students, later observed, most people "drew a clear line between 'history' and their own lives. 'History' was often remote 'book learning'—Columbus, Abe Lincoln, Henry VIII, the Norman Conquest—the 'boring stuff from school.' "[1]

Such comments persuaded us that if we were genuinely interested in the relationship between the past and the present in Americans' lives, we should use the term that they found more immediate and meaningful. When it came time to do the survey in the late spring of 1994, we announced this as clearly as possible to the people we called. The interviewers began by explaining: "We're conducting a nationwide study funded by the National Endowment for the Humanities to find out how people understand and use the past in their everyday lives." Then when interviewers began the questioning they explained, "I am going to ask you some questions about the past. By the past, we mean everything from the very recent past to the very distant past, from your personal and family past to the past of the United States and other nations."

Framing our survey in these inclusive terms gave us different answers than if we had focused more narrowly on "history," but since we set out to understand the past as our respondents understood and defined it—and not as professional historians did—this was the best phrasing. Our pilot surveys, which sought reactions to a number of terms ("history," "tradition," "heritage," "the past"), had shown us that "the past" was the most accessible term—one that left respondents with the greatest latitude to describe their engagements on their own terms. We are aware, of course, that some readers, perhaps professional historians in particular, will not share the capacious definition of the past used in this study, but our respondents think about the past in these elastic terms. To the charge that our instructions and questions encouraged people to talk about the past in more expansive and less professionally conventional terms, we plead guilty—by design.

Our piloting and pretesting taught us a second, related lesson. On the one hand, questions whose answers could be easily quantified—ones that were answered with a "yes" or a "no" or a numeric score—were valuable in developing benchmarks for participation in and attitudes toward past-related activities. But on the other hand, a study that restricted itself to such closed-ended inquiries would never yield the richer and deeper (if sometimes perplexing) insights into how the past figured in people's lives that had emerged in the open-ended interviews during the piloting of the survey. Although we asked a number of conventional, closed-ended questions (e.g., "During the last 12 months, have you visited any history museums or historic sites?"), we confined them to only about one third of a typical interview. We realized that we had to find out why someone had gone to a museum and what they had gotten from the experience.

Follow-up questions told us more, but they required some compromises in the survey design. We could not ask follow-up questions about everything (for instance, why people did each of ten different activities) without exhausting our relatively modest budget for long-distance telephone calls and interviewers' wages—or, for that matter, exhausting the patience of our respondents. In such situations, our survey research colleagues advised us, it was conventional to ask certain questions of only a limited—but randomly selected—portion of our larger sample. For example, only 27 percent of people who said they had been to a history museum were also asked to talk about the occasions or reasons for doing so. In addition, we included some open-ended questions—for instance, "What about the past do you think is important for children to know?"—that went to a portion of the sample (about one tenth in this case).[2] Some follow-up questions only went to people who offered specific answers; for instance, those who rated a source as particularly trustworthy or particularly untrustworthy were asked about the basis of their rating, but those who gave a middling rating weren't.

Even so, merely asking conventional survey follow-up questions frequently evoked brief and vague answers. In collaboration with the staff at the CSR, we developed less conventional probing strategies that borrowed from techniques of ethnography and oral history. We encouraged interviewers to use their own experiences and natural curiosity in questioning respondents. If a respondent talked about a hobby that the interviewer was familiar with, he or she could use that familiarity to prompt further comments. As one interviewer later explained, "by simply saying 'any other?' we usually do not get to the heart of the matter, and this study, with its open probing, allowed us to do so. Because the tone was so conversational, I feel people opened up to us more. . . . I think they felt I was genuinely interested in what they had to say."

Our goal was to convince the people we called that we were interested in their perspectives. We sought to elicit what mattered to respondents, not interviewers, even when interviewers shared their own experiences and feelings as part of the strategy for getting people to talk more openly. As Christopher Botsko and John M. Kennedy later observed in a paper given at the annual meeting of the American Association for Public Opinion Research: "The interviewing process was far more collaborative between the interviewing staff, the study managers, and the investigators than a standardized survey. It was also more labor intensive." But the results seemed to justify the effort. In the same paper, Botsko and Kennedy recommended these innovative techniques to other survey researchers, arguing that "nonstandardized techniques permit the use of survey research beyond the method's reach when only standardized techniques are used."[3]

A postsurvey survey of interviewers found that they too endorsed the open-ended questions and the nonstandard probing. On the one hand, every interviewer described the interviewing techniques and the "experience with respondents" as different from those of other surveys in which they had participated. And about three quarters of the interviewers called their work on the survey "much" or "somewhat" "more difficult than most other surveys" (only one said it was "less difficult"). Yet on the other hand, all but two found it "more rewarding than other studies you have worked on." Most interviewers specifically praised the open-ended questions and the unconventional probing techniques. "The main difference" between this and other surveys, explained an interviewer who had worked on at least eight other CSR surveys, "was that the respondents in history were sharing a *lot* of themselves, the different things they did and why they did these things, while in other studies we just are getting facts or numbers to be analyzed. Many times at the end of an interview I would feel like I had actually met the respondent." He and many other interviewers attributed this quality of "real sharing" to the "more personal" nature of the questions, to the open-ended follow-up questions, and to their ability to ask more natural questions as part of the probing. One interviewer nicely summarized the "different probing technique" as "the ability to respond to the respondent in a more human fashion. For example, if the respondent told a hilarious joke, we could laugh, which would make the respondent open up more, instead of giving generic feedback and going on."

Not surprisingly, some interviewers at first worried (as did we) that this interview approach would be "directive" or less "scientific." Yet after they were finished, they decided it wasn't. One noted, for example, that despite the "more personal, even intimate conversations," interviewers could maintain "a comparable professionalism (respect, neutrality, listening skills, and consideration) with other surveys." Some argued that this approach actually made the study more objective and complete. What one called "history-style probing" gave "more complete and more specific information." The ability to "follow up on what they [respondents] were saying," explained another experienced interviewer, "made them realize more acutely that I was actually listening and not just hoping that they would fit their answer into my category so that I could finally move on." Still another long-term CSR interviewer commented that this study differed from the nine others that she had done because she could converse "with the respondent as if we were both human beings" and didn't have to force all "answer[s] into a category like we usually make people do." Over and over, interviewers used words like "rapport," "sharing," "conversation," and "communication" to describe these interviews. One older interviewer who had taken part in ten different CSR surveys spoke for many when she concluded, "I always felt I got more information for the client than in any other study."

Because of the particularly demanding nature of this survey and the use of unconventional probing techniques, the CSR selected experienced interviewers with the strongest performance records on previous projects. More than half had worked at the CSR for over a year; one third had been there for two or more years. Even so, we and the CSR intensively trained the interviewers for this project. They learned about the background of the study and about the techniques of probing for answers. Then they watched supervisors role-play interviews and practiced interviewing each other. In addition, the CSR took unusual steps to monitor the interviewers and ensure the quality of the data collected. For example, both we and project manager Barbara Hopkins reviewed answers to open-ended questions and gave the interviewers feedback on which probes were most successful. In the first few weeks of the study, the interviewers and their supervisors held regular postshift meetings to talk about problems they were encountering and approaches they found effective in getting respondents to report on their own thoughts and experiences. Supervisors also held individual discussions with interviewers to talk about the pros and cons of different approaches. The interviewers' insights from the field played a central role in developing survey procedures that would encourage interviewees to open up.

Formulating the Questions

These general lessons about the need for framing questions in broad terms and for following up and probing guided us as we composed the actual survey, but that process still required difficult decisions. Our questions reflected our interest in two general areas: activities and attitudes. We wanted to carry out a census of behaviors, attitudes, and experiences related to the past. Then we wanted to map and understand the multiple ways that Americans value, use, and experience their pasts. After much discussion and debate, we decided that we could get at activities and attitudes through questions organized in four areas: "activities related to the past," "trustworthiness of sources of information about the past," "how connected to the past people feel on certain occasions," and "the importance of various pasts." (See Web site for the complete questionnaire.)

Our method for deciding what to ask about activities was typical of how we developed all the questions. In piloting, we had questioned people in a more open-ended way, asking in the Arizona study, for example, "What activities in your life are related to the past?" From such questioning, we made a checklist of more than thirty items. Since we did not want to devote more than one third of the interview to questions about activities, we had to limit ourselves to ten questions that incorporated the range of what people do but also emphasized the most important areas of activities. Thus, we asked whether they had encountered the past as it was synthesized and presented by others in historical films and television programs, in history books, and at historic sites and museums. We also asked whether they had constructed, documented, or preserved the past themselves by working on hobbies or collections, participating in historical groups or organizations, writing in diaries and journals, taking photos, or investigating the history of their family. And because we knew from piloting that the past was often encountered in intimate circles of family and friends, we asked whether people had, in the past twelve months, looked at photos with family or friends or attended a family reunion or a reunion of some other group of people with whom they shared a common experience.

These ten items embodied the broad definition of historymaking that we had sought, but they also reflected some inevitable compromises. We would have preferred to ask separately about fiction and nonfiction books, documentary films and Hollywood features, hobbies and collections, and historic sites and history museums. But such distinctions would have greatly lengthened the interviews. Moreover, one advantage to asking the questions in a less specific format was that respondents could, in follow-up questions, make the distinctions among books and films that mattered to them. Other, more specific activities—membership in a reenactment group or attendance at historical lectures, for instance—would have been interesting to know about, but piloting and pretesting told us that the number of positive responses would have been too small to be genuinely useful. Information on frequency of participation—hours per week or number of times per year—would also have been valuable, though very time-consuming to collect and perhaps of questionable reliability, given the difficulty respondents have in remembering such specific information. Our general remedy was the use of follow-up questions to gather more impressionistic data on things that we could not ask systematically of the entire sample.

The most important demonstration of the relevance of our checklist to popular historymaking is found in what our respondents said rather than in what we thought. When we followed up on our simple questions about whether or not people had done any of these ten things in the past year and asked why, when, or how they pursued the past in these ways, their answers indicated that most implicitly shared our broad definition of historymaking. Some respondents even worried that we might not share their own expansive view of significant historical work. A 39-year-old lawyer from Alabama, for example, described in detail his hobby of building model warships, which he had become interested in through his father and his grandfather. "You might not consider it the past, but I do," he noted.

The questions about "trustworthiness" of sources were also directed at learning about historymaking broadly construed. We began with a problem familiar to all professional historians: How do you evaluate different sources from and perspectives on the past? Then, in the pilot, we questioned people in a more open-ended way that might allow them to tell us whether their historical methodology was similar to or different from that of professional historians. For example, we simply asked people to "list what source(s) you trust for information about the past."

From the long list we compiled, we selected for the phone survey seven areas in which people reported they had encountered the past—museums, movies, television programs, personal accounts from relatives, conversations with eyewitnesses, and interactions with high school and college history teachers. (College history classes were a less widely shared arena of experience than the other six, but we decided that once we, as college professors ourselves, opened high school history to critical scrutiny, we could hardly exempt ourselves.) In order to facilitate the comparisons that we thought were essential to this section of the survey, we asked people to rate trustworthiness of sources on a 10-point scale—a standard measuring stick in phone surveys.

Our piloting also suggested that the word "trust" (as compared, for example, to "accurate" or "valuable" or "authentic") was most likely to evoke our respondents' sense of what they did and didn't value about a particular source or authority. This was especially important in the follow-up questions, where we asked a percentage of those who rated a source as especially trustworthy or untrustworthy why they had given that rating.

Our questions about "connectedness" were also intended to make comparisons among different modes and arenas for historymaking. Using a 10-point scale, a conventional approach for survey research, allowed us to compare the intensity of engagement with the past that people felt celebrating holidays, visiting history museums or historic sites, gathering with their family, watching a movie or TV program about the past, studying history in school, and reading a book about the past. In part, these questions were meant to build upon the activities questions, gauging intensity of participation and degree of emotional investment. We asked about some of the same arenas (e.g. movies, museums, books), but also added others (e.g., holiday celebrations and schools) that would not have made sense in an inventory of activities over the past year.

As with other closed-ended questions, we asked follow-up questions in a proportion of the cases—between one eighth and one half. The precise wording of these questions varied depending on what the pretesting had shown to be most effective. For example, we asked simply, "How does gathering with your family make you feel connected to the past?" But for museums, films, and books, we found that we needed a more concrete follow-up like "Please give me an example of a museum or historic site that made you feel connected to the past. Why did that museum or historic site make you feel that way?" Perhaps because our phrasing probed the emotional content of the experience, the follow-up questions on the connectedness series elicited some of the richest and most detailed answers in the survey.

The final group of questions focused on the relative importance of various pasts. The only one of these queries that was phrased in a closed-ended way asked people to say which of four areas of the past (family, racial or ethnic group, current community, and the United States) was "most important" to them. We later added an open-ended question about whether the "past of any other area or group" is "very important to you." This proved an economical way of picking up answers that we might have otherwise missed.

We also tried a different way of getting at the same subject by asking people "What about the past is important for children to know?" Our advisers had generally responded enthusiastically to this question, but the answers in pretesting were somewhat disappointing. As a result, we decided to ask the question of only about one tenth of our sample. In general, our guiding principle in deciding which questions to ask (and how often to ask them) was whether or not they seemed to provide useful insights into popular historymaking. (See tables on Web site for information on how many people were asked each question.)

Still another way of assessing what respondents found important about the past was to ask who or what had affected them. We deliberately phrased this question as openly as possible so that people would have the opportunity to describe either Lincoln or their grandmother as the person from the past "who has particularly affected you" and either the Vietnam War or the divorce of their parents as the event from "the past that has most affected you." The follow-ups to these two questions, which asked what the respondent had learned from the person or event, allowed us to probe the ways that people both used and interpreted the past. We knew from piloting, moreover, that the concept of "learning from the past" emerged frequently in discussions about the past, and these questions offered a focused way of investigating what people meant by that phrase.

One question that greatly interested us was whether popular historymaking had changed over time. Unfortunately, surveys conducted at one point in time are not particularly useful for measuring change and continuity. Nevertheless, we tested out various questions—e.g., "In what ways do you believe your knowledge or understanding of the past is similar to and different from your parents?"—that might give us clues. None of them provided particularly telling responses. We did get some useful answers to the question we ultimately asked: "In what ways do you think differently about the past now than you did when you were younger?" That respondents generally answered this question in terms of changes in their personal development instead of changes in the world around them was itself an intriguing finding that could be the subject of another survey.

In deciding on the questions, we consulted extensively with historians and sociologists who study African Americans, Mexican Americans, and American Indians. They encouraged us to develop some additional questions for the minority samples, which are described below. Thus, in those samples we asked African Americans about their sense of connection to the past on Martin Luther King Jr.'s birthday, and we questioned Mexican Americans about Cinco de Mayo, which celebrates the Battle of Puebla on May 5, 1862, in which French forces were defeated near Mexico City. (We tried, however, to phrase these questions in a neutral fashion that would not suggest an expected answer.) We also asked both groups (as well as American Indians) about their views on the relationship of their history to the history of other Americans—for example, "How much of a common history do you think you share with other Americans?" Trying to get at the relationship of African Americans to Africa and Mexican Americans to Mexico, we asked minority respondents: "Is the past of any other place in the world more important to you than the past of the United States?" and then followed up if they said "yes." These additional questions—as well as our decision to ask certain questions of a higher percentage of minority respondents—partially explain why the three minority samples averaged between forty-seven and fifty-nine minutes, whereas the interviews in the national sample averaged thirty minutes.[4]

Choosing Respondents

Since one of our most important goals was to use a survey as a baseline for future investigations, we needed a random and representative national survey. Here we followed standard survey practice that considers samples as small as 800 people adequate for a national sample from which to make statistically valid comparisons among large subgroups within the population—e.g., men and women, high school graduates and college graduates, people under 30 and those over 65. Although earlier chapters discuss those statistical variations, some readers will be particularly interested in the more detailed tables of cross-tabulations and regressions provided in appendix 2 and especially on our Web site.

To ensure that a random sample of Americans would be called, the CSR did random-digit dialing to a list of phone exchanges randomly selected from all phone exchanges in the United States. This approach is more expensive than calling numbers drawn from a phone directory, but it does not exclude people with unpublished or new listings. In other words, any household in the continental United States with a telephone could have been called as part of the national sample.[5] In order to make sure that anyone within that household could be part of the sample, we took additional steps. First, we called to determine that it was a residence; many of the randomly generated phone numbers, as expected, were businesses or numbers not in service. Second, we asked the person who answered the phone to tell us the number of people over the age of eighteen in the household. The interviewer's computer then randomly selected the actual respondent from this group. Since some people are more likely to answer the phone than others, this procedure enabled us to have a group of respondents that better represented the overall population in terms of age, sex, and household status.

Our piloting had suggested that members of "minority" groups had some distinctive responses to our questions about the past. Melissa Keane, for example, described the Arizona pilot interviews with nonwhite respondents as particularly "compelling."[6] Moreover, because debates about the place of history in our national culture—specifically about how history should be taught in the schools—have focused, in part, on the relationship between minority and majority cultures, we thought it especially important to hear the voices of members of minority groups. We wanted to know about bases for developing a common curriculum as well as, more generally, about the possible relationship between cultural background on the one hand, and attitudes toward and experiences of the past on the other hand. Unfortunately, a nationwide random sample will not provide sufficient numbers to do that fully. Our 808 national interviews, for example, included 76 African Americans, but only 20 who identified themselves as Native Americans, 33 as Latinos, and 13 as Asian Americans.

We decided, therefore, to develop three minority samples (African Americans, Mexican Americans, and American Indians), using procedures that would give us the most representative samples within the constraints of our budget. For each group we wanted to interview about 200 additional people, since samples of this size provide sufficient statistical precision to compare different minority groups, though not to make fine-grained analyses of them. For African Americans, our initial plan was to keep the same random-digit dialing we used for the national sample but to make a higher percentage of calls in areas with high concentrations of African Americans. Interviewers would begin by asking about age, education, and race (questions that came at the end of the national sample questionnaire). If we learned that the interviewee was not an African American, Mexican American, or American Indian, we would ask four brief questions about the past and then terminate the interview. This approach would make it possible for any African American with a telephone to be included in the survey, even though some (those living in areas with lesser concentrations of black residents) would have a smaller chance of being included.

Using a system developed by a commercial firm, Genesys Sampling Systems of Ft. Washington, Pennsylvania, we randomly generated a list of telephone exchanges and then used demographic data to divide them into three groups—exchanges where the black population was greater than 75 percent; exchanges where it was between 50 and 75 percent; and exchanges where it was below 50 percent. Unfortunately, making calls to phone exchanges with black concentrations of under 50 percent proved prohibitively expensive. We completed only one interview after 400 phone calls in low-concentration exchanges. As a result, we decided to focus our efforts on the medium- and high-concentration exchanges, and as time and money pressures became more intense, we did most of our calling in the high-concentration exchanges. Of the 224 completed interviews in the black sample, 161 were done in high-concentration exchanges and 48 in the medium-density areas. (We also included 14 African Americans whom we reached while making calls in Mexican American and American Indian areas.)

The African Americans in our minority sample were thus atypical in that they were more likely than African Americans in general to live in areas with high concentrations of black residents. (About 15.9 percent of African American households in the United States with telephones are in areas of high-concentration African American telephone exchanges; another 13.6 percent are in medium-concentration exchanges.) Because patterns of black-white segregation extend across class lines, our sample was not dominated by poorer and "inner-city" blacks. We did not, for example, interview any black residents of Fairfax County, a middle-class suburb of Washington, D.C. with a heavily white population, but we did interview residents of Prince George's County, a middle-class suburb of Washington with a majority black population. A more systematic way of demonstrating this point is to compare the 224 black respondents in the minority sample with the black population of the United States. Kennedy and Botsko did this in their AAPOR paper and concluded that our "sampling methods resulted in a diverse group of respondents that came fairly close to approximating the national population of African Americans."[7]

Our sample and the overall population differed most in place of residence. Whereas only one fifth of the American black population lives in the Midwest, one third of our respondents came from that region. On the other hand, 9 percent of blacks live in the West, but only 4 percent of our respondents were from the West. These differences reflect the greater concentration of high-density black areas in the Midwest as well as the generally greater difficulty in reaching respondents in the West.[8] To a lesser degree, our minority sample underrepresented men, younger and older people, the less educated, and the poor. Many of these differences, however, were relatively modest. For example, 47.7 percent of our sample had household incomes under $25,000 per year versus 59.3 percent of the overall black population; 12.2 percent of our sample (versus 17.7 percent of the African American population) was 18–24 years old; 62.8 percent of our sample (compared to 54.5 percent of the black population) was female. More important, these differences are typical of all phone surveys. The bias toward the better educated and more affluent, for example, results partly from the large proportion (an estimated 15.6 percent) of African American households without telephone service.[9]

The respondents in our special black sample were not only reasonably representative of the nation's black population in sociodemographic terms, they also seem likely to have answered our questions in the same ways as the more broadly drawn black sample. Here, our basis of comparison is the 76 black Americans we reached as part of the national sample. Although African Americans who lived in high concentrations with other African Americans might be expected to think differently about the past (or experience the past differently) than those who lived primarily among whites, they actually gave strikingly similar answers to those of blacks in the national sample. We read and analyzed the text of the 76 interviews with black respondents before the special black sample was undertaken. The subsequent interviews confirmed our initial hypotheses based on reading the open-ended answers given in the national sample.

The answers that black respondents in the two different samples gave to closed-ended, quantifiable questions were also quite similar. In 18 of the 24 questions for which we have quantifiable answers, black respondents in both samples stood in the same relation to the national sample. For example, black respondents in the national sample gave a 8.0 "trust" score to history museums and those in the minority sample gave an 8.1 score; both were lower than the overall result in the national sample (8.4). In six cases there were divergences; they were usually small. For instance, black respondents in the national sample gave a 7.1 "connectedness" score to holiday celebrations, which was higher than the overall national sample (7.0) and blacks in the minority sample (6.9), but obviously not by very much.

Even when the differences between the samples appear greater, they do not turn out to be statistically significant except in one case. For example, more blacks in the national sample than in the black sample (81.8 percent versus 71.3 percent) said that they had seen a film or television program about the past in the previous year. But using a "difference of proportions test"—a standard technique for measuring the statistical significance of the difference between independent samples—we find that this difference is not significant at the .05 level. (To be significant at the .05 level would mean that in only 5 out of 100 samples like the ones used here would we find a difference as large as the one we observe if the populations from which the samples were drawn were, in fact, identical. In other words, a statistically significant difference in our data is one that is unlikely to have occurred simply because of the random fluctuation inherent in survey samples.)

That same test also belies the statistical significance of seeming differences in answers to the question about which area of the past respondents considered most important. In the national sample 18.4 percent put "the past of your ethnic or racial group" first; 28.1 percent of the respondents in the African American sample did the same. It is plausible to speculate that on this question the different manner of creating the samples affected the answers and that those who live in areas with higher concentrations of black residents are more likely to see the past of black America as important. But the difference of proportion test tells us that we would need a difference of 11.3 percent (rather than 9.7 percent) for it to be considered statistically significant.[10]

The connectedness and trust questions, because they were done on a 1–10 scale, permit us to use a more sensitive "difference of means" test to compare the samples. Even so, the differences in the samples turn out to be statistically significant in only one case—the question about how connected to the past respondents felt when studying history in school. Blacks in the minority sample gave schools a lower connectedness score than the national mean (4.9 versus 5.7), but blacks in the national sample gave a slightly higher number (6.0). Could this be the result of the different schooling experiences that African Americans in heavily black areas might have? This is highly speculative, since we don't know for sure that people who currently live in integrated neighborhoods went to school in similar neighborhoods.

Another possible explanation for this difference had to do with some small differences in the questionnaires. For example, because the screening process required us to ask the respondent's race early in the questionnaire and because the minority sample included an additional question comparing Martin Luther King Jr.'s birthday with other holidays, the respondent might have been thinking in more racially inflected terms by the time we got to this question.[11] It is also possible, of course, that this difference is just a statistical accident—in comparing differences between the samples on twenty-four different questions, it would not be implausible for one to be a "false positive."[12]

Because the special black sample was not particularly different (either in their demographic composition or their answers) from the African Americans in the national sample, we have not distinguished between the two groups in most of the book. When we report on the open-ended responses to questions, we don't indicate whether they came in the national sample or the minority sample. This procedure seems defensible because we are most interested in giving a flavor of different black voices that we heard, because each of the black respondents is offering an individual perspective, and because we didn't find any systematic differences among the black respondents in the two samples. We have also combined the quantifiable answers of the two groups, because this makes the data much easier to follow and separating the answers would not add much to the argument.

We had initially planned a sample of Latinos, but after consulting with survey specialists and experts on Latino Americans, we decided that it made more sense to focus on a particular Latino group. We selected Mexican Americans, who make up 61 percent of the nation's Hispanic population. We used a similar sampling approach to the one employed for African Americans, but focused on high-concentration (70 percent or more) Hispanic-surnamed phone exchanges in Arizona, New Mexico, Colorado, California, and Texas. We chose the states and this approach based on the sampling strategy used in the Latino National Political Survey. That survey spent about $1,000,000 to develop a plan for efficiently surveying Mexican Americans.[13] Although we did most of the calls in the high-concentration phone exchanges, we made some calls to a sample of numbers from all exchanges in the five states.

Once again, the greatest difference between our Mexican American respondents and the Mexican American population of the United States involved place of residence. About 16 percent of the nation's 13.5 million Mexican Americans live outside the five states where we surveyed, but only 2 percent of our sample did. (These six people were picked up in doing the African American and Indian samples and then included in the overall Mexican American sample.) But a more important difference had to with the five states where we made our calls. Although only 29 percent of all Mexican Americans live in Texas, 63 percent of our survey respondents did. By contrast, whereas California is home to 45 percent of all Mexican Americans, only 29 percent of our respondents lived there. One reason for the discrepancy is the large number of high-concentration Mexican American areas in Texas, particularly south Texas. Another reason was the higher response rate in Texas than in California. The lower response rate in California probably stems from the generally greater difficulty in reaching respondents in California and the concurrent campaign for the passage of anti-illegal-immigrant Proposition 187 in that state, which probably made Mexican Americans less responsive to calls from non-Hispanic interviewers.

Despite these geographic discrepancies, our Mexican American sample matched the overall Mexican American population in a number of other ways. We had similar numbers of low-income respondents as in the overall population (about 31 percent in both cases had incomes under $15,000, for example). And the match in ages was quite close. Our survey included fewer high-income Mexican Americans, perhaps a result of doing more interviews in south Texas and fewer in California. Women, as in the black sample, were overrepresented (61 percent versus 48 percent). People born in the United States also appear to have been overrepresented (62 percent versus 54 percent), but given general uneasiness over questions of citizenship, our numbers may overstate the number of native-born respondents.

In order to include the experiences of recent Mexican immigrants, we asked Mexican American respondents whether they were more comfortable conversing in Spanish or English and had a Spanish speaker call those who preferred Spanish. We did more than one quarter of the 196 Mexican American interviews in Spanish.

We faced a more serious challenge as we tried to implement our original plan of doing a nationwide sample of American Indians. As we consulted with specialists, we learned that this would require an extraordinary number of phone calls. We also gradually realized that such a sampling would distort the experience of distinctive and often widely scattered tribes.[14] On the advice of leading American Indian scholars, we decided to focus instead on a single reservation and selected the Pine Ridge reservation in southwestern South Dakota, home of the Oglala Sioux.

Pine Ridge, the second-largest reservation in the United States, covers two million acres—an expanse bigger than Connecticut or Rhode Island—and is home to 25,000 people.[15] We developed a technique for randomly calling phone numbers in one major section of Pine Ridge. (We are not specifying that area here in order to preserve as much anonymity as possible for our respondents.) Our sample differed from the overall Pine Ridge population in some ways that are similar to the other samples—for example, we talked to more women, fewer people under 30, and more people over 65. More significantly, three fifths of our sample reported that they had household incomes under $25,000 per year, whereas the census described more than four fifths as being in this category. (The disparity was even greater for those with household incomes under $15,000 per year.)

Moreover, the general population of Pine Ridge seems to include three times as many non-high school graduates as our sample, and our sample had five times as many college graduates as the overall population. We would speculate that lack of telephones may have had a greater effect in biasing results on Pine Ridge toward the better educated and more affluent than in any of our other samples. We don't have figures for phone service, but about 16 percent of Pine Ridge homes have no electricity and 20 percent have no plumbing; probably the number without phone service is higher.[16] Even so, the notion of affluence is relative; most of our respondents, like most Pine Ridge residents, were poor. The Pine Ridge residents we interviewed were more than twice as likely as respondents in the national sample to have income under $25,000 a year. Indeed, Pine Ridge reservation is one of the poorest places in the United States; estimates of unemployment run as high as 75 percent, and Shannon County, South Dakota (which lies entirely within the reservation) is the fourth poorest county in the nation.[17]

Although this sample can only claim to be reasonably representative of the Oglala Sioux residents of Pine Ridge in telephone households and not of all American Indians, this was the most cost-effective way to incorporate the perspective of at least one major group of American Indians. Further, we thought readers might find the perspectives of the Pine Ridge Sioux particularly intriguing, since that reservation had acquired much national visibility through protests and films and the presence of the Wounded Knee memorial.

To have a limited basis of comparison to the 186 Sioux residents of Pine Ridge, we also called 28 American Indian residents of the Minneapolis area because Minneapolis is the city with the highest proportion of Indians among its inhabitants. (In addition, we interviewed eleven people who identified themselves as American Indians from other parts of the country whom we reached when calling Mexican Americans and African Americans, as well another twenty Native Americans we called in the national sample.) Indeed, another reason for selecting Pine Ridge was that it was near the only major city that had particular census tracts where more than 50 percent of the population was made up of American Indians. In addition to calling people from those census tracts (using reverse phone directories), we also called people from some lists of Minneapolis-area

Indians that we were able to obtain. It had been our original intention to call 100 Indian residents of Minneapolis, but the calls to the census tracts proved more difficult to complete than we had anticipated, and we decided that it would instead be worthwhile to have a larger sample of Pine Ridge residents.

We had also initially planned on surveying a sample of Asian Americans, possibly focusing on Chinese Americans. But we could not readily come up with a cost-effective way to sample this group. One problem is that Chinese Americans are a much smaller group (about 1.6 million people in 1990) than Mexican Americans (13.5 million) or African Americans (30 million). And while there are concentrations of Chinese Americans in particular areas, the data on such concentrations in specific telephone exchanges are not readily available and the differences between the Chinese American populations of particular areas (in terms of income, education, and place of birth) are often great. Moreover, we faced the additional problem of locating a sufficient number of qualified survey interviewers in Bloomington, Indiana who could conduct interviews in Mandarin and Cantonese. We reluctantly canceled that portion of the study.

Besides close studies of other groups within the United States, we also need to find out whether these patterns are replicated in other nations and cultures. Attempts by colleagues in Britain (Patricia Clavin) and Australia (Paula Hamilton and her team) to develop surveys of how people in those countries understand and use the past are encouraging. The largest significance of our findings can only become clear when similar studies have been done elsewhere.[18]

Facing up to the Realities of Telephone Surveys

Although our survey topic and some of our survey methods were unconventional, we faced many of the same problems and limitations as any telephone survey. The questions you ask and the way you ask them will affect the answers you receive. That was just as true in our survey as in any other. For instance, asking about "the past" rather than "history" emphasized certain answers over others. If we had asked people to name an important historical figure we would have received a different set of answers than we did from asking people to "name a person, either a historical figure or one from your personal past, who has particularly affected you."

As with all surveys, responses were also shaped by the context in which the questions were asked. Without another systematic study, there is no way to know which contextual factors may have affected the responses we received. Some of those factors are common to all phone surveys—for example, what confidences are people prepared to offer a distant stranger? Others would have been shared by almost any survey carried out by the Center for Survey Research at Indiana University—for example, did it matter that the calls came from a university in the Midwest or that most of interviewers sounded young (almost three quarters were under 25), white, and female (more than three quarters were women), and started out by speaking in English?[19]

Probably the best known of these potential "interviewer effects" are those involving cross-racial interviewing. We were concerned about that since only one of our interviewers was nonwhite (an African American woman), and we did a substantial number of interviews among nonwhite populations. We have no way of knowing whether this procedure influenced the answers we received. Survey researchers who have studied the effect of the interviewer's race generally conclude that it makes little difference in regard to nonracial subjects. Thus, it is unlikely that the answers to our questions about, for example, what activities people did in the previous year or how connected to the past they felt on different occasions were affected by having a largely white interviewing staff. A few of our questions (e.g., Which area of the past is most important to you?) did touch on race, and respondents did talk extensively about race in their open-ended answers. But they did not necessarily get into the areas that researchers find most affected by the race of the interviewer—for instance, expressions of hostility or closeness to whites by black respondents.[20]

Since we are arguing that black and Sioux respondents expressed a significant amount of racial feeling and racial distinctiveness, the use of white interviewers probably only served to understate the degree of that feeling. In other words, we suspect that the use of African American or Indian interviewers would further strengthen rather than undercut our conclusions. It is possible that these interviewer effects also understated ethnic distinctiveness in the answers given by Mexican Americans, but we suspect that the larger impact in that sample, as we note in chapter 5, was to encourage more patriotic answers among people worried about current anti-immigrant feeling.

Presumably, the particular time that we called also made a difference. (Almost all the calls in the national sample were made in April and May of 1994. We began the minority samples in June 1994, but did not complete the last of those interviews until mid-November of that year.) Calling in 1994 probably meant that we were a bit more likely to hear about *Schindler's List*, which won the Academy Award for Best Picture in March of that year, or about Richard Nixon and Jacqueline Kennedy, both of whom died while we were doing the survey. Similarly, people in the national sample, who were generally called in the spring, might have been more likely to talk about Easter, just as Mexican Americans, some of whom were called in the fall, might have been more likely to mention Thanksgiving. The appearance of Proposition 187 on the California ballot in the fall of 1994 may have influenced some of the Mexican Americans' answers, even though only one person mentioned it explicitly.[21] There is no way to do survey research insulated from particular historical or social contexts, and this survey, like all others (and indeed like all forms of social and historical research) was inevitably shaped by the people who carried it out and the times in which they lived.

Another important way that our survey was shaped by the realities of the moment had to do with the problem of getting people to spend time on the phone with strangers. As survey researchers know all too well (and anyone with a telephone probably recognizes), this problem has gotten much worse in the recent past along with the explosion in telemarketing and telephone soliciting for charities and causes. Americans have grown increasingly irritated with being interrupted by unrequested phone calls, and their response has increasingly been to simply hang up. We admit to having done the same thing.

Since one of the goals of surveys like ours is to get a random sample of views, these hang-ups ("refusals" as the survey researchers call them) are a potential problem. The worry, of course, is that the people who are willing to talk are in some way unrepresentative. We don't think that this was a particular problem in our survey, but we should acknowledge that many people refused to talk with us.

In the national sample, for example, the CSR called 2,105 different phone numbers (not counting the calls to numbers that were determined to be either businesses or out of service) to complete the 808 interviews. They classified these 1,300 uncompleted interviews into four categories. Despite at least eight different attempts (including twice each during a weekday morning, afternoon, and evening and the weekend), 250 people "never answered." Another 121 people were away during the entire survey period, were ill, or didn't speak English or Spanish.[22] The CSR categorized another 211 people as "persistently unavailable" when repeated attempts (at different times of the day) to contact the selected respondent failed. Finally, in 772 cases, people who answered the phone refused to participate despite at least two attempts by the CSR to win their coopera-tion. These include 187 hang-ups that occurred before our interviewers were even able to establish that they were speaking to a residence.

In these and other cases, it is difficult to discern the reasons for the refusals, even though the interviewers recorded detailed notes on their efforts. In our rough count of responses, the most common explanation for refusing to participate was a generic comment like "not interested" that people often use when trying to get off the phone quickly. For example, on Sunday, April 24, 1994, an interviewer reached a woman, who listened to the background information about the confidentiality of the survey and then responded that "she wasn't interested." The interviewer tried to explain the importance of getting everyone's opinions and then offered to call back if this was a bad time. She said it was, and the interviewer arranged to call back the next day. The interviewer's notes record her frus-tration: "I identified myself, and the female respondent remembered talk-ing to us before. However, after she stated remembering our previous calls, she politely, but firmly, said she still wasn't interested and hung up. I was not able to explain the purpose of the interview or do much in the way of conversion." The interviewer tried one more time five days later; the respondent repeated once again that she "wasn't interested" and hung up.

Overall, minority respondents were more likely to refuse to be inter-viewed—a pattern well known to survey researchers.[23] Some of these refusals no doubt reflected the suspicion that a Mexican American in south Texas or an African American in Brooklyn might have about a call from an obviously white interviewer from Indiana. And, indeed, many of the minority refusals came almost immediately. We had 348 refusals (and 165 completions) in calls to high-density African American phone exchanges, but 170 of those refusals came before we could establish the identity of the potential respondent. Similarly, the Mexican American sample included 207 completions with 407 refusals—168 of these coming before residency was established. American Indians from Pine Ridge were, however, more receptive to our calls; we had 186 completions and only 126 refusals.

Our immediate concern was whether our refusal rate was "high." John Kennedy said the refusal rate for this survey was the same as for other sur-veys of this length that CSR conducted at the same time. Our survey was unusually long; respondents were told that they would likely devote thirty minutes to the survey, and this scared away some people. After "not interested," probably the next most common comment among those who refused to be interviewed was "not enough time."[24] And we did our interviews at a time when refusal rates were rising, presumably because of the boom in telemarketing. Our refusal rates might have been high five years earlier, but not in 1994.[25] Although we would have liked to talk to all the people we called, we have no reasons to suspect that those who were willing to talk with us differed significantly from those who refused.

Our interviewers used some methods employed by ethnographers and oral historians, but this study was neither a true ethnography nor an oral history. Such studies would supply enormously rich insight into particular people, but they cannot readily offer the representativeness of a national telephone sample that reaches a much wider range of people. Still, that search for representativeness meant we were required to follow some of the standard features of phone interviews, in which interviewers rapidly type out the responses from respondents and repeat them back for accuracy in recording. Not surprisingly, such techniques result in a less freely flowing conversation than would occur in an oral history interview.

Moreover, the pressure of quickly getting down respondents' words inevitably results in typing errors. Because this survey required considerable typing by interviewers, "keeping up with what the respondent was saying in typing down text" was one of the most frequent difficulties cited by interviewers in the postsurvey interviews. As a result, we have occasionally taken the liberty of silently adding missing words and correcting errors in order to get the respondents' words into something closer to what they actually said and to improve the flow of the words. We tried hard, however, not to alter the meanings or even the nuances of the answers.

Although our survey shared the limitations of all telephone survey research and the possible biases introduced by the method should always be in the reader's mind, we do not believe that the answers we received were unusually unrepresentative or distorted. Quite the contrary, we (and the interviewers as well) were often quite surprised by the fullness and candor with which people answered these inquiries.

Tables

General Findings by Racial/Ethnic Group

National Sample Findings by Demographic Characteristics

The first twenty tables presented here include cross-tabulations between the closed-ended questions asked and major sociodemographic categories. The last three tables offer regressions, which allow us to sort out the effects of different variables. For example, in some cases, an apparent relationship between participation in an activity and income is really the result of educational differences. For more discussion of the samples and the tables, see appendix 1. For more detailed tables, see http://chnm.gmu.edu/survey.

TABLE 1

Participation in Activities That Relate to the Past—by Racial/Ethnic Group

We asked our respondents if they had participated in each of 10 "activities related to the past . . . during the last 12 months." The table below reports the percentage of respondents in our national sample and each of four racial/ethnic groups who reported participating in the activities in the far left column. The numbers in parentheses indicate how many respondents in each group answered the given question. In this and the next three tables, the Mexican American and Pine Ridge figures come from separate "minority" samples; the African American figures combine the minority and national samples, as explained in appendix 1.

| During the last 12 months, have you . . . | Racial/Ethnic Groups | | | | |
	National Sample	White American	African American	Mexican American	Pine Ridge Oglala Sioux
Looked at photographs with family and friends?	91% (808)	92% (624)	88% (300)	87% (195)	82% (184)
Taken any photographs or videos to preserve memories?	83 (808)	85 (624)	71 (300)	76 (195)	66 (182)
Watched any movies or television programs about the past?	81 (803)	82 (620)	74 (298)	68 (195)	72 (185)
Attended a family reunion or reunion of some other group with whom you have a shared experience?	64 (808)	63 (624)	63 (300)	68 (195)	59 (182)
Visited any history museums or historic sites?	57 (807)	58 (623)	46 (300)	46 (195)	65 (182)
Read any books about the past?	53 (805)	54 (621)	45 (300)	35 (195)	45 (185)
Participated in any hobbies or worked on any collections related to the past?	39 (807)	40 (623)	30 (300)	25 (193)	37 (182)
Looked into the history of your family or worked on your family tree?	36 (807)	36 (623)	29 (300)	26 (195)	54 (185)
Written in a journal or diary?	29 (808)	29 (624)	24 (300)	16 (195)	20 (183)
Participated in a group devoted to studying, preserving, or presenting the past?	20 (808)	20 (624)	21 (300)	15 (194)	25 (182)

TABLE 2

Trustworthiness of Sources of Information About the Past—
by Racial/Ethnic Group

We asked our respondents for the following information about seven "places where people might get information about the past": "Please tell [us] how trustworthy you think each is as a source of information about the past using a 1 to 10 scale, where 1 means not at all trustworthy and 10 means very trustworthy." The table below reports the mean score our national sample and four racial/ethnic groups gave the sources of information in the far left column. The numbers in parentheses indicate the number of respondents on which each mean is based.

How trustworthy do you think _____ are as a source of information about the past?	Racial/Ethnic Groups				
	National Sample	White American	African American	Mexican American	Pine Ridge Oglala Sioux
Museums	8.4	8.5	8.1	8.6	7.1
	(778)	(608)	(283)	(185)	(176)
Personal accounts from your grandparents or other relatives	8.0	8.0	8.4	8.3	8.8
	(789)	(615)	(289)	(189)	(181)
Conversation with someone who was there	7.8	7.8	7.9	8.2	8.0
	(790)	(611)	(290)	(188)	(177)
College history professors	7.3	7.4	7.0	8.3	7.1
	(692)	(537)	(261)	(172)	(161)
High school history teachers	6.6	6.7	6.2	7.5	5.9
	(771)	(594)	(293)	(189)	(178)
Nonfiction books	6.4	6.4	5.6	6.6	5.4
	(747)	(583)	(278)	(181)	(169)
Movies or television programs about the past	5.0	4.9	5.2	6.0	4.2
	(783)	(610)	(291)	(189)	(180)

TABLE 3

Connectedness to the Past on Six Occasions—
by Racial/Ethnic Group

We asked our respondents for the following information about six "occasions": "On a scale of 1 to 10, where 1 means you felt no connection to the past and 10 means you felt a strong connection to the past, please tell [us] how connected to the past you felt on the following." The table below reports the mean score our national sample and four racial/ethnic groups gave the occasions in the far left column. The numbers in parentheses indicate the number of respondents on which each mean is based.

How connected to the past do you feel when ...	Racial/Ethnic Groups				
	National Sample	White American	African American	Mexican American	Pine Ridge Oglala Sioux
Gathering with your family?	7.9	7.8	8.3	7.7	7.6
	(795)	(615)	(291)	(192)	(180)
Visiting a museum or historic site?	7.3	7.4	6.5	6.9	6.7
	(782)	(609)	(270)	(180)	(177)
Celebrating holidays?	7.0	7.0	7.0	7.5	6.5
	(797)	(616)	(295)	(193)	(177)
Reading a book about the past?	6.5	6.7	6.0	6.1	5.5
	(775)	(602)	(280)	(179)	(166)
Watching a movie or television program about the past?	6.0	6.0	6.1	6.2	4.6
	(778)	(603)	(288)	(189)	(177)
Studying history in school?	5.7	5.7	5.2	5.8	4.1
	(788)	(610)	(290)	(183)	(180)

TABLE 4

Most Important Pasts—by Racial/Ethnic Group

We asked each of our respondents the following question: "Knowing about the past of which of the following four areas or groups is most important to you: the past of your family, the past of your racial or ethnic group, the past of the community in which you now live, or the past of the United States?" The table below reports the percentage of respondents in our national sample and four racial/ethnic groups who choose each of the pasts in the far left column.

Knowing about the past of which of the following four areas or groups is most important to you?	Racial/Ethnic Groups				
	National Sample	White	African American	Mexican American	Pine Ridge Oglala Sioux
Your family	66%	69%	59%	61%	50%
Your racial or ethnic group	8	4	26	10	38
The community in which you now live	4	3	4	7	7
The United States	22	24	11	22	5
	N=796	N=616	N=297	N=191	N=176

TABLE 5

Participation in Activities That Relate to the Past by Age—National Sample

We asked our respondents if they had participated in each of 10 "activities that relate to the past . . . during the last 12 months." The table below divides the national sample into four age groups, and reports the percentage of respondents who participated in the activities listed in the far left column. The numbers in parentheses indicate the number of respondents of the given age group who answered the question.

   In this table and the next sixteen, the chi-square significance test in the far right column measures the likelihood that the observed association between the independent variable (in the table below, "age") and the dependent variable (in the table below, "participation in the given activity") is caused by chance. Among statisticians a chi-square of .05 is a conventionally accepted threshold of statistical significance; values of less than .05 are commonly referred to as "statistically significant." In practical terms, a chi-square of less than .05 means that if, in fact, there was no association in the population between the independent and dependent variables, the observed association would be expected to occur by chance fewer than 5 times in 100 samples of the type we used. Thus, when the chi-square is less than .05, we can be confident in rejecting the possibility that no association exists between the independent and dependent variables. NS indicates that the chi-square is not significant using the .05 threshold.

During the last 12 months, have you . . .	Age				
	Total National Sample	18 to 29	30 to 44	45 to 64	65 and Older	Significance Test
Looked at photographs with family and friends?	91% (808)	95% (154)	91% (308)	93% (219)	85% (121)	.02
Taken photographs or videos to preserve memories?	83 (808)	94 (154)	88 (308)	84 (219)	60 (121)	< .001
Watched any movies or television programs about the past?	81 (803)	80 (153)	82 (305)	85 (219)	76 (121)	NS
Attended a family reunion or a reunion of some other group of people with whom you have a shared experience?	64 (808)	64 (154)	63 (308)	63 (219)	70 (121)	NS
Visited any history museums or historic sites?	57 (807)	56 (154)	61 (307)	56 (219)	50 (121)	NS
Read any books about the past?	53 (805)	49 (154)	51 (307)	58 (219)	52 (119)	NS
Participated in any hobbies or worked on any collections related to the past?	39 (807)	43 (154)	38 (308)	41 (128)	36 (121)	NS

TABLE 5 (Continued)
Participation in Activities That Relate to the Past by Age—National Sample

During the last 12 months, have you ...	Age					
	Total National Sample	18 to 29	30 to 44	45 to 64	65 and Older	Significance Test
Looked into the history of your family or worked on your family tree?	36 (807)	30 (154)	38 (308)	35 (219)	42 (120)	NS
Written in a journal or diary?	29 (808)	42 (154)	31 (308)	23 (219)	22 (121)	< .001
Participated in a group devoted to studying, preserving, or presenting the past?	20 (808)	23 (154)	19 (308)	18 (219)	23 (121)	NS

TABLE 6

Participation in Activities That Relate to the Past by Gender—National Sample

We asked our respondents if they had participated in each of 10 "activities that relate to the past . . . during the last 12 months." The table below divides the national sample by gender, and reports the percentage of respondents who participated in the activities listed in the far left column. The numbers in parentheses indicate the number of respondents of each gender who answered the question.

During the last 12 months, have you . . .	Gender Groups			
	Total National Sample	Men	Women	Significance Test
Looked at photographs with family and friends?	91%	90%	92%	NS
	(808)	(369)	(439)	
Taken photographs or videos to preserve memories?	83	82	84	NS
	(808)	(369)	(439)	
Watched any movies or television programs about the past?	81	83	80	NS
	(803)	(367)	(436)	
Attended a family reunion or reunion of some other group with whom you have a shared experience?	64	59	68	.01
	(808)	(369)	(439)	
Visited any history museums or historic sites?	57	61	53	.02
	(808)	(369)	(438)	
Read any books about the past?	53	52	53	NS
	(805)	(368)	(437)	
Participated in any hobbies or worked on any collections related to the past?	39	39	39	NS
	(807)	(369)	(438)	
Looked into the history of your family or worked on your family tree?	36	29	42	< .001
	(807)	(368)	(439)	
Written in a journal or diary?	29	24	34	.00
	(808)	(369)	(439)	
Participated in a group devoted to studying, preserving, or presenting the past?	20	18	22	NS
	(808)	(369)	(439)	

TABLE 7
Participation in Activities That Relate to the Past by Education—
National Sample

We asked our respondents if they had participated in each of 10 "activities that relate to the past . . . during the last 12 months." The table below divides the national sample into four education groups and reports the percentage of respondents who participated in the activities listed in the far left column. The numbers in parentheses indicate the number of respondents of the given education group who answered the question.

During the last 12 months, have you . . .	Education					
	Total National Sample	No High School Diploma	High School Diploma	Some College	4-Year Degree and Up	Signi-ficance Test
Looked at photographs with family and friends?	91% (808)	84% (86)	90% (207)	94% (213)	92% (300)	.03
Taken photographs or videos to preserve memories?	83 (808)	65 (86)	81 (207)	91 (213)	85 (300)	< .001
Watched any movies or television programs about the past?	81 (803)	66 (86)	77 (205)	85 (212)	86 (298)	< .001
Attended a family reunion or reunion of some other group with whom you have a shared experience?	64 (808)	62 (86)	56 (207)	65 (213)	70 (300)	.01
Visited any history museums or historic sites?	57 (807)	33 (86)	43 (207)	59 (212)	72 (300)	< .001
Read any books about the past?	53 (805)	30 (86)	39 (207)	62 (211)	63 (299)	< .001
Participated in any hobbies or worked on any collections related to the past?	39 (807)	30 (86)	36 (206)	43 (213)	41 (300)	NS
Looked into the history of your family or worked on your family tree?	36 (807)	26 (85)	33 (207)	41 (213)	38 (300)	NS
Written in a journal or diary?	29 (808)	16 (86)	17 (207)	40 (213)	34 (300)	< .001
Participated in a group devoted to studying, preserving, or presenting the past?	20 (808)	12 (86)	14 (207)	21 (213)	27 (300)	< .001

TABLE 8

Participation in Activities That Relate to the Past by Income—National Sample

We asked our respondents if they had participated in each of 10 "activities that relate to the past . . . during the last 12 months." The table below divides the national sample into six income groups, and reports the percentage of respondents who participated in the activities listed in the far left column. The numbers in parentheses indicate the number of respondents of the given income group who answered the question.

During the last 12 months, have you . . .

	Total National Sample	$0 to $14,999	$15,000 to $24,999	$25,000 to $34,999	$35,000 to $49,999	$50,000 to $74,999	$75,000 and Up	Significance Test
						Income		
Looked at photographs with family and friends?	91% (808)	87% (92)	87% (123)	92% (162)	95% (149)	94% (125)	92% (118)	NS
Taken photographs or videos to preserve memories?	83 (808)	63 (92)	71 (123)	86 (162)	89 (149)	92 (125)	92 (118)	< .001
Watched any movies or television programs about the past?	81 (803)	78 (91)	75 (122)	81 (161)	87 (149)	85 (124)	84 (117)	NS
Attended a family reunion group of people with or reunion of some other whom you have a shared experience?	64 (808)	59 (92)	63 (123)	63 (162)	63 (149)	70 (125)	67 (118)	NS
Visited any history museums or historic sites?	57 (807)	48 (92)	50 (123)	52 (162)	60 (149)	63 (124)	72 (118)	.00

TABLE 8 (continued)

Participation in Activities That Relate to the Past by Income—National Sample

During the last 12 months, have you . . .

	Total National Sample	Income						Significance Test
		$0 to $14,999	$15,000 to $24,999	$25,000 to $34,999	$35,000 to $49,999	$50,000 to $74,999	$75,000 and Up	
Read any books about the past?	53 (805)	40 (90)	49 (123)	54 (162)	56 (149)	58 (125)	62 (117)	.02
Participated in any hobbies or worked on any collections related to the past?	39 (807)	39 (92)	42 (123)	35 (161)	40 (149)	44 (125)	38 (118)	NS
Looked into your family history or worked on your family tree?	36 (807)	30 (92)	33 (122)	36 (162)	36 (149)	36 (125)	42 (118)	NS
Written in a journal or diary?	29 (808)	25 (92)	27 (123)	31 (162)	32 (149)	28 (125)	31 (118)	NS
Participated in a group devoted to studying, preserving, or presenting the past?	20 (808)	21 (92)	16 (123)	21 (162)	21 (149)	22 (125)	19 (118)	NS

TABLE 9

Trustworthiness of Sources of Information About the Past by Age—
National Sample

We asked our respondents for the following information about seven "places where people might get information about the past": "Please tell [us] how trustworthy you think each is as a source of information about the past using a 1 to 10 scale, where 1 means not at all trustworthy and 10 means very trustworthy." The table below divides the national sample into four age groups, and reports the mean score those four groups gave each of the seven sources of information about the past listed in the far left column. The numbers in parentheses indicate the number of respondents of the given age group who answered the question.

How trustworthy do you think _____ are as a source of information about the past?	Age				
	Total National Sample	19 to 29	30 to 44	45 to 64	65 and Older	Significance Test
Museums	8.4 (778)	8.4 (151)	8.5 (304)	8.5 (213)	8.2 (105)	NS
Personal accounts from your grandparents or other relatives	8.0 (789)	8.0 (152)	7.9 (306)	8.1 (212)	8.4 (114)	.03
Conversation with someone who was there	7.8 (790)	7.9 (154)	7.9 (303)	7.7 (214)	7.6 (113)	NS
College history professors	7.3 (692)	7.6 (136)	7.3 (275)	7.2 (187)	7.1 (89)	NS
High school history teachers	6.6 (771)	6.4 (153)	6.5 (304)	6.5 (212)	7.0 (96)	NS
Nonfiction books	6.4 (747)	6.8 (147)	6.4 (296)	6.3 (206)	6.1 (93)	.04
Movies and television programs about the past	5.0 (783)	4.8 (153)	5.0 (306)	4.9 (212)	5.2 (107)	NS

TABLE 10

Trustworthiness of Sources of Information About the Past by Gender— National Sample

We asked our respondents for the following information about seven "places where people might get information about the past": "Please tell [us] how trustworthy you think each is as a source of information about the past using a 1 to 10 scale, where 1 means not at all trustworthy and 10 means very trustworthy." The table below divides the national sample by gender, and reports the mean score each gender gave each of the seven sources of information about the past listed in the far left column. The numbers in parentheses indicate the number of respondents of each gender who answered the question.

How trustworthy do you think _____ are as a source of information about the past?	Gender			
	Total National Sample	Men	Women	Significance Test
Museums	8.4	8.1	8.6	< .001
	(778)	(360)	(418)	
Personal accounts from your grandparents or other relatives	8.0	7.8	8.2	< .001
	(789)	(361)	(428)	
Conversation with someone who was there	7.8	7.6	8.0	.01
	(790)	(363)	(427)	
College history professors	7.3	7.1	7.5	.02
	(692)	(363)	(363)	
High school history teachers	6.6	6.4	6.7	.04
	(771)	(354)	(417)	
Nonfiction books	6.4	6.4	6.4	NS
	(747)	(398)	(398)	
Movies or television programs about the past	5.0	4.7	5.1	.01
	(783)	(362)	(421)	

TABLE 11

Trustworthiness of Sources of Information About the Past by Education—
National Sample

We asked our respondents for the following information about seven "places where people might get information about the past": "Please tell [us] how trustworthy you think each is as a source of information about the past using a 1 to 10 scale, where 1 means not at all trustworthy and 10 means very trustworthy." The table below divides the national sample into four education groups, and reports the mean score those four groups gave each of the seven sources of information about the past listed in the far left column. The numbers in parentheses indicate the number of respondents of the given education group who answered the question.

How trustworthy do you think _____ are as a source of information about the past?	Education					
	Total National Sample	No High School Diploma	High School Diploma	Some College	4-Year Degree and Up	Signi-ficance Test
Museums	8.4 (778)	8.1 (76)	8.5 (194)	8.4 (210)	8.4 (297)	NS
Personal accounts from your grandparents or other relatives	8.0 (789)	8.1 (80)	8.3 (203)	8.1 (211)	7.8 (294)	.03
Conversation with someone who was there	7.8 (790)	8.1 (82)	7.9 (204)	7.9 (206)	7.6 (296)	.04
College history professors	7.3 (692)	7.9 (67)	7.4 (151)	7.1 (194)	7.2 (279)	.02
High school history teachers	6.6 (771)	7.1 (80)	6.7 (198)	6.3 (203)	6.5 (288)	.02
Nonfiction books	6.4 (747)	5.4 (66)	6.2 (190)	6.5 (205)	6.7 (285)	< .001
Movies or television programs about the past	5.0 (783)	5.5 (80)	5.0 (201)	5.0 (211)	4.7 (290)	.03

TABLE 12

Trustworthiness of Sources of Information About the Past by Income—
National Sample

We asked our respondents for the following information about seven "places where people might get information about the past": "Please tell [us] how trustworthy you think each is as a source of information about the past using a 1 to 10 scale, where 1 means not at all trustworthy and 10 means very trustworthy." The table below divides the national sample into six income groups, and reports the mean score those six groups gave each of the seven sources of information about the past listed in the far left column. The numbers in parentheses indicate the number of respondents of the given income group who answered the question.

How trustworthy do you think _____ are as a source of information about the past?	Total National Sample	Income						Significance Test
		$0 to $14,999	$15,000 to $24,999	$25,000 to $34,999	$35,000 to $49,999	$50,000 to $74,999	$75,000 and Up	
Museums	8.4 (778)	8.3 (82)	8.1 (120)	8.3 (155)	8.8 (146)	8.3 (123)	8.5 (117)	.01
Personal accounts from your grandparents or other relatives	8.0 (789)	8.2 (85)	8.1 (121)	8.2 (160)	8.2 (147)	7.9 (123)	7.6 (117)	NS
Conversation with someone who was there	7.8 (790)	7.9 (85)	8.0 (119)	7.7 (162)	7.8 (147)	7.8 (123)	7.5 (117)	NS
College history professors	7.3 (692)	7.6 (67)	7.4 (104)	7.4 (143)	7.5 (125)	7.0 (112)	7.1 (113)	NS
High school history teachers	6.6 (771)	6.7 (86)	6.6 (116)	6.6 (159)	6.7 (141)	6.4 (122)	6.5 (115)	NS
Nonfiction books	6.4 (747)	5.5 (73)	6.2 (112)	6.6 (156)	6.4 (137)	6.6 (121)	6.5 (115)	.00
Movies or television programs about the past	5.0 (783)	5.1 (84)	5.1 (116)	4.9 (161)	5.2 (146)	4.7 (125)	4.7 (116)	NS

TABLE 13

Connectedness to the Past on Six Occasions by Age—National Sample

We asked our respondents for the following information about six "occasions": "On a scale of 1 to 10, where 1 means you felt no connection to the past and 10 means you felt a strong connection to the past, please tell [us] how connected to the past you felt on the following." The table below divides the national sample into four age groups, and reports the mean score each of those four groups gave the six occasions listed in the far left column for connectedness. The numbers in parentheses indicate the number of respondents of the given age group who answered the question.

How connected to the past do you feel when ...	Age				
	Total National Sample	19 to 29	30 to 44	45 to 64	65 and Older	Significance Test
Gathering with your family?	7.9 (795)	7.6 (152)	7.8 (306)	8.2 (214)	8.0 (117)	NS
Visiting a history museum or historic site?	7.3 (782)	7.1 (151)	7.3 (304)	7.2 (214)	7.5 (108)	NS
Celebrating holidays?	7.0 (797)	6.4 (154)	7.0 (308)	7.3 (217)	7.4 (113)	.01
Reading a book about the past?	6.5 (775)	6.2 (152)	6.4 (299)	6.6 (211)	7.0 (107)	NS
Watching a movie or television program about the past?	6.0 (778)	5.9 (153)	6.0 (303)	5.9 (213)	6.3 (103)	NS
Studying history in school?	5.7 (788)	5.5 (154)	5.6 (308)	5.6 (214)	6.5 (106)	.00

TABLE 14

Connectedness to the Past on Six Occasions by Gender—National Sample

We asked our respondents for the following information about six "occasions": "On a scale of 1 to 10, where 1 means you felt no connection to the past and 10 means you felt a strong connection to the past, please tell [us] how connected to the past you felt on the following." The table below divides the national sample by gender, and reports the mean score each gender gave the six occasions listed in the far left column for connectedness. The numbers in parentheses indicate the number of respondents of each gender who answered the question.

How connected to the past do you feel when . . .	Gender			
	Total National Sample	Men	Women	Significance Test
Gathering with your family?	7.9	7.4	8.3	< .001
	(795)	(363)	(432)	
Visiting a history museum or historic site?	7.3	7.4	7.2	NS
	(782)	(359)	(423)	
Celebrating holidays?	7.0	6.3	7.6	< .001
	(797)	(363)	(434)	
Reading a book about the past?	6.5	6.6	6.5	NS
	(775)	(360)	(415)	
Watching a movie or television program about the past?	6.0	5.9	6.1	NS
	(778)	(358)	(420)	
Studying history in school?	5.7	5.8	5.7	NS
	(788)	(360)	(428)	

TABLE 15

Connectedness to the Past on Six Occasions by Education—National Sample

We asked our respondents for the following information about six "occasions": "On a scale of 1 to 10, where 1 means you felt no connection to the past and 10 means you felt a strong connection to the past, please tell [us] how connected to the past you felt on the following." The table below divides the national sample into four education groups, and reports the mean score each of those four groups gave the six occasions listed in the far left column for connectedness. The numbers in parentheses indicate the number of respondents of the given education group who answered the question.

How connected to the past do you feel when ...	Education					
	Total National Sample	No High School Diploma	High School Diploma	Some College and Up	4-Year Degree	Significance Test
Gathering with your family?	7.9 (795)	8.0 (82)	8.2 (203)	8.1 (211)	7.5 (297)	.01
Visiting a history museum or historic site?	7.3 (782)	6.5 (74)	7.2 (198)	7.2 (213)	7.5 (296)	.01
Celebrating holidays?	7.0 (797)	7.1 (85)	7.4 (205)	7.0 (209)	6.7 (297)	.04
Reading a book about the past?	6.5 (775)	6.1 (75)	6.5 (195)	6.8 (207)	6.5 (296)	NS
Watching a movie or television program about the past?	6.0 (778)	5.9 (76)	6.0 (203)	6.2 (206)	5.8 (291)	NS
Studying history in school?	5.7 (788)	6.4 (80)	5.6 (202)	5.8 (211)	5.5 (293)	.04

TABLE 16
Connectedness to the Past on Six Occasions by Income—National Sample

We asked our respondents for the following information about six "occasions": "On a scale of 1 to 10, where 1 means you felt no connection to the past and 10 means you felt a strong connection to the past, please tell [us] how connected to the past you felt on the following." The table below divides the national sample into six income groups, and reports the mean score each of those six groups gave the six occasions listed in the far left column for connectedness. The numbers in parentheses indicate the number of respondents of the given income group who answered the question.

How connected to the past do you feel when . . .	Income							
	Total National Sample	$0 to $14,999	$15,000 to $24,999	$25,000 to $34,999	$35,000 to $49,999	$50,000 to $74,999	$75,000 and Up	Signi- ficance Test
Gathering with your family?	7.9 (795)	7.8 (89)	8.0 (119)	8.1 (161)	7.7 (147)	8.0 (124)	7.4 (117)	NS
Visiting a history museum or historic site?	7.3 (782)	6.3 (83)	7.3 (119)	7.1 (158)	7.6 (147)	7.3 (124)	7.6 (118)	.00
Celebrating holidays?	7.0 (797)	6.5 (88)	7.2 (121)	7.3 (162)	7.1 (147)	6.9 (125)	6.6 (117)	NS
Reading a book about the past?	6.5 (775)	6.0 (83)	6.7 (119)	6.5 (158)	7.0 (142)	6.6 (121)	6.1 (117)	.02
Watching a movie or television program about the past?	6.0 (778)	6.3 (84)	6.2 (117)	6.0 (156)	6.3 (147)	5.7 (122)	5.6 (117)	NS
Studying history in school?	5.7 (788)	6.0 (85)	6.0 (119)	5.8 (161)	5.7 (147)	5.6 (123)	5.1 (117)	NS

TABLE 17
Most Important Pasts by Age—National Sample

We asked each of our respondents the following question: "Knowing about the past of which of the following four areas or groups is most important to you: the past of your family, the past of your racial or ethnic group, the past of the community in which you now live, or the past of the United States?" The table below divides the national sample into four age groups, and reports the percentage of respondents who chose each of the pasts listed in the far left column. Totals in this and the next three tables do not always add up to 100% because of rounding.

Knowing about the past of which of the following four areas or groups is most important to you?	Age				
	Total National Sample	18 to 29	30 to 44	45 to 64	65 and Older
Your family	66%	69%	66%	65%	66%
Your racial or ethnic group	8	12	8	6	3
The community in which you now live	4	5	3	6	3
The United States	22	13	24	23	28
	N=796	N=154	N=306	N=214	N=116

Chi-square = .02

TABLE 18
Most Important Pasts by Gender—National Sample

We asked each of our respondents the following question: "Knowing about the past of which of the following four areas or groups is most important to you: the past of your family, the past of your racial or ethnic group, the past of the community in which you now live, or the past of the United States?" The table below divides the national sample by gender and reports the percentage of respondents who chose each of the pasts listed in the far left column.

Knowing about the past of which of the following four areas or groups is most important to you?	Gender		
	Total National Sample	Men	Women
Your family	66%	58%	73%
Your racial or ethnic group	8	9	7
The community in which you now live	4	4	4
The United States	22	29	16
	N=796	N=363	N=433

Chi-square = < .001

TABLE 19
Most Important Pasts by Education—National Sample

We asked each of our respondents the following question: "Knowing about the past of which of the following four areas or groups is most important to you: the past of your family, the past of your racial or ethnic group, the past of the community in which you now live, or the past of the United States?" The table below divides the national sample into four education groups and reports the percentage of respondents who chose each of the pasts listed in the far left column.

Knowing about the past of which of the following four areas or groups is most important to you?	Education				
	Total National Sample	No High School Diploma	High School Diploma	Some College	4-Year Degree and Up
Your family	66%	52%	70%	68%	67%
Your racial or ethnic group	8	15	6	3	9
The community in which you now live	4	6	4	5	2
The United States	22	26	19	24	22
	N=796	N=84	N=201	N=212	N=297

Chi-square = .01

TABLE 20

Most Important Pasts by Income—National Sample

We asked each of our respondents the following question: "Knowing about the past of which of the following four areas or groups is most important to you: the past of your family, the past of your racial or ethnic group, the past of the community in which you now live, or the past of the United States?" The table below divides the national sample into six income groups and reports the percentage of respondents who chose each of the pasts listed in the far left column.

Knowing about the past of which of the following four areas or groups is most important to you?	Total National Sample	Income				
		$0 to $14,999	$15,000 to $24,999	$25,000 to $34,999	$35,000 to $49,999	$50,000 to $74,999	$75,000 and Up
Your family 62%	66%	72%	64%	65%	68%	65%	
Your racial or ethnic group	8	10	6	10	4	10	7
The community in which you now live	4	6	7	4	3	5	1
The United States	22	12	23	20	24	21	31
	N=796	N=89	N=120	N=162	N=146	N=125	N=117

Chi-square = .13

TABLE 21

Regressions for Activity Series—National Sample

We asked our respondents if they had participated in each of 10 "activities that relate to the past . . . during the last 12 months." The table below reports the OLS (ordinary least squares) Coefficients for regressions of participation in each of the 10 activities listed under the table. These regressions are a statistical method for measuring the extent to which one or more variables (e.g., demographic characteristics like age or gender) affect another variable (e.g., participation in past-related activities). The standard errors for the coefficients are in parentheses. In this table and the next two, asterisks indicate the results of the chi-square significance tests. These significance tests measure the likelihood that the association between the independent and dependent variables is caused by chance. Among statisticians a chi-square of .05 is a conventionally accepted threshold of statistical significance; values less than .05 are commonly referred to as "statistically significant." In practical terms, a chi-square of less than .05 means that if, in fact, there was no association in the population between the independent and dependent variables, the observed association would be expected to occur by chance fewer than 5 times in 100 samples of the type we used. Thus, when the chi-square is less than .05, we can be confident in rejecting the possibility that no association exists between the independent and dependent variables. In this table and the next two, one asterisk (*) indicates a chi-square of less than .05 and two asterisks (**) indicates a chi-square of less than .001.

Dependent Variables—Activity Series

Independent Variables in the Model	A1	A2	A3	A4	A5	A6	A7	A8	A9	A10
Age	(-).002*	(-).007**	.000	.001	(-).002	.002*	(-).001	.001	(-).004**	(-).000
(Actual)	(.00)	(.00)	(.00)	(.00)	(.00)	(.00)	(.00)	(.00)	(.00)	(.00)
Gender	(-).021	(-).066**	.016	(-).104*	.028	(-).035	(-).015	(-).136**	(-).122**	(-).059*
(0=Women, 1=Men)	(.02)	(.03)	(.03)	(.04)	(.04)	(.04)	(.04)	(.03)	(.03)	(.03)
Education	.000	.004	.017*	.013	.044**	.038**	.015*	.018*	.029**	.023**
(0 to 20 years completed)	(.00)	(.00)	(.01)	(.01)	(.01)	(.01)	(.01)	(.01)	(.01)	(.01)
Income	.011	.055**	.007	.016	.019	.018	(-).008	.014	(-).004	(-).011
(6 categories)	(.01)	(.01)	(.01)	(.01)	(.01)	(.01)	(.01)	(.01)	(.01)	(.01)

TABLE 21 (continued)
Regressions for Activity Series—National Sample

Independent Variables in the Model	Dependent Variables—Activity Series									
	A1	A2	A3	A4	A5	A6	A7	A8	A9	A10
R-square (Adjusted)	.010	.153	.014	.016	.076	.054	.002	.028	.056	.021
Constant	.961	.912	.549	.391	-.053	-.156	.246	.059	.113	-.040

*p < .05   **p < .001

A1 = Looked at photographs with family/friends
A2 = Took photos/videos to preserve memories
A3 = Watched movies/television programs about the past
A4 = Attended family or other reunion
A5 = Visited history museums/historic sites
A6 = Read books about the past
A7 = Participated in hobbies/collections
A8 = Looked into family history/tree
A9 = Wrote in journal/diary
A10 = Participated in history-related group

TABLE 22
Regressions for Trustworthiness Series—National Sample

We asked our respondents for the following information about seven "places where people might get information about the past": "Please tell [us] how trustworthy you think each is as a source of information about the past using a 1 to 10 scale, where 1 means not at all trustworthy and 10 means very trustworthy." The table below reports the OLS Coefficients for regressions of the trustworthiness of the seven sources of information about the past listed under the table. The standard errors for the coefficients are in parentheses.

Independent Variables in the Model	Dependent Variables—Trustworthiness Series						
	T1	T2	T3	T4	T5	T6	T7
Age	(-).003	.009*	(-).008	(-).009	.005	(-).015*	.004
(Actual)	(.00)	(.00)	(.00)	(.00)	(.00)	(.00)	(.00)
Gender	(-).548**	(-).391*	(-).342*	(-).273	(-).255	(-).044	(-).322*
(0=Women, 1=Men)	(.12)	(.13)	(.14)	(.15)	(.16)	(.15)	(.15)
Education	(-).014	(-).020	(-).044	(-).020	(-).031	.082*	(-).062*
(0 to 20 years completed)	(.02)	(.03)	(.03)	(.03)	(.03)	(.03)	(.03)
Income	.109*	(-).065	(-).022	(-).081	(-).014	.097	(-).033
(6 categories)	(.04)	(.04)	(.05)	(.05)	(.05)	(.05)	(.05)
R-square (Adjusted)	.029	.024	.013	.011	.003	.032	.013
Constant	8.60	8.32	8.99	8.39	6.95	5.56	5.89

$*p < .05$ $**p < .001$

T1 = Museums
T2 = Personal accounts from grandparents or other relatives
T3 = Conversation with someone who was there
T4 = College history professors
T5 = High school history teachers
T6 = Nonfiction books
T7 = Movies and television programs about the past

TABLE 23
Regressions for Connectedness Series—National Sample

We asked our respondents for the following information about six "occasions": "On a scale of 1 to 10, where 1 means you felt no connection to the past and 10 means you felt a strong connection to the past, please tell [us] how connected to the past you felt on the following." The table below reports the OLS Coefficients for regressions of the 1 to 10 ratings respondents gave each of the six occasions listed under the table for feeling connected to the past. The standard errors for the coefficients are in parentheses.

Independent Variables in the Model	Dependent Variables—Connectedness Series					
	C1	C2	C3	C4	C5	C6
Age	.009	.008	.017*	.018*	.007	.018*
(Actual)	(.01)	(.01)	(.01)	(.01)	(.01)	(.01)
Gender	(-).854**	.094	(-)1.157**	.190	(-).181	.166
(0=Women, 1=Men)	(.17)	(.18)	(.19)	(.17)	(.17)	(.19)
Education	(-).060	.075*	(-).069	.036	.016	.002
(0 to 20 years completed)	(.03)	(.03)	(.04)	(.03)	(.03)	(.04)
Income	(-).002	.126*	.075	(-).017	(-).119*	(-).168*
(6 categories)	(.06)	(.06)	(.07)	(.06)	(.06)	(.06)
R-square (Adjusted)	.041	.017	.059	.011	.005	.018
Constant	8.72	5.30	7.49	5.22	5.98	5.43

*p < .05   **p < .001
C1 = Gathering with your family
C2 = Visiting a history museum or historic site
C3 = Celebrating holidays
C4 = Reading a book about the past
C5 = Watching a movie or television program about the past
C6 = Studying history in school

Introduction: Scenes from a Survey

1. Michael Frisch, "Cracking the Nutshell: Making History-Making," unpublished document, 20 September 1989, in possession of authors.

2. Lynne V. Cheney, *American Memory: A Report on Humanities in the Nation's Public Schools* (National Endowment for the Humanities, undated but published in September 1987), 5. (Cheney is approvingly quoting the poet Czelaw Milosz.) See also Chester Finn Jr. and Diane Ravitch, "Survey Results: U.S. 17-Year-Olds Know Shockingly Little About History and Literature," *The American School Board Journal* 174 (Oct. 1987): 31–33, as quoted in Dale Whittington, "What Have 17-Year-Olds Known in the Past?" *American Educational Research Journal* 28 (Winter 1991): 763; Diane Ravitch and Chester Finn Jr., *What Do Our 17-Year-Olds Know? A Report on the First National Assessment of History and Literature* (New York: Harper & Row, 1987). There is a large literature debating the work of Ravitch and Finn. For one brief critique, see William Ayers, "What Do 17-Year-Olds Know? A Critique of Recent Research," *Education Digest* 53 (Apr. 1988): 37–39.

3. David Thelen, "How Do Americans Understand Their Pasts? A Second Working Draft," unpublished paper, April 1989, in possession of authors.

4. See, for example, the essays in *Journal of American History* 75 (4) (March 1989) (special issue on "Memory and American History") and in Susan Porter Benson, Steve Brier, and Roy Rosenzweig, *Presenting the Past: Essays on History and the Public* (Philadelphia: Temple University Press, 1986).

5. See, for example, Janice Radway, *Reading the Romance: Women, Patriarchy, and Popular Literature* (Chapel Hill: University of North Carolina Press, 1984). See also Robert Merton, *Mass Persuasion: The Social Psychology of a War Bond*

Drive (New York: Harper and Brothers, 1946); David Morley, *The Nationwide Audience: Structure and Decoding* (London: British Film Institute, 1980); Doris A. Graber, *Processing the News: How People Tame the Information Tide* (New York: Longman, 1984); Patricia Palmer, *The Lively Audience: A Study of Children Around the TV Set* (Sydney and Boston: Allen and Unwin, 1986); John Fiske, *Television Culture* (London: Methuen, 1987), chapter 6.

1. The Presence of the Past

1. As with all the numbers in this (and any other) survey, methodological cautions are in order. Some respondents may have "telescoped" their responses in a way that made one year into a longer unit; others may have interpreted activities related to the past very broadly; still others may have given us responses they thought we wanted. See appendix 1 for a fuller discussion of methodological issues.

2. As noted, we are here arbitrarily—but not without justification—using 8 points on a 10-point scale as a description of feeling "very strongly" connected to the past.

3. After family reunions, the next largest categories were friends (11 percent) and school (7 percent).

4. Spontaneous comments on "reading" the past: look at photos—8; movies/TV—11; museums—35; books—21; average—18.75.

Spontaneous comments on "writing" the past: take photos—26; reunions—35; hobby—31; family history—61; journal—24; group—24; average—33.5.

The count for reunions is complicated because interviewers routinely asked respondents for the type of reunion they attended. Our estimate is that about 35 of the 196 comments were offered spontaneously rather than as the result of direct questions.

5. The statistical technique known as "regression" offers one way to gauge which social and demographic factors predict particular behaviors. (A regression is a statistical technique for estimating the effects of one or more variables on another variable. For example, you might use a regression to measure how much fertilizer affects the height of corn when you control for sunlight and rainfall.) In effect, regression equations permit us to ask whether knowing someone's age, income, education level, race, and gender would allow us to predict if they were likely to visit a museum, write in a diary, or watch a history film.

Even when added together, the five social and demographic characteristics (age, income, education, race, and gender) we used explain only a small part of the variations in the ways that individuals answered the activities questions. For eight of the ten activities, these characteristics explain less than 6 percent of what statisticians call "the variance." (The variance measures the variability from one person to the next in their propensity to do these activities. If these social and demographic characteristics perfectly predicted whether or not someone did a particular activity, they would explain 100 percent of the variance.) For example, only 2.3 percent (a tiny amount) of the variance in the degree to which people have investigated the history of their family is explained by demographic variables. Virtually none (less than .1 percent) of the variance in whether people have a hobby or collection related to the past can be attributed to those same variables. Even in the two cases—visiting museums and taking photos—where demography matters more, the variance is still modest: just 7.5 percent and 14 percent.

It is possible, of course, that a different set of questions might have yielded more differences, e.g., if we had asked about different kinds of hobbies, if we had mapped frequency, or if we had separated museums from historic sites.

6. When you control for education, income, age, and gender, taking photos is the only statistically significant difference in black and white patterns among the ten activities we asked about. (If you combine numbers from the special African American sample with the blacks in the national sample, blacks also appear to be statistically less likely to participate in hobbies and collections related to the past.) Blacks and whites are, for instance, equally likely to investigate the history of their families or visit museums and historic sites. Adding race to our regression equations thus only slightly enhances our ability to predict whether or not an individual will participate in most activities related to the past.

7. It is more difficult to compare activity patterns for Native Americans and whites and for Mexican Americans and whites because the samples are not strictly comparable. Still, based on what we can see after controlling for other variables (especially education), the differences among these groups are either negligible or relatively easy to explain. For example, although 16 percent of Mexican Americans (as opposed to 29 percent of white Americans) report writing in journals or diaries, these differences largely disappear if you compare people of the same educational level. Even when race or ethnicity does make a difference, it is still a relatively modest difference. For example, social background (including race) never explains more than 13 percent of the variance when the Sioux and white responses are combined, and only on two activities (visiting museums and sites and taking photographs) does it even explain as much as 7 percent.

8. These five differences hold up when we control for other variables like income, gender, and age. Thus, based purely on cross-tabulations, education also correlates with looking at and taking photos, attending reunions, and watching movies about the past. But these differences disappear when we use regressions to control for other variables. On the other hand, the modest difference in levels of participation in hobbies and collections emerges as statistically significant in the regression equations. Compare tables 7 and 21 in appendix 2.

9. Based on the regressions in table 23, only the relationship between education and a feeling of connectedness in visiting history museums is statistically significant. Race, income, age, education, and gender together explain only 1.7 per-

cent—an almost trivial amount—of the variance in the answers that people gave to our questions about connectedness. On only two of the questions (family gatherings and holiday celebrations) does social background explain more than 1.6 percent of the variance in answers to the connectedness question, and in those cases it still explains only 7.1 percent and 5.7 percent.

10. As table 6 indicates, the differences for attending reunions, working on family history, and writing in a diary are statistically significant based on a chi-square significance test. The regressions presented in table 21, which control for income, education, and age, confirm the significance of these three differences in levels of participation in activities. The regressions, in fact, suggest two additional differences are also statistically significant (e.g., taking photos and participating in history-related groups). Another way of comparing differences is to use logistic regressions. By that method, which holds other demographic variables constant, women were 50 percent more likely than men to have investigated the history of their family (the probability of a man doing this was .28 and for a woman .42), 55 percent more likely to have written in a journal or diary (men: .22 and women: .34), and 17 percent more likely to have attended a reunion (men: .59 and women: .69).

11. For men: 86 family; 24 nonfamily but also nonpublic figures (friends, etc.); 99 public figures. For women: 166 family; 34 other nonpublic figures; 74 public figures.

12. These categorizations are necessarily subjective; to control for this, they (and similar counts) were done independently by one of the authors (Rosenzweig) and our research assistant (Andy Draheim) with similar results. Men were more likely than women to offer reasons for keeping diaries or journals like tracking work procedures, exercise schedules, and skill progress.

13. The average age of the 14 women was 55.

14. Women also tended to collect domestic objects, and favored hobbies in which they made rather than just collected objects.

15. Jane Clarke, Market Research Director, History Book Club, letter to David Wilson, 3 May 1994, in possession of authors.

16. Sixteen of the 44 people asked this follow-up question offered a specific title. Another 5 people mentioned titles without a follow-up question. Hence, only 21 of 653 people who said that they watched a film or television program about the past gave us a specific title.

17. To be sure, many people also make quite deliberate trips—even pilgrimages—to specific sites and museums in order to honor a particular history, to instill patriotism in their children, to understand current problems, or to retreat from the present by visiting the past. Below is a breakdown of the reasons given for visits to museums and historic sites: travel—50; proximity—11; visiting relative/friend—11; taking child—10; leisure—9; personal connection/interest—7; school trip—7; research—5; ethnic connection—4; activism/museum work—3;

work-related—2; local history interest—2; understand the present—2; escape the present—1; saw movie—1; other—9.

18. Brook Hindle argues that "modern man is separated more firmly from the realities of his own world than was man in earlier periods of history." Thus, "man's need to touch the past has increased rather than decreased." "How Much Is a Piece of the True Cross Worth?" in Ian M. G. Quimby, ed., *Material Culture and the Study of American Life*, (New York: Norton, 1978), 5. See also Greg Dening, *Mr. Bligh's Bad Language: Passion, Power and Theatre on the Bounty* (New York: Cambridge University Press, 1992), 339–40.

19. The rough estimate is based on 192 million people over 18 multiplied by 39.6 percent.

20. Below is a breakdown of the types of groups devoted to studying, preserving, or presenting the past in which interviewees participated during the previous year: school-related—26; church/religious—22; local history/local preservation—17; ethnic or racial—12; hobbyist/collector—12; environmental—11; genealogical—9; family/friends—12; work-related—6; civic/community—6; art museum—5; veterans—4; reenactor—3; therapy—3; fraternal—2; tourism—2.

21. This interview was done in pretesting; unless otherwise noted, all quotes come from the main study.

22. The average times were probably longer, according to John Kennedy of the Center for Survey Research, because it is more difficult to keep an accurate time count during long interviews (because of starting and stopping).

2. Using the Past to Live in the Present

1. John R. Gillis, *A World of Their Own Making: Myth, Ritual, and the Quest for Family Values* (New York: Basic Books, 1996).

2. Two accounts that place intermarriage increasingly at the center of American life and explore how it may recast issues of cultural identity are Gary B. Nash, "The Hidden History of Mestizo America," *Journal of American History* 82 (Dec. 1995): 941–64, and David Hollinger, *Postethnic America: Beyond Multi-culturalism* (New York: Basic Books, 1995).

3. George Sánchez, *Becoming Mexican American: Ethnicity, Culture, and Identity in Chicano Los Angeles, 1900–1945* (New York: Oxford University Press, 1993).

4. "Experience Is the Best Teacher"

1. Table 4.1 shows percentages of people who answered each question. The total number of answers varies from question to question. For example, many people didn't comment on college professors, but most people did comment on museums.

2. We asked 76 respondents to give a single word to describe their high school experience with history. (We had intended to ask this question of a larger percentage of respondents but stopped asking when their answers turned out to be very similar.) The results: boring, irrelevant—26; incomplete, biased, ignorant—15; interesting—14; educational and useful—6; vaguely favorable—9; vaguely unfavorable—3; average or okay—3.

5. Beyond the Intimate Past

1. We coded these responses in two ways: we counted the number of people who selected an event as their primary response (either by mentioning it first or by speaking at length about it) as well as the number who simply mentioned an event. Using the second method (in which an individual could be counted more than once), 40 people mentioned World War II.

2. To argue for the significance of an absence—of a dog that didn't bark in the night—is to leave yourself open to the charge that you didn't listen hard enough or that you didn't listen to enough people (or dogs). Many questions we didn't ask might have elicited a different set of answers. And the limitations of a sample of 624 white Americans leads us to generalize about them as a "group" when we are well aware of distinctions within white America. Certainly, other patterns might have become apparent if we had sampled particular subgroups—Orthodox Jews in Brooklyn, lesbian feminists in Ann Arbor, Armenian farmers in Fresno, or Civil War buffs in Virginia. We hope that others will test some of our hypotheses by more closely questioning white Americans—and especially subgroups within that population—about their complex relationships to the past.

3. We did speak with a few people, like an Albuquerque contractor, who located themselves within trajectories based on the histories of their communities; he talked of his "respect" for the architectural styles of the 1920s and the "men and women who built my neighborhood." Yet very few others offered community history as a fundamental reference point.

4. There were very few exceptions: one person talked about a film on Jimmy Hoffa; one mentioned a father who was a union leader; one noted that he was a union electrician; one said he went to a reunion of teacher union members. When we asked people to name a historical figure who profoundly affected them, only one person mentioned anyone from labor history—socialist leader Eugene V. Debs. There were only two mentions of "class" in a sociological sense: one person talked about an interest in the upper class in early modern England and one about a "white middle-class" version of the past. One can have a language of class without the word, but that was not present either.

5. On the notion of "residual" culture, see Raymond Williams, *Marxism and Literature* (Oxford: Oxford University Press, 1977), 121–27.

6. Other recent studies discern the waning and blurring of white ethnic histor-

ical consciousness. In the region around Albany, New York, Richard Alba found that white Americans had little political, social, or cultural "ethnic solidarity" and had reduced "ethnic identity . . . to largely personal and family" expressions. Only about one fifth of white Americans in his study reported "practicing customs or traditions" of their "ethnic background"; 15 percent reported teaching their children about their ethnic background and 10 percent said they had visited their homelands. Richard Alba, *Ethnic Identity: The Transformation of White America* (New Haven: Yale University Press, 1990), 79, 300.

Mary Waters, who closely studied the ancestry question in the 1980 census and conducted in-depth interviews with sixty third- and fourth-generation white ethnics in the suburbs of San Jose, California, and Philadelphia, Pennsylvania, concluded that "ethnicity is increasingly a personal choice of whether to be ethnic at all, and, for an increasing majority of people, of which ethnicity to be." Waters argues that this "symbolic ethnicity" means that people "cling tenaciously to their ethnic identities," even though that identity "does not matter" in most important respects. Mary C. Waters, *Ethnic Options: Choosing Identities in America* (Berkeley: University of California Press, 1990), 147.

7. Almost four fifths of the native-born whites in Alba's study reported "no experience" of feeling "a special sense of relationship to someone based on common ethnic background." A similar percentage never or almost never discussed their ethnic backgrounds with others. Rather, they tied their ethnic identities to a sense of personal family histories and not to any sense of some larger social group. "This amounts," Alba concludes, "to a privatization of ethnic identity—a reduction of its expression to largely personal and family terms." *Ethnic Identity*, 129, 300.

8. High rates of intermarriage have fostered the waning, blurring, and fracturing of white ethnic particularism. Of those white Americans who told census-takers in 1980 that they had an ethnic ancestry, 37 percent described that ancestry as mixed. The same census showed that three quarters of marriages of white Americans involved some degree of what Alba calls "ethnic border crossing" and about half are between people with entirely dissimilar ancestries. Stanley Lieberson and Mary C. Waters, *From Many Strands: Ethnic and Racial Groups in Contemporary America* (New York: Russell Sage Foundation, 1988), 249; Alba, *Ethnic Identity*, 12.

9. Historian George Chauncey finds the roots of this effort to create a gay past in early twentieth-century New York. "One prime way" that gay men sought to "undermine the authority of the dominant culture" and "create affirmative conceptions of themselves," he writes in *Gay New York*, "was to create gay histories, and in particular to claim that heroic figures from the past were gay." This project of reclaiming a gay past was difficult because not only was the history of homosexuality not part of "formal history instruction," it also "had no place in the family-centered oral traditions available to other disenfranchised groups." Instead, gay New Yorkers transmitted their understanding of the gay past through "day-

to-day" interactions in the gay world, passing it on "in bars and at cocktail parties, from friend to friend, from lover to lover, and from older men serving as mentors to younger men just beginning to identify themselves as gay." As Chauncey points out, "one of the major ways groups of people constitute themselves as an ethnic, religious, or national community is by constructing a history that provides its members with a shared tradition and collective ancestors. . . . By imagining that they had collective roots in the past, they asserted a collective identity in the present." Chauncey, *Gay New York: Gender, Urban Culture, and the Making of the Gay Male World, 1890–1940* (New York: Basic Books, 1994), 283, 285–86.

This project of gay historical reclamation has continued—and indeed greatly accelerated—in more recent years. See, for example, Lisa Duggan, "History's Gay Ghetto: The Contradictions of Growth in Lesbian and Gay History," in Benson, Brier, and Rosenzweig, eds., *Presenting the Past*, 281–92.

10. We asked this question of all respondents and 57 percent said yes, but we asked only 231 people in the national sample to say what their particular interest was. Forty-five of those respondents gave answers about religion or the church.

11. Without entering into definitional debates about traditions within Christianity, we are including Mormons and Jehovah's Witnesses among evangelical Christians since they also emphasize spreading the word of Jesus. In any case, our categorization of respondents as "evangelical Christians" must be very loose, since we did not ask any explicit questions about religious affiliation.

12. By most measures, of course, evangelical Christians make up more than 5 percent of the American population; the 5 percent figure represents those in our sample who spontaneously gave evidence of the way their religious beliefs influenced their view of the past.

13. The notion that the future was foretold in the past and recorded in the Bible is really "prophecy" rather than "history," as historians would define it. Thus, at least viewed from a conventional definition of history, fundamentalist Christians (including many evangelicals) turn the past into a sacred narrative that makes "history" irrelevant. Fundamentalists, religious historian Robert Orsi argues, subscribe to "pre-given plots" that can "drain away curiosity about specific moments in history" and can "override" what might be conventionally called "history." Robert Orsi, e-mail to Roy Rosenzweig, 16 September 1995.

14. Orsi, for example, points out that there are really a "cluster of terms for various Christian notions" about history: " 'salvation history,' which is the story of the world told teleologically from creation to fall to redemption in Jesus to his final triumph at the end of time; 'prophecy,' which is a reading of the signs of the times, past and present, to determine the nature of the future; 'millennialism,' understandings of the end of the world in relation to a narrative about the movement of the world toward that end (which includes a reading of history); 'apostolic history,' the notion among Reformed Protestant churches that their way of being Christian is in complete conformity with the earliest history of the Christian com-

munity around Jesus, the example of which had been lost after Constantine and only recovered in later centuries with the rise of Protestant churches." Ibid.

15. E. J. Hobsbawm, "Ethnicity and Nationalism in Europe Today," *Anthropology Today* 8 (Feb. 1992): 3. See also, for example, Benedict Anderson, *Imagined Communities: Reflections on the Origins and Spread of Nationalism* (London: Verso, 1991); Prasenjit Duara, *Rescuing History from the Nation: Questioning Narratives of Modern China* (Chicago: University of Chicago Press, 1995). For a brief summary of the debate on the History Standards, see Jon Wiener, "History Lesson," *New Republic* 212 (2 Jan. 1995): 9–11. A recent book treats the controversy in detail: Gary B. Nash, Charlotte Crabtree, and Rose E. Dunn, *History on Trial: Culture Wars and the Teaching of the Past* (New York: Knopf, 1997).

16. There is plenty of other evidence that Americans are quite familiar with the basic icons of our national history. Historian Michael Frisch, for instance, questioned more than 1,000 university students about the names they associated with U.S. history and found that they almost uniformly cited the standard "great men," from Washington to Lincoln to Jefferson. And when the History Channel asked a cross section of Americans which "historical figures" they "most admired," 9 of the top 15 choices were presidents. Even in our own survey, in which history was defined much more broadly, respondents routinely brought up these standard names. Michael Frisch, "American History and the Structure of Collective Memory: A Modest Exercise in Empirical Iconography," reprinted in Frisch, *A Shared Authority: Essays on the Craft and Meaning of Oral and Public History* (Albany: State University of New York Press, 1990), 29–54; Roper Starch Worldwide, "American Attitudes Toward History," conducted for the History Channel, April 1995.

17. Counts of responses to open-ended questions are inevitably subjective. It also seems likely that our question, which asked about an event or period that affected the person, encouraged respondents to draw personal connections.

David Glassberg, in a perceptive analysis of letters written to filmmaker Ken Burns about his PBS series *The Civil War*, finds a similar pattern of taking national events and understanding them as part of personal and family history; many letter-writers thanked Burns for helping them understand their own families, and others talked about "how they learned about the war from their families." According to Glassberg, "nearly one-third of the letters Burns received mentioned family members, suggesting that these viewers saw the national history presented in the film through the lens of their family history." "Public History and the Study of Memory," *Public Historian* 18 (Spring 1996): 17. See also "Dear Ken Burns: Letters to a Filmmaker," *Mosaic* 1 (Fall 1991): 1, 8.

18. Of white Americans, 126 of 369 or 34 percent chose a public figure; 25 choose non-U.S. figures, so 101 of 369 or 27 percent made selections from the national past. The top choices were: father—52; mother—43; grandmother—34;

Kennedy—24; grandfather—23; friend—20; parents—16; teacher—16; Lincoln —14; Christ—14.

19. As with many other counts here, this is subjective. Andy Draheim and Roy Rosenzweig both counted these and came up with somewhat different numbers. These are Draheim's numbers.

20. For example, that women are less likely than men to put U.S. history first may well be the flip side of women's strong connection to family history and their traditional responsibility for maintaining the family. In this loose division of labor, preserving national history falls more into the male domain. Race also affected attitudes toward national history. Black Americans and Native Americans are significantly more likely to list racial or ethnic history as most important to them. The unstated premise that the American past is "white" is as powerful as the framing assumption that our national past is "male." For an empirical study of gender-based framing assumptions about history, see Janice E. Fournier and Samuel S. Wineburg, "Picturing the Past: Gender Differences in the Depiction of Historical Figures," *American Journal of Education* 105 (Feb. 1997): 160–85. Based on a study of fifth and eighth graders, they conclude: "In girls' minds, women in history are blurry figures; in boys' minds, they are virtually invisible."

21. For perceptive (and sometimes conflicting) perspectives on the history of patriotism and nationalism, see John Bodnar, ed., *Bonds of Affection: Americans Define Their Patriotism* (Princeton: Princeton University Press, 1996). Harvey Kaye provides a perceptive account of the "crisis of the grand-governing narratives" in Britain and America in the 1970s and 1980s in *The Powers of the Past: Reflections on the Crisis and the Promise of History* (Minneapolis: University of Minnesota Press, 1992), 40–119. See also John R. Gillis's introduction to his edited volume *Commemorations: The Politics of National Identity* (Princeton: Princeton University Press, 1994) in which he argues that "by the late 1960s, the era of national commemoration was clearly drawing to a close" and that "the nation is no longer the site or frame of memory for most people and therefore national history is no longer a proper measure of what people really know about their pasts" (13, 17).

22. In this case, we are counting the number of people who made any mention of an event in answering this question; thus a single individual could be counted for more than one event. On the relationship of generation and memory, see Howard Schuman and Jacqueline Scott, "Generations and Collective Memories," *American Sociological Review* 54 (June 1989): 359–81.

Saul Wisnia, "Moments to Remember? A Tough Question for Generation X," *Washington Post*, 26 July 1994, makes the point that unlike baby boomers, who recall the assassinations of JFK, RFK, and MLK, the landing on the moon, or Watergate, "there appears to be little that current 20-somethings deem dramatic enough to impress a permanent stamp on their minds."

23. A survey by the History Channel provides some further support for this

conclusion about a generation-based skepticism about government actions. The survey questioned people on whether three government actions were justified (the United States' role in Vietnam, Gerald Ford's pardon of Richard Nixon, and the dropping of the atomic bomb on Hiroshima). Only slightly more than a quarter of Americans thought American actions in Vietnam were justified, but baby boomers (35–49 years old) were the group least likely to support government policy. Moreover, whereas 80 percent of those over 55 supported the dropping of the atomic bomb, only 55 percent of those between 35 and 49 took the same position. Roper Starch Worldwide, "American Attitudes Toward History."

24. The 1990 population of the United States and Canada minus Texas, California, New Mexico, Arizona, and Colorado is approximately 220 million. On the circular migration patterns between Mexico and the United States, see, for example, Roger Rouse, "Mexican Migration and the Social Space of Postmodernism," *Diaspora* 1 (1991): 8–23, as reprinted in Dave Gutierrez, ed., *Between Two Worlds* (Wilmington, Del.: Scholarly Resources, 1996), 247–63.

25. The proximity of other Mexican Americans and of Mexico may have biased our sample; perhaps Mexican Americans in other parts of the United States are even less conscious of their ethnic background and their links to their native land.

26. The Mexican Americans interviewed in Spanish (almost all of whom were born in Mexico) were more likely to choose the past of the United States than white, European Americans. Whether that is the result of some defensive patriotism is hard to determine.

27. Note that these are figures for English-language interviews. Subsequent to the completion of the survey we learned from one of the two interviewers who did the Spanish interviews that this question was generally misunderstood in Spanish translation. According to that interviewer: "It was almost inevitably interpreted . . . as 'How much history do you share with Americans in the sense of talking with Americans?' " And it was answered: "I don't talk about it much." As a result, we have not used the Spanish-language data for this question.

28. We asked only a limited number of people (26) whether they felt more connected to the past on July fourth or Cinco de Mayo. Of those, 4 chose Cinco de Mayo; 18 chose July fourth; 3 said they felt equally connected; and 1 said neither. We did not ask about September sixteenth, which celebrates the day in 1810 when Father Hildalgo called for liberation from Spain and is thus more comparable to July fourth. Seven people did mention that holiday. All but one of those were interviewed in Spanish—one case where we could note a difference between the Spanish-language interviews and those done in English.

29. The differences on movies and high school and college teachers are statistically significant, but such tests are, of course, hazardous since we are comparing different samples.

30. In percentage terms, Mexican American participation rates are lower than the national sample on every question except reunions. But regression equations

offer the basis for arguing that the differences are really due to lower education levels and income levels among Mexican Americans. Using regressions, writing in diaries and visiting museums or historic sites are the only activities on which Mexican Americans have a significantly lower participation rate.

As noted in chapter 1, it is also possible that the slightly higher figure for reunions is the result of not having worded the question carefully enough for Mexican Americans. "Reunion" in Spanish is spelled the same as in English. But, according to Ricardo Romo, "reunion" in Spanish means gathering. It does not mean "reunion" in the sense of a more formal meeting or organized function. Nevertheless, there is ample evidence of the importance of transnational reunions in Mexican American life. For example, a recent report describes a seasonal pattern in which Mexican Americans return to their villages in Mexico in December to celebrate Christmas, marriages, and christenings. It estimates that one million Mexican Americans return from California to Mexico each Christmas, depopulating public school classrooms across the state. See "Home for the Holidays," *Los Angeles Times*, 25 December 1997, A3 and "Students Pack Homework for Trips South," *Los Angeles Times*, 29 December 1997, A16.

31. Sánchez, *Becoming Mexican American*, 9 (includes Anzaldúa quote).

6. History in Black and Red

1. As explained in appendix 1, we have combined the two black samples in reporting results because they are so similar. For example, 29 percent of the special black sample of 224 people said that they had looked into the history of their family in the past year; among the 76 African Americans in the national sample, it was 31 percent. In the few cases where there is some significant difference between the samples, we have noted them.

2. It is not clear the degree to which the widespread use of the term "roots" by African Americans predates the Alex Haley book and the resulting television program. There is no doubt, however, that the book and TV show have had a major impact on how black Americans talk about their pasts.

3. As noted in appendix 1, the percentage in the national sample (18 percent) was lower than in the minority sample (28 percent), but the difference was not statistically significant.

4. Few people offered family stories about Reconstruction; most family narratives were about slavery, sharecropping, Jim Crow, or the civil rights movement. But apparently in earlier generations, Reconstruction stories were more common. In the first third of the twentieth century, when a racist interpretation dominated the historical profession, Eric Foner points out, it was "only in the family traditions and collective folk memories of the black community . . . [that] a different version of Reconstruction survive[d]." Eric Foner, *Reconstruction: America's Unfinished Revolution, 1863–1877* (New York: Harper & Row, 1988), 610–11. On

Murray, see William L. Clay, *Just Permanent Interests: Black Americans in Congress, 1870–1991* (New York: Amistad, 1992), 382.

5. Of course, some African Americans would describe Christ as black. In the special black sample, 89 of 102 chose a "historic" figure: 43 of those chose King; 8 chose Christ; 13 chose other white figures, including Kennedy, Nixon, and Lincoln. The death of Nixon a few months before these interviews probably accounts for his being selected by more people (4) than Lincoln (2). These same patterns occur in the interviews with African Americans in the national sample. We had been concerned that asking the minority sample a specific question about Martin Luther King Jr.'s birthday might bias the results. But in the national sample, which did not include a question about King's birthday, an almost identical percentage of African Americans who talked about a historical figure selected King as the figure who most affected them.

6. In the national sample, 111 whites chose a parent; 103 chose a national historical figure. In the black sample, 43 chose King; the largest personal choice was mother, selected by 17 people; 37 people chose either a parent or just "parents."

The disparity in the choice of historic figures between whites and blacks is even greater if we focus on figures from American history—with 41 percent of African Americans (in the minority sample) choosing a figure from the U.S. past and 27 percent of white Americans in the national sample making a similar selection.

7. Alwyn Barr, "Juneteenth," in Charles Reagan Wilson and William Ferris, eds., *Encyclopedia of Southern Culture* (Chapel Hill: University of North Carolina Press, 1989), 216.

8. These differences are for the combined total of the black sample and African Americans in the national sample. As appendix 1 notes, blacks in the national sample rated connectedness in schools higher than blacks in the minority sample and very slightly higher than whites (although the second difference was not statistically significant). African Americans gave films and television slightly higher trustworthiness and connectedness ratings than whites; perhaps this is because they were particularly thinking about *Roots*.

9. Some respondents, aware that they were talking to white interviewers, may have consciously sought to find common ground. Yet overall, black respondents did not hesitate to give frank answers, as the quotes in this chapter indicate.

10. Respondents in the minority sample were asked what county they lived in, what year they were born, and what their highest grade or level of education was. Then the interviewer said: "Is your race or ethnic background:" and gave respondents five choices. "Black or African American" was the third choice and if respondents selected that, they were included in the minority sample. In the national sample, they were offered the same five choices but at the end of the interview.

11. Such comments acknowledge the complexity of racial identity in American society and indicate what historian Earl Lewis has called the "multipositional"

nature of identity formation among African Americans. Earl Lewis, "To Turn on a Pivot: Writing African Americans into a History of Overlapping Diasporas," *American Historical Review* 100 (June 1995): 783–84.

12. On Drew, see Charles E. Wynes, *Charles Richard Drew: The Man and the Myth* (Urbana: University of Illinois Press, 1988); Spencie Love, "Noted Physician Fatally Injured: Charles Drew and the Legend That Will Not Die," *Washington History* 4 (Fall/Winter 1992–93): 4–19, and *One Blood: The Death and Resurrection of Charles R. Drew* (Chapel Hill: University of North Carolina Press, 1996).

13. Black Americans did also offer narratives of moral decline and rising crime that we heard from white Americans, but they were counterbalanced by this optimistic narrative of group progress.

14. There is a rich historical, anthropological, and journalistic literature on the Sioux and on Pine Ridge. See, for example, Michael F. Steltenkamp, *Black Elk: Holy Man of the Oglala* (Norman: University of Oklahoma Press, 1993); Raymond J. DeMallie, *The Sixth Grandfather: Black Elk's Teachings Given to John G. Neihardt* (Lincoln: University of Nebraska Press, 1984); Joe Starita, *The Dull Knifes of Pine Ridge: A Lakota Odyssey* (New York: G. P. Putnam, 1995); Mary Crow Dog and Richard Erdoes, *Lakota Woman* (New York: HarperPerennial, 1991); Raymond J. DeMallie and Douglas R. Parks, eds., *Sioux Indian Religion: Tradition and Innovation* (Norman: University of Oklahoma Press, 1987); Peter Matthiessen, *In the Spirit of Crazy Horse* (New York: Penguin, 1983).

15. As Michael Steltenkamp has noted, the Sioux or Lakota are "a people whose very name has elicited controversy and confusion." We have generally followed our respondents in using "Oglala" or "Oglala Sioux." For a brief discussion of some of the naming issues, see Steltenkamp, *Black Elk*, 3–6.

16. For an incisive discussion of "hybridity" among the Pine Ridge Sioux, see Philip J. Deloria, "Sioux Christianity, Traditional Religion, and Politics on the Northern Plains, 1933–1972," unpublished paper presented to Japanese American Studies Association Annual Meeting, Aichi University, June 1997. Deloria makes clear the way that Sioux historical narratives have changed over time and particularly since the 1960s. We obviously only captured those narratives at one moment in time—one that was itself decisively shaped by prior events, particularly the rise of the American Indian Movement and the occupation at Wounded Knee in 1973.

17. Ben Black Elk was the son of Black Elk, whose teachings were recorded by John Neihardt in the widely read book *Black Elk Speaks*. Ben Black Elk, who died in 1973, was, as Michael Steltenkamp notes, known for years "as the 'other face' on Mount Rushmore because of his popularity with tourists." On Black Elk, see, for example, Steltenkamp, *Black Elk*; DeMallie, *The Sixth Grandfather*; John G. Neihardt, *Black Elk Speaks: Being the Life Story of a Holy Man of the Ogalala Sioux* (New York: William Morrow, 1932).

18. For the death of Crazy Horse, see Dee Brown, *Bury My Heart at Wounded Knee: An Indian History of the American West* (New York: Henry Holt, 1970), 312;

Eleanor H. Hinman, ed., "Oglala Sources on the Life of Crazy Horse," *Nebraska History* (Spring 1976): 1–51. For a discussion of current views on Crazy Horse among the Oglala Sioux, see Martin Walker, "Still Crazy," *Guardian*, 7 Dec. 1996, T38.

19. The treaty, a peace accord between the Sioux and the U.S. government, established a vast reservation "for the absolute and undisturbed use and occupation of the Indians herein named." But when whites discovered gold in the Black Hills six years later, prospectors started mining land that the Sioux regarded as sacred. In 1876, the government coerced the Sioux to give up their rights to the Black Hills. But this agreement was signed by only 10 percent of adult Sioux males rather than the three quarters mandated by the treaty. In 1980, the U.S. Supreme Court upheld a federal claims court decision that "a more ripe and rank case of dishonorable dealings will never, in all probability, be found in our history." The courts awarded the Sioux $122 million in compensation. They have, however, refused the money (now worth more than $300 million with interest), insisting that they want the land returned instead. See Starita, *Dull Knifes*, 320–21; Peter Carlson, "The Unfashionable," *Washington Post Magazine*, 23 Feb. 1997, W06.

20. For an excellent discussion of the contested understandings of the Battle of Little Bighorn, see Edward Tabor Linenthal, *Sacred Grounds: Americans and Their Battlefields* (Urbana: University of Illinois Press, 1993), 127–71.

21. The Sioux (like African Americans) are more likely than white Americans to cite figures from American history as having influenced them: 38 percent of Sioux selected figures from American history as having influenced them, compared to 41 percent of African Americans (in minority sample) and 27 percent of white Americans.

22. The reference is presumably to the execution of 38 Santee Sioux on December 26, 1863. Lincoln approved the executions, although he angered local and military officials who wanted to execute 303 Sioux. See Brown, *Bury My Heart at Wounded Knee*, 59–61. The executions took place in Mankato, Minnesota; the association of the event with Mandan, North Dakota probably reflects the fact that when George Custer led his men into the Battle of Little Bighorn in 1876, they started out from Fort Abraham Lincoln in Mandan.

23. White Americans gave oral sources an overall rating of 7.9 and nonoral sources a rating of 6.8; for the Pine Ridge Sioux, it was 8.4 and 5.9.

24. Ninety-four of 186 Pine Ridge respondents brought up Wounded Knee; it was mentioned 137 times (not counting multiple mentions in a single question). It should be noted, however, that they were not always talking exclusively about the 1890 massacre. For example, of the 94, 32 made reference to the 1973 occupation as well as or instead of the earlier massacre. In some cases, respondents just said "Wounded Knee," and we can't know for sure whether they were talking about the massacre, the occupation, or the historic site—or, most likely, all three.

Wounded Knee is not a single event for Pine Ridge Sioux Indians; it is a massacre, an occupation, and a nearby location. This, in fact, accounts for some of its great power and importance for Pine Ridge residents.

25. See American Automobile Association, *North Central Tourbook* (Heathrow, Fla.: AAA, 1995).

26. Sharp divisions remain today, although they have somewhat diminished in the 1990s. For accounts of conflict at Pine Ridge, see Matthiessen, *In the Spirit of Crazy Horse*; Starita, *Dull Knifes*, 296–302; William Clairborne, "Drained by Internecine War, Oglala Sioux Look to Past with Hope," *Washington Post*, 11 Nov. 1992, A3; Daniel Golden, "The Legacy of Wounded Knee," *Boston Globe Magazine*, 26 Nov. 1989, 22ff.

27. One estimate is that alcohol abuse at Pine Ridge is ten times the national rate (Clairborne, "Drained by Internecine War"). Fetal alcohol syndrome is twenty times the national average (Starita, *Dull Knifes*, 343). For a recent discussion of the uses of the past to combat alcoholism at Pine Ridge, see Dirk Johnson, "Reversing Reservation's Pattern of Hard Drink and Early Death," *New York Times*, 23 December 1997, A16.

28. For discussions of the cultural changes and revivals (e.g., changes in education, the growing interest in Lakota language and traditional medicine, revivals of the Sun Dance, and the use of Indian names), see, for example, Golden, "The Legacy of Wounded Knee"; Clairborne, "Drained by Internecine War"; Walker, "Still Crazy"; Starita, *Dull Knifes*, 315–17. Golden notes, for instance, that in 1972, there was only one Sun Dance at Pine Ridge (for a tourist carnival); in the summer of 1989, there were thirty. For a perceptive discussion of earlier remakings of Sioux culture "within the constraints of American rules and regulations," see Philip Deloria, " 'I Am of the Body': Thoughts on My Grandfather, Culture, and Sports," *South Atlantic Quarterly* 95 (Spring 1996): 325.

29. In 1992, Melvin Lone Hill, then tribal vice-president and a former AIM activist, told a reporter: "As young warriors, we never took part in preserving spiritual and cultural values like the young people are doing today, preserving what you call religion and we call a way of life. That's the hope for the future that I see, the younger people getting involved in preserving their past." Clairborne, "Drained by Internecine War."

Afterthoughts

Roy Rosenzweig: Everyone a Historian

1. Louis R. Harlan, "The Future of the American Historical Association," *American Historical Review* 95 (Feb. 1990): 3.

2. Carl Becker, "Everyman His Own Historian," *American Historical Review* 37 (Jan. 1932): 233–55.

3. Ibid., 252–53. Gerald Figal notes that Japanese "self-histories" (a written form of personal histories that have become popular in Japan since the early 1970s) share this tendency to relate past and present, "shifting easily from a chronology of the past to a commentary on the past and its ramifications for the present and future." "How to *jibunshi*: Making and Marketing Self-histories of Shōwa Among the Masses in Postwar Japan," *Journal of Asian Studies* 55 (November 1996): 902–33.

4. See, for example, Mike Wallace, *Mickey Mouse History and Other Essays on American Memory* (Philadelphia: Temple University Press, 1996); Edward T. Linenthal and Tom Engelhardt, *History Wars: The Enola Gay and Other Battles for the American Past* (New York: Henry Holt, 1996).

5. For example, in her *Wall Street Journal* op-ed piece of October 20, 1994, which launched the assault on the national history standards, Lynne Cheney complained that Harriet Tubman was "mentioned six times," whereas Paul Revere, Robert E. Lee, and Thomas Edison received nary a reference. Similarly, columnist John Leo slammed the standards for asking students to learn about such allegedly trivial figures as Mercy Otis Warren ("a minor poet and playwright" included only "so the founders of the nation won't seem so distressingly male") and Ebenezer MacIntosh, a shoemaker and leader of the Stamp Act demonstrations ("a brawling street lout of the 1760s" mentioned merely because he was "anti-elitist"). National Center for History in the Schools, *National Standards for United States History: Exploring the American Experience* (Los Angeles, 1994); Wiener, "History Lesson," 9–11; Hugh Dellios, "Battle over History May Itself Prove Historic," *Chicago Tribune*, 30 October 1994, Perspective Section, 1; John Leo, "The Hijacking of American History," *U.S. News & World Report* 117 (Nov. 14, 1994): 36. For a recent comprehensive discussion of the controversy, see Nash, Crabtree, and Dunn, *History on Trial*.

6. For some perceptive comments on the decline of nationalism, see Gary Gerstle, "Blood and Belonging," *Tikkun* 9 (Nov. 1994): 68ff. and Kaye, *The Powers of the Past*, 40–119.

7. For recent defenses of liberal nationalism, see, for example, Michael Lind, *The Next American Nation: The New Nationalism and the Fourth American Revolution* (New York: Free Press, 1995); David A. Hollinger, "National Solidarity at the End of the Twentieth Century: Reflections on the United States and Liberal Nationalism," *Journal of American History* 84 (Sept. 1997): 559–69. The case for postnationalism and transnationalism is made in such works as Arjun Appadurai, "Sovereignty Without Territoriality," in Patricia Yaeger, ed., *The Geography of Identity* (Ann Arbor: University of Michigan Press, 1996) and Saskia Sassen, *The Global City: New York, London, Tokyo* (Princeton: Princeton University Press, 1991).

8. See Duara, *Rescuing History from the Nation*.

9. Alice Garrett, "Teaching High School History Inside and Outside the

Historical Canon," in Lloyd Kramer et al., eds., *Learning History in America: Schools, Cultures, and Politics* (Minneapolis: University of Minnesota Press, 1994), 75.

10. David Kobrin, Ed Abbott, John Ellinwood, and David Horton, "Learning History by Doing," *Educational Leadership* (Apr. 1993): 39, 40; Kobrin, "It's My Country, Too: A Proposal for a Student Historian's History of the United States," *Teachers College Record* 94 (Winter 1992): 334. See also David Kobrin, *Beyond the Textbook: Teaching History Using Documents and Primary Sources* (Portsmouth, N.H.: Heinemann, 1996).

11. *New York Times*, 5 Apr. 1995.

12. National Education Association 1916 report on *The Social Studies in Secondary Education*, as quoted in Hazel Whitman Herzberg, "The Teaching of History" in Michael Kammen, ed., *The Past Before Us: Contemporary Historical Writing in the United States* (Ithaca: Cornell University Press, 1980), 476.

13. Frisch, *A Shared Authority*, xx, xxii.

14. John Kuo Wei Tchen, "Creating a Dialogic Museum: The Chinatown History Museum Experiment," in Ivan Karp, Christine Mullen Kreamer, and Steven D. Lavine, eds., *Museums and Communities: The Politics of Public Culture* (Washington, D.C.: Smithsonian Institution Press, 1992), 286, 301; Tchen, "Back to the Basics: Who Is Researching and Interpreting for Whom?" *Journal of American History* 81 (Dec. 1994): 1007.

15. Barbara Franco, "Doing History in Public: Balancing Historical Fact with Public Meaning," *AHA Perspectives* (May/June 1995): 5–8.

16. Sandra Marwick, "Learning from Each Other: Museums and Older Members of the Community—the People's Story," in Eileen Hooper-Greenhill, ed., *Museum, Media, Message* (New York: Routledge, 1995), 140–50. For a Canadian project, see Laurence Grant, " 'Her Stories': Working with a Community Advisory Board on a Women's History Exhibition at a Canadian Municipal Museum," *Gender & History* 6 (Nov. 1994): 410–18.

17. For an overview of some of these projects, see Roy Rosenzweig, " 'People's History' in den Vereinigten Staaten," in Hans Heer and volker Ullrich, eds., *Geschicte entdecken* [History Discovered] (Rowohlt, 1985), 46–57. See also, for example, Jeremy Brecher, "A Report on Doing History from Below: The Brass Workers History Project"; Duggan, "History's Gay Ghetto"; Sonya Michel, "Feminism, Film, and Public History"; Jeffrey C. Stewart and Faith Davis Ruffins, "A Faithful Witness: Afro-American Public History in Historical Perspective, 1828–1984"; James R. Green, "Engaging in People's History: The Massachusetts History Workshop," all in Benson, Brier, and Rosenzweig, eds., *Presenting the Past*, 267–359; and Arthur A. Hansen, "Oral History and the Japanese American Evacuation," *Journal of American History* 82 (Sept. 1995): 625–39.

18. Michael O'Malley and Roy Rosenzweig, "Brave New World or Blind

Alley? American History on the World Wide Web," *Journal of American History* 84 (June 1997): 132–55.

19. Franco, "Doing History in Public," 8.

20. See Paul Thompson, *The Voice of the Past: Oral History*, 2nd edition (Oxford: Oxford University Press, 1988), 22–71.

21. Microhistorians set the everyday stories of particular individuals against larger "historical" events. For one promising example, see Dening, *Mr. Bligh's Bad Language*. Professional scholarship, of course, does reflect fundamental moral judgments, even while eschewing explicit discussions of moral conduct or character. On the relationship of historical narrative and moral judgments, see, for example, Hayden White, "The Value of Narrativity in the Representation of Reality," in W. J. T. Mitchell, ed., *On Narrative* (Chicago: University of Chicago Press, 1980), 1–23; William Cronon, "A Place for Stories: Nature, History, and Narrative," *Journal of American History* 78 (Mar. 1992): 1347–1376. But on the ways that "the tradition of scholarly detachment," and professional training in general, lead historians to avoid "the emotional places of history" and "the feelings of pride, anger, and loss that accompanies reflecting on the personal past," see David Glassberg, "A Sense of History," *Public Historian* 19 (Spring 1997): 70.

22. For a series of perceptive essays focused on the ways that power shapes history, see Wallace, *Mickey Mouse History*.

23. Megan Rosenfeld, "Clothing Industry Rips into Planned Sweatshop Exhibit," *Washington Post*, 12 Sept. 1997, C1; Irwin Molotosky, "Furor Builds Over Sweatshop Exhibition," *New York Times*, 30 Sept. 1997, 20; Kristin Young, "Debate over Smithsonian Exhibit Heats Up," *Apparel News*, 29 Aug. 1997, 8.

24. Quoted in Franco, "Doing History in Public," 7.

25. Linda Shopes, "Oral History and Community Involvement: The Baltimore Neighborhood Heritage Project," in Benson, Brier, and Rosenzweig, eds., *Presenting the Past*, 249–63.

26. *Mission Hill and the Miracle of Boston* (Boston: Cine Research, 1979).

27. Robert D. Putnam, "Bowling Alone: America's Declining Social Capital," *Journal of Democracy* 6 (Jan. 1995): 65–78. Putnam's work raises a host of complex questions that go well beyond this discussion. For some perceptive critiques, see, for example, Michael Schudson, "What If Civic Life Didn't Die?" and Theda Skocpol, "Unravelling from Above," both in *American Prospect* 25 (Mar./Apr. 1996): 17–25.

28. I draw this phrase from David Hollinger, "How Wide the Circle of We? American Intellectuals and the Problem of Ethnos Since World War II," *American Historical Review* 98 (Apr. 1993): 317–37. Hollinger is concerned with the narrowing from a universalist species-centered discourse to an ethnos-centered discourse, and my own focus is on a further narrowing of the "we" to the family.

29. I borrow this phrase from Anderson, *Imagined Communities*. My thanks to

Nancy Grey Osterud and Ken Cmiel for suggestions that shaped ideas in this paragraph and some other sections of these afterthoughts.

30. Joan W. Scott provides a well-known critique of the category of "experience" in "Experience," *Critical Inquiry* 17 (Summer 1991): 773–97. For a perceptive effort to examine more empirically how experience might be mediated by language and culture, see Regina Kunzel, "Pulp Fictions and Problem Girls: Reading and Rewriting Single Pregnancy in the Postwar United States," *American Historical Review* 100 (Dec. 1995): 1465–1487.

31. Shopes, "Oral History," 252. Shopes also notes that "people's sense of their own history is private, personal, and grounded in the family and therefore not congenial to institutional frameworks."

32. Harvey Kaye offers some thoughtful comments on the ways that "the powers of the past" can break "the tyranny of the present" in chapter 5 of *The Powers of the Past*.

David Thelen: A Participatory Historical Culture

I am indebted to Ken Cmiel, Michael Frisch, Harvey Kaye, Bruno Ramirez, Roy Rosenzweig, Esther Thelen, and Jennifer Thelen for helping me to formulate and express the ideas in this essay.

1. David Thelen, "History After the *Enola Gay* Controversy: An Introduction," *Journal of American History* 82 (Dec. 1995): 1029–1035.

2. Pierre Nora, "General Introduction: Between Memory and History," in Lawrence D. Kritzman, ed., *Realms of Memory: Rethinking the French Past*, vol. 1 (New York: Columbia University Press, 1996), 1–20.

3. Dening, *Mr. Bligh's Bad Language*. For other examples, see Kim Chernin, *In My Mother's House: A Daughter's Story* (New Haven: Ticknor & Fields, 1983) and Jonathan Schell, *History in Sherman Park: An American Family and the Reagan-Mondale Election* (New York: Knopf, 1987).

4. For examples, see William I. Thomas and Florian Znanecki, *The Polish Peasant in Europe and America* (1918; reprint [Eli Zaretsky, ed.], Urbana: University of Illinois Press, 1984); Elton Mayo, *The Human Problems of an Industrial Civilization* (1933; reprint, New York: Viking, 1966); Samuel Stouffer et al., *The American Soldier* (Princeton: Princeton University Press, 1949); Edward Shils, "The Study of the Primary Group," in Harold Lasswell and Daniel Lerner, eds., *The Policy Sciences: Recent Developments in Scope and Method* (Stanford: Stanford University Press, 1951), 44–69; Elihu Katz and Paul F. Lazarsfeld, *Personal Choice: The Part Played by People in the Flow of Mass Communications* (Glencoe: Free Press, 1955), chs. 2–6; Fiske, *Television Culture*, ch. 5; Palmer, *Lively Audience*; Jack Whalen and Richard Flacks, *Beyond the Barricades: The Sixties Generation Grows Up* (Philadelphia: Temple University Press, 1989); David Thelen, *Becoming Citizens in the Age of Television* (Chicago: University of Chicago Press, 1996).

5. Charles Horton Cooley, *Social Organization: A Study of the Larger Mind* (New York: Scribner's, 1909); Zygmunt Bauman, *Modernity and the Holocaust* (Ithaca: Cornell University Press, 1989); Arne Vetlesen, "Why Does Proximity Make a Moral Difference? Coming to Terms with a Lesson Learned from the Holocaust," *Praxis International* 12 (Jan. 1993): 371–86.

6. Norbert Elias, *What Is Sociology?* (New York: Columbia University Press, 1978); Sánchez, *Becoming Mexican American*. For a case study of changing constructions and applications of identities as they affect citizenship, see Lisa Lowe, *Immigrant Acts: On Asian American Cultural Politics* (Durham: Duke University Press, 1996).

7. For an excellent example of how individuals suddenly felt a burst of connection even as they constructed very different trajectories around that connection, see Alissa J. Rubin, "Black Women March as One in Philadelphia," *Los Angeles Times*, 26 Oct. 1997, A1.

8. For a recent collection of nine brief statements connecting history and nation, see "Teaching American History," *The American Scholar* (Winter 1998): 91–106.

9. For a case study of how opinion managing came to displace citizens and how citizens fought back, see Thelen, *Becoming Citizens*. See also Susan Herbst, *Numbered Voices: How Opinion Polling Has Shaped American Politics* (Chicago: University of Chicago Press, 1993).

10. William Greider has observed that no elected government, left or right, in any developed country could provide a definition of the national interest that could persuade its electorate. See Greider, *One World, Ready or Not: The Manic Logic of Global Capitalism* (New York: Simon & Schuster, 1997), 18.

11. Kevin Phillips, *Arrogant Capital: Washington, Wall Street, and the Frustration of American Politics* (Boston 1994), 7; Steven J. Rosenstone et al., "American National Election Study" (1994, computer file; in possession of Indiana University Political Science Laboratory); William Schneider, " 'Off With Their Heads': The Confidence Gap and the Revolt Against Professionalism in Politics," in Gary Marks and Larry Diamond, eds., *Reexamining Democracy: Essays in Honor of Seymour Martin Lipset* (Newbury Park: Sage Publications, 1992).

12. Kaye, *The Powers of the Past*.

13. Clifford Geertz, *Local Knowledge: Further Essays in Interpretive Anthropology* (New York, 1983), 151.

14. Ralph Waldo Emerson, "History," in *Essays: First Series* (London: George Routledge and Sons, n.d.), 9.

15. For a spirited elaboration of this perspective, see David Harlan, *The Degradation of American History* (Chicago: University of Chicago Press, 1997).

16. Adam Smith, *The Theory of Moral Sentiments* (1759), Part First, section 1, chapter 1.

Appendix 1. How We Did the Survey

1. "The Pilot Study Report: People and the Past," and Melissa Keane, "Asking Questions About the Past," both in *Mosaic* (Spring/Summer 1992).

2. We sometimes raised or lowered the percentage of people getting particular questions as we began to see which questions produced the richest answers.

3. Christopher Botsko and John M. Kennedy, "Exploring the Past Using Survey Research: Procedures and Problems." Paper presented at the Annual Meeting of the American Association for Public Opinion Research, Fort Lauderdale, Florida, May 1995.

4. The average times were: Oglala Sioux—59 minutes; African American—48 minutes; Mexican American—47 minutes.

5. Because of time zone differences, we did not include Hawaii in the sample.

6. Keane, "Asking Questions About the Past," 8.

7. Kennedy and Botsko, "Exploring the Past," 5.

8. Survey researchers find that response rates for surveys are significantly lower in California; they attribute this pattern to the greater degree of mobility among Californians, the tendency to spend more time out of doors, and a general attitude of "noncompliance" toward surveys.

9. Owen T. Thornberry and James T. Massey, "An Overview of Telephone Coverage," in R. M. Groves et al., eds., *Telephone Survey Methodology* (New York: Wiley, 1988), 30. (Only 5.8 percent of white households lack phone service.)

10. We recognize that because the samples we are comparing are relatively small, the power of our tests of significance is fairly low. Thus, observed differences among the samples must be large in order to be judged as statistically significant.

11. Minority respondents were also asked how much of a common history they thought they shared with other Americans and whether the past of any other place in the world was more important to them than the past of the United States. But these questions came after the question about how connected the respondents felt studying history in school.

12. One other factor may have affected the differences. Blacks who did not graduate from high school gave a higher rating on connectedness to the past when studying history in school, and the national sample had a higher proportion of non-high school graduates (22 percent) than the black sample (12.4 percent).

13. See "A Methodological Report on the Latino National Political Survey (Partial Draft)" prepared by Robert Santos (University of Michigan) and Carolyn Rahe and Ann Shinefeld (Temple University). See also Rodolfo del Garza et al., *Latino Voices: Mexican, Puerto Rican, and Cuban Perspectives on American Politics* (Boulder: Westview Press, 1992).

14. For a discussion of the distortions introduced by aggregating data from different groups of Native Americans as well as some of the other methodological and ethical problems in surveying Native Americans, see Fred Solop, "Surveying

American Indians: Rethinking the Boundaries of Western Methodology," unpublished paper given to authors by Professor Solop, Department of Political Science, Northern Arizona University.

15. Peter T. Kilborn, "For Poorest Indians, Casinos Aren't Enough," *New York Times*, 11 June 1997, A1.

16. Jim Naughton, "The Sioux and the Soil: The Black Hills Battle," *Washington Post*, 24 March 1988, C1. Solop, "Surveying American Indians" reports that "according to tribal officials, 79 percent of homes on the Navajo reservation do not have telephones."

17. Kilborn, "For Poorest Indians."

18. As this book was in press, we learned of the very interesting study of "youth and history" in Europe, based on 30,000 interviews with adolescents in twenty-seven countries. The findings have some intriguing similarities to ours. European adolescents, for example, were much more interested in the pasts of their families than of their nations. They trusted museums and historical places more than other sources; found school textbooks less engaging than other sources; and were highly critical of the same features of their history classes that troubled our respondents: rote memorization of textbooks and facts. See Magne Angvik and Bodo von Borries, eds., *Youth and History: A Comparative European Survey on Historical Consciousness and Political Attitudes Among Adolescents* (2 vols., Hamburg: Koerber-Stiftung, 1997). References are to Volume A, pp. 74, 76, 86, 87, 88, 96.

19.Twenty-six of the 36 interviewers on whom we have information were under 25; most of them were college or graduate students.

20. See Barbara Anderson, Brian D. Silber, and Paul Abramson, "The Effects of the Race of the Interviewer on Race-Related Attitudes of Black Respondents in SRC/CPS National Election Studies," *Public Opinion Quarterly* 52 (Fall 1988): 289–342. See also, for a brief summary of previous research, Steven E. Finkel, Thomas Guterbock, and Marian J. Borg, "Race-of-Interviewer Effects in a Pre-election Poll, Virginia 1989," *Public Opinion Quarterly* 55 (Fall 1991): 313–30.

21. The interviewers who did most of the Spanish-language interviews thought that immigration concerns affected the response rate among Mexican Americans.

22. Janice Sebold, "Survey Period Length, Unanswered Numbers, and Non-response in Telephone Surveys," in Groves, *Telephone Survey Methodology*, 251–53, cites studies showing that 38 to 47 percent of unanswered calls are to non-residential numbers. According to John Kennedy, language problems accounted for very few uncompleted interviews.

23. See Thornberry and Massey, "Trends in United States Telephone Coverage," 48, for evidence of lower response rates among African Americans as well as men, those under 25 and over 65, and those with less education.

24. One British study found refusal rates of 14 percent for a forty-minute questionnaire and 9 percent for a twenty-minute version. Martin Collins, et al.,

"Nonresponse: The UK Experience" in Groves, *Telephone Survey Methodology*, 229. See also Robert M. Groves and Lars E. Lyberg, "An Overview of Non-response Issues in Telephone Surveys" in the same volume, 191–211.

25. For a study showing "disturbingly high" and increasing refusal rates for surveys in the mid-1990s, see "CMOR Refusal Rates and Industry Image Survey (Summary of Results)," *Survey Research 28* (Winter-Spring 1997): 1–4.